Lincoln's
Defense of Politics

Shades of Blue and Gray Series
Edited by Herman Hattaway and Jon L. Wakelyn

The Shades of Blue and Gray Series offers Civil War studies for
the modern reader—Civil War buff and scholar alike. Military
history today addresses the relationship between society and
warfare. Thus biographies and thematic studies that deal with
civilians, soldiers, and political leaders are increasingly important to a larger public. This series includes books that will appeal
to Civil War Roundtable groups, individuals, libraries, and aca-
demics with a special interest in this era of American history.

Lincoln's
Defense of Politics

The Public Man and

His Opponents in the

Crisis over Slavery

Thomas E. Schneider

University of Missouri Press   Columbia and London

Library of Congress Cataloging-in-Publication Data

Schneider, Thomas E., 1963–
  Lincoln's defense of politics : the public man and his opponents in the crisis over
slavery / Thomas E. Schneider.
    p. cm.
  Summary: "Examines six of Lincoln's key opponents (states' rights constitutionalists
Alexander H. Stephens, John C. Calhoun, and George Fitzhugh; and abolitionists
Henry David Thoreau, William Lloyd Garrison, and Frederick Douglass) to illustrate
the broad significance of the slavery question and to highlight the importance of
political considerations in public decision making"—Provided by publisher.
  Includes bibliographical references and index.
  ISBN-13: 978-0-8262-1606-9 (alk. paper)
  ISBN-10: 0-8262-1606-4 (alk. paper)
    1. Lincoln, Abraham, 18091865—Views on slavery. 2. Lincoln, Abraham,
1809–1865—Adversaries. 3. Slavery—Political aspects—United States—History—
19th century. 4. Slavery—Southern States—Justification. 5. Antislavery movements—United States—History—19th century. 6. Slaves—Emancipation—United
States. 7. United States—Politics and government—1861–1865. I. Title.

  E457.2.S37 2005
  306.'3620973—dc22
                                                                    2005026927
∞™ This paper meets the requirements of the
American National Standard for Permanence of Paper
for Printed Library Materials, Z39.48, 1984.

Designer: Jennifer Cropp
Typesetter: Foley Design
Printer and binder: Thomson-Shore, Inc.
Typefaces: Minion and Bodoni

*The University of Missouri Press offers its grateful acknowledgment
to an anonymous donor whose generous grant in support of the
publication of outstanding dissertations has assisted us with this volume.*

Contents

Preface

Retrospective endorsement of the historic achievements of Abraham Lincoln's administration—ending slavery and maintaining the integrity of the Union—has tended to overshadow misgivings about the manner in which those achievements were realized. Among Lincoln's contemporaries, however, such misgivings were rife, and they have never altogether disappeared.

On one hand, emancipation came about through a proclamation, "warranted by the Constitution upon military necessity," that, to cite Richard Hofstadter's well-known description, "had all the moral grandeur of a bill of lading." Frederick Douglass was even more pointed when he said of the Emancipation Proclamation, a year after its issuance, "I have applauded that paper and do now applaud it, as a wise measure—while I detest the motive and principle upon which it is based. By it the holding and flogging of Negroes is the exclusive luxury of loyal men." Lincoln could exempt the people of the loyal slave states from his proclamation because it was directed not at slaveholders as such, but at rebels.[1]

On the other hand, conservative Unionists worried that Lincoln had freighted the cause of restoring the constitutional authority of the federal government with an unnecessary and dangerous moral commitment. "And now . . . in such a crisis as this—must the question of the extinguishment of African slavery be forced upon the country?" asked Representative Henry Grider of Kentucky. Referring to what he called the "pretense" of attacking the rebellion through a proclamation against slavery, Grider predicted that "when the judicial authorities of the country, the great bulwark of human liberty, shall review these times, 'military necessity' and abolition aggression must meet their doom"; all would then see "that our system in its majesty and strength can stand the shock of faction and treason." In Lincoln's view, the question to be decided by the war was not simply whether "our system" could endure but whether "any nation so conceived and so dedicated, can long endure"—any nation "conceived in Liberty, and dedicated to the proposition that all men are created equal."[2]

Would-be admirers of Lincoln the emancipator or Lincoln the Union-saver have been correct to perceive a tension between his moral and constitutional aims. It is difficult to avoid the impression, however, that Lincoln saw something valuable in the political life of the nation that has escaped their attention—something neither independent of morality and law nor reducible to either. This study is an effort to shed light on that political "something" by examining the alternatives. Accordingly, it is as much about those I call Lincoln's opponents as it is about Lincoln himself. The opposition of moral reformers and conservative constitutionalists to what Lincoln stood for ran deeper than the opposition of a political rival such as Stephen Douglas. These groups were fundamentally opposed to any political settlement of the slavery question.

Although he would win the presidency in 1860, Lincoln lost the series of debates that preceded the 1858 Illinois senatorial election—at least in the sense that he failed to unseat his Democratic rival. A number of historical causes might be assigned for the loss of the election. But was Douglas's argument for popular sovereignty was stronger than Lincoln's argument for congressional exclusion of slavery from the territories? This is a question for political scientists rather than for historians. Harry V. Jaffa has said of his study *Crisis of the House Divided: An Interpretation of the Issues in the Lincoln-Douglas Debates* that it "was not meant to be a book about American history, except incidentally."[3] The question that Jaffa's book considers is not why Lincoln lost or won the debates in the electoral sense but whether he deserved to lose or win them. My concern is similarly with a particular historical instance of a problem that I take to be timeless. The difference is that the debates I examine are ones in which the opponents did not directly confront each other. Lincoln never debated an abolitionist or a southern states' rights man in the formal way that he debated Stephen Douglas, but by his words and deeds he made sufficiently clear his view of their positions, as they did their views of his.

Crisis of the House Divided adopts the perspective of voters in the 1858 Illinois senatorial campaign who were called upon to endorse one of the two alternatives represented by the candidates. Sensible as this procedure is, it imposes severe limits on the scope of the study. Jaffa is prevented from giving more than passing consideration to the abolitionists or the proslavery states' rights party.[4] One advantage of a broader perspective comes to light in the work of another political scientist attentive to philosophical aspects of the slavery question, Herbert J. Storing.

Storing makes it clear that the existence of slavery in a *republic* brought politics itself into question. In two essays, "Frederick Douglass" and "The Case against Civil Disobedience," he revisited the dispute between William Lloyd Garrison and Frederick Douglass that was occasioned by the latter's embrace of political abolitionism.[5] In doing so, Storing was primarily concerned with defending Douglass's break with the Garrisonians, who for his purposes included Thoreau—a break that amounted to a rejection of civil disobedience in favor of political action against slavery. Storing regarded civil disobedience, whether in its nineteenth-century abolitionist form or in the form practiced by Martin Luther King and his followers in the twentieth century, as an untenable station between politics and revolution.

Storing's criticism of Douglass, then, is necessarily muted. He defends Douglass's constitutional views insofar as they made it possible for Douglass, beginning in 1851 when he announced his change of opinion, to demand "of every American citizen, whose conscience permits him so to do, to use his *political* as well as his *moral* power for [slavery's] overthrow." Although clearly superior in Storing's view to the moral-suasionist stance he had repudiated, Douglass's acceptance of the constitutional framework, qualified as it was by his wish to maintain the purity of the antislavery cause, led to problems that "well illustrate the apparent dilemma of the reformer in politics."[6] If the dilemma is only an apparent one, then Douglass's problems were in part of his own making. He wavered between supporting moderate antislavery Free-Soil or Republican candidates and supporting the unelectable candidates put forward by the political abolitionists. Douglass's ambivalence about politics, even after 1851, makes his dispute with the Garrisonians less revealing as to the fundamental alternatives than the Garrisonians' disputes with Lincoln, whose faith in politics was more robust.

This study first saw the light as a doctoral dissertation, so it is fitting that I acknowledge those who served on my committee (all of the Department of Political Science at Boston College): Dennis Hale, Christopher Bruell, and especially Robert Faulkner, my *Doktorvater*. David L. Townsend of St. John's College gave valuable encouragement to my work at the time of my first encounters with some of these authors. I was also encouraged in my studies by Laurence Berns. My study of Lincoln began in a serious way in a course at Boston College with David Lowenthal. In making revisions to the dissertation, I benefited from comments by Robert Scigliano and Erik Dempsey. Revisions were begun in a postdoctoral year supported by the Lynde and Harry Bradley Foundation, for which I am grateful.

Debts of a more personal kind are by no means forgotten, though they go unrecorded here.

Abbreviations

The following abbreviations refer to works cited parenthetically in the text. Full references are located in the bibliography.

CA	George Fitzhugh, *Cannibals All!*
MBMF	Frederick Douglass, *My Bondage and My Freedom*
Reform Papers	Henry D. Thoreau, *Reform Papers*
Second Treatise	John Locke, *Second Treatise of Government*
SS	George Fitzhugh, *Sociology for the South*
SSW	Frederick Douglass, *Selected Speeches and Writings*
Works	John C. Calhoun, *The Works of John C. Calhoun*

Lincoln's
Defense of Politics

Part I

Introduction

Lincoln's Opponents

Where is the philosophy or statesmanship which assumes that you can quiet that disturbing element in our society which has disturbed us for more than half a century, which has been the only serious danger that has threatened our institutions—I say, where is the philosophy or the statesmanship based on the assumption that we are to quit talking about it, and that the public mind is all at once to cease being agitated by it? Yet this is the policy here in the North that Douglas is advocating.

Abraham Lincoln, 1858

Chapter 1

A Divided Lincoln?

In view of the sweeping changes that occurred during the presidency of Abraham Lincoln, especially after the Emancipation Proclamation went into effect on January 1, 1863, it is easy to forget the relatively moderate character of the platform that won him that office. No doubt the Republican nonextension program appears more moderate in retrospect than it did at the time. Many Americans did find Lincoln's party too radical; but others faulted it because its opposition to slavery did not in their view go far enough. Until Lincoln's election and the subsequent disruption of the Union, through a decade marked, in the words of Don E. Fehrenbacher, by "the submergence of other public business in the all-absorbing controversy over Negro slavery," one thing did not change: "Constitutional restraints and political necessity confined the sectional controversy to narrow limits." Despite its sectional basis, the Republican Party "proposed to circumscribe the slaveholding system, not destroy it."[1]

What separated Lincoln's party from the Democrats was a constitutional question: did Congress have the lawful power to exclude slavery from the federal territories? The Republican Party, like its rival, disclaimed any power under the Constitution to interfere with slavery in the states. Lincoln personally took this position as early as 1854, before

1

the Republican Party had even been founded. He would repeat it in 1861 in his inaugural address, quoting from the opening debate with Stephen Douglas: "I have no purpose, directly or indirectly, to interfere with the institution of slavery in the States where it exists. I believe I have no lawful right to do so, and I have no inclination to do so."[2]

There was a wider debate about slavery in the United States, but it took place mostly on the political margins. The abolitionists were determined not to let the Constitution have the last word. The seeming arbitrariness of the distinction between territories and states fed suspicions among abolitionists that Lincoln and the Republicans had simply bowed to political necessity. Surely, the abolitionists insisted, the Republican and Democratic positions did not exhaust the alternatives. If it was politically necessary for mainstream parties to confine the debate to terms set by the Constitution, political necessity after all was not the same thing as simple necessity. A deeper question had been ignored: Why this constitution and not another? Indeed, why any constitution at all? The error of "all men of expediency," Henry David Thoreau said, lay in considering not whether a law "is right, but whether it is what they call *constitutional*." To abolitionists like Thoreau, the real question was "not whether you or your grandfather" in accepting the Constitution "did not enter into an agreement to serve the devil . . . but whether you will not now, for once and at last, serve God."[3]

There is an alluring directness in the view that the abolitionists took of slavery—also in the view taken by the proslavery Democrats, the group that responded most directly to the abolitionists' challenge. The acknowledged spokesman of the proslavery Democrats until his death in 1850 was John C. Calhoun. In 1837 a Senate colleague from Virginia, William C. Rives, disputed Calhoun's contention that slavery could be a positive good: at best it might be a lesser evil, he said. Rives insisted, however, that whatever the moral status of slavery, he would defend the constitutional rights of the states where the institution existed. Calhoun replied, "The gentleman from Virginia held [slavery] an evil. Yet he would defend it. Surely if it was an evil, moral, social, and political, the Senator, as a wise and virtuous man, was bound to exert himself to put it down."[4] An abolitionist might have replied to Lincoln in the same way: You hold slavery to be an evil, yet you defend the rights of the slave states. Surely if it is an evil as you say, you are bound to exert yourself to put it down there as well.

At times, abolitionists even acknowledged that they shared common ground with proslavery Democrats in opposing the moderate antislavery position. Frederick Douglass wrote in an 1855 editorial entitled "The True Ground upon Which to Meet Slavery,"

> Free Soilism is lame, halt and blind, while it battles against the spread of slavery, and admits its right to exist anywhere. . . . There is much reason in the logic of the late John C. Calhoun. If slaves are property in the eye of the constitution of the United States, they are subject to the same condition of all other property contemplated in that instrument, and their owners are entitled to all the advantages of this property equally with other citizens in their property—We repeat, slaves are property, or they are not property.

According to William Lloyd Garrison biographer Henry Mayer, the abolitionist "came to respect Calhoun's bold and forthright defiance and preferred his candor to the equivocal positions taken by men like [Henry] Clay"—of whom Lincoln is reported to have told a Missouri congressman in 1864, "I never had an opinion upon the subject of slavery in my life that I did not get from him."[5]

The defenders of slavery were by no means averse to constitutional arguments, but they could not make their final appeal to the authority of the Constitution—the very thing that was in dispute. Like the abolitionists, they had to argue outside the Constitution. According to George Fitzhugh, notable for his intention to take the "highest ground of defence" against northern critics, "the great difficulty in defending Slavery has arisen from the fear that the public would take offence at assaults on its long-cherished political axioms"—such as those expressed in the Declaration of Independence—"which, nevertheless, stood in the way of that defence." But instead of introducing new axioms in place of the old, Fitzhugh maintained that "a 'frequent recurrence to fundamental principles' is at war with the continued existence of all government."[6] Lincoln did not think that recurrence to such principles endangered the American government. On his way to Washington in 1861 the president-elect stopped at Independence Hall in Philadelphia, and in a brief speech there he evoked "the great principle or idea" that had sustained the American Revolutionaries in their struggle: "something in that Declaration giving liberty, not alone to the people of this country, but hope to the world."[7] The conclusions Lincoln drew from that principle, however, alarmed the South even while they failed to satisfy northern abolitionists.

The view of Lincoln that prevailed in the South in 1860 has been characterized by Robert W. Johannsen as follows: "having proclaimed slavery to be a moral evil, Lincoln would be untrue to his own principles if he did not bend all of his power and energy to its elimination." An editor writing for a Kentucky newspaper, citing a campaign speech for Lincoln by William Henry Seward, whom he called "the ablest expositor and most distinguished embodiment of the principles of the party that supports Mr. Lincoln as its candidate," put the matter this way:

> The country is told that Mr. Lincoln's sole claim in the estimation of his supporters to the high seat he aspires to is that he confesses his obligation to "the higher law," that he holds himself bound by an anti-slavery law in his own soul above the laws and constitution of the United States and independent of them, that he considers himself at liberty to trample all the statutes of the land and the decisions of all the tribunals of the land under his feet when they are at variance with his own private judgment and sense of right.

The views ascribed to the candidate by the editor were not necessarily those Lincoln had actually expressed, but they were "in strict keeping with the doctrines put forth by him in his Illinois [senatorial] campaign" in 1858—precisely the doctrines that Lincoln in November 1860 urged southerners who had questions about his position on slavery to acquaint themselves with. It was a question not of Lincoln's integrity as a man—"We have a favorable opinion of the personal and even the political integrity of Abraham Lincoln"—but of the logical tendency of his principles. Lincoln disavowed the term *higher law* that Seward had made famous, but he seemed to many in the South to hold himself bound by the equivalent of such a law. How could he oppose the extension of slavery on moral grounds and yet be willing to leave it alone in the states where it existed? Lincoln acknowledged the constitutional rights of the southern people in regard to their slaves; should he not have had moral reservations about the Constitution? How could he acknowledge those rights "not grudgingly, but fully, and fairly," as he said? At the start of his senatorial campaign, Lincoln had asserted that to "arrest the further spread" of slavery would "place it where the public mind shall rest in the belief that it is in course of ultimate extinction." A New York editor proposed the term *extinctionist* to distinguish Lincoln's approach from that of the abolitionists. Johannsen offers this comment: "Abolitionist or extinctionist? To most Americans"—presumably the majority that would vote for candidates other than Lincoln in 1860—"it was a distinction without a difference."[8]

Along with those who opposed Lincoln because they could not see the difference between extinctionism and abolitionism, there was the small but committed group that opposed him because they ascribed the highest importance to this distinction—the abolitionists themselves. Johannsen quotes a southern clergyman as expressing the view of his section: "When Lincoln is in place, Garrison will be in power." The clergyman was actually quoting Wendell Phillips's more nuanced judgment on Lincoln's election: "Not an abolitionist, hardly an anti-slavery man, Mr. Lincoln consents to represent an anti-slavery idea. . . . Lincoln is in place, Garrison in power." But if some abolitionists saw Lincoln in 1860 as representing *their* antislavery idea, they would soon be disabused; Phillips, in fact, proved to be one of Lincoln's harshest critics. Writing after Lincoln's death, Garrison's coadjutor Oliver Johnson took a more generous view of the Republicans' antislavery motives than most abolitionists did while the president was alive, but he remained puzzled by their willingness to "fight their battle while wearing the shackles imposed upon them by the compromises of the Constitution." They could take the oath to support the law "only with mental reservations which exposed them to embarrassing imputations of insincerity from the pro-slavery side." Clearly, Lincoln and his party were exposed to imputations of insincerity from the antislavery side as well. At best, if Johnson is right, Lincoln was divided against himself. Johnson wrote that the constitutional restraints "galled [Lincoln's] anti-slavery spirit, compelling him . . . to seek to win back the South to her allegiance to the Union by a zealous enforcement, in the first months of his administration, of the fugitive slave law, which he hated and loathed from the bottom of his heart." But if Lincoln had succeeded in winning back the southern states, the result would only have been that "they could remain in the

Union with the perfect assurance that their diabolical system would be preserved from harm."[9]

James M. McPherson has spoken of the Emancipation Proclamation as having "liberated Abraham Lincoln from the agonizing contradiction between his 'oft-expressed *personal* wish that all men everywhere could be free' and his oath of office as president of a slaveholding republic," quoting from Lincoln's well-known August 1862 letter to the editor Horace Greeley. McPherson seems to agree with Oliver Johnson as to the "moral degradation" involved in Lincoln's assumption of the constitutional duties of the presidency in 1861. Lincoln would find it convenient to account for his action or inaction concerning slavery by distinguishing between his personal wish and his "view of *official* duty" in writing to the abolitionist-minded Greeley, or between an "official act" and his "abstract judgment and feeling," in an 1864 letter to a Kentucky man who had spoken with Lincoln about dissatisfaction in that state over the enlistment of slaves as soldiers there. In seeking to conciliate both extremes of loyal opinion, Lincoln lent credence to those who would see him as divided against himself. But Lincoln gave every indication of his willingness to live in peace with the "agonizing contradiction" between his moral beliefs and his constitutional duties. The war that ended slavery had not begun when he took the oath of office—"with no mental reservations," he claimed—and months afterward, he expressed a hope that it might be brought to a conclusion before it should "degenerate into a violent and remorseless revolutionary struggle" destructive of established rights. "We should not be in haste," Lincoln warned, "to determine that radical and extreme measures, which may reach the loyal as well as the disloyal, are indispensable."[10]

In 1854, Lincoln had declared that if slavery could be turned "from its claims of 'moral right,' back upon its existing legal rights, and its arguments of 'necessity'"—returned "to the position our fathers gave it"— then it might safely be left to "rest in peace" for the foreseeable future. On the same occasion, he also admitted, "if all earthly power were given me, I should not know what to do, as to the existing institution." By 1858, however, Lincoln seemed to retreat somewhat from the necessity argument: "When our government was established, we had the institution of slavery among us. We were in a certain sense compelled to tolerate its existence. It was a sort of necessity." "We had slave[s] among us, we could not get our Constitution unless we permitted them to remain in slavery, we could not secure the good we did if we grasped for more." Toleration of slavery had not been a necessity in the strictest sense, but the price paid for union. There is some basis for Garrison's complaint that "our fathers were intent on securing liberty to themselves, without being very scrupulous as to the means they used to accomplish their purpose." If the price of union was not too high in the 1780s when, Lincoln said, slavery had been expected to die out, it might be doubted whether the bargain was still a good one in the 1850s. By that time, he conceded, the "spirit which desired the peaceful extinction of slavery, has itself become extinct."[11]

Lincoln's commitment to the principle of the ultimate extinction of slavery in the United States certainly did not mean that he thought such an event was near. Fehrenbacher wrote that for Lincoln

> the paramount importance of the Republican anti-extension program lay in its symbolic meaning as a commitment to the principle of ultimate extinction. Some later generation, he thought, would then convert the principle into practice. What this amounted to, in a sense, was antislavery tokenism, but it also proved to be a formula for the achievement of political power, and with it, the opportunity to issue a proclamation of emancipation.

This is an illustration of what Lord Charnwood calls Lincoln's "wise and nobly calculated opportunism." If Lincoln had not been in office he could not have issued the Emancipation Proclamation, and he could not have got into office if his stand on slavery had been more radical.[12] For Lincoln the candidate, however, political power could not have been looked to as an opportunity to issue such a proclamation; it was the military authority of the president in the extraordinary circumstances of civil war that brought that step within view. If Lincoln's term of office had passed as peacefully as the terms of all his predecessors, the opportunity to free the slaves by proclamation would never have arisen. Nor could it have arisen for Lincoln as a member of the Senate, if his candidacy for that body in 1854 or 1858 had been successful.

Lincoln's moderate stance situated him between what he referred to as the "dangerous extremes" on the slavery question. From either of these vantage points, it was Lincoln's openness to politics that presented the real danger. Abolitionists charged that his course on slavery was dictated by what they liked to call "mere expediency"—Lincoln was a moderate when something more than moderation was demanded.[13] Southerners charged him with an expedient disregard for the Constitution. The basis for both charges is Lincoln's majoritarianism. The abolitionists liked to think of themselves as the yeast that would leaven the whole lump. Indeed, majorities are often not drivers but resisters of social change; by the same token, their conservatism is not necessarily grounded in a respect for the law. Fehrenbacher concurs with Lincoln as to the importance of majority rule, but he admits to differing about why. He argues that the "two dynamic elements in any effort at major social change are usually two intensely hostile minorities, one supporting the change and the other resisting it. The function of the majority . . . is to restrain, delay, moderate, and finally absorb the dynamic force of change and then bring it to bear, gradually but insistently, on the dynamic force of resistance." Fehrenbacher does not go as far as some writers who rank the agitator or social reformer, unhampered as such by constitutional restraints or majority sentiment, above the politician; but his reasoning is broadly consistent with theirs. Similar considerations have led other commentators to question the sincerity of Lincoln's constitutionalism.[14]

The argument of Lincoln's opportunism in a less noble sense—his success at appearing to have reconciled what were in fact irreconcilably opposed points of view on the slavery issue—has been made famous by Richard Hofstadter. As Hofstadter presents it, these opposites were not moral and legal justice: Lincoln's success was actually due to his having taken the slavery question "out of the realm of moral and legal dispute." Hofstadter charges Lincoln with having put concern with his own electoral prospects ahead of justice for the slave or even "intellectual consistency." "To please the abolitionists," Lincoln "kept saying slavery was an evil thing; but for the material benefit of all Northern white men"— many of them Negrophobes—"he opposed its further extension." He does not claim that Lincoln defended Negrophobia. One of Lincoln's accusations against the Democrats was that they "so far as possible, crush all sympathy for [the Negro], and cultivate and excite hatred and disgust against him." In stressing the Negrophobia that Lincoln did not defend, Hofstadter neglects the constitutional views that he did defend; it was these views, much more than his own or his auditors' racial sentiments, that Lincoln cited in expressing his reservations about abolitionism. Although Hofstadter gives little attention to the constitutional aspect of the slavery question, and his sympathies clearly lie with the abolitionists, his evaluation of Lincoln's career is consistent with the accusation that Lincoln undermined the inherited constitutional order.[15]

The only certain way to protect the integrity of the law is to place it beyond the reach of political action. Lincoln did not take the prospect of amending the Constitution lightly; in one early speech, he even suggested that it would be a good thing to "habituate ourselves to think of it, as unalterable." No degree of antislavery sentiment insufficiently broad and permanent for formal amendment could affect a clear constitutional obligation such as the obligation to deliver up fugitive slaves. Lincoln insisted, however, that it was proper for electoral majorities to determine the bearing of the Constitution on great national questions such as the extension of slavery, where the law left room for legitimate disagreement. "The Constitution does not expressly say" how Congress may legislate in regard to slavery in the territories. "From questions of this class spring all our constitutional controversies, and we divide upon them into majorities and minorities. If the minority will not acquiesce, the majority must, or the government must cease."[16]

The writers and orators treated here were not necessarily the most influential voices in their time. Thoreau's most famous political essay, for example, appeared during his lifetime only in a short-lived periodical called *Aesthetic Papers*, where it attracted little attention. Nevertheless, his worthiness to be included in a study on the case for politics with reference to slavery is not likely to be disputed. (If Lincoln read Thoreau— there is no way to know—he is most likely to have done so in connection with John Brown. The pro-Brown collection *Echoes of Harper's Ferry*, edited by the radical journalist James Redpath, opens with Thoreau's "A Plea for Captain John Brown," followed by selections from better-known figures such as Theodore Parker and Ralph Waldo Emerson.) Thoreau rejected politics because politicians and, what is sometimes forgotten, their constituents have permitted such injustices as slavery to continue.

By contrast, few scholars of the Civil War period have regarded

George Fitzhugh as worthy of their attention (even though Lincoln did read him), unless it has been, in the words of Eugene D. Genovese, "as an eccentric and a curiosity." Fitzhugh himself acknowledged that his fellow southerners, though well disposed in feeling, were inclined to think him "heretical." Among the scholars who have taken Fitzhugh seriously, judgment on his work has not been uniformly favorable. According to Louis Hartz, southern would-be conservatives such as Fitzhugh were unable to overcome this fundamental difficulty: since America had always been liberal, they could not attack liberalism without thereby ceasing to be conservative. The problem is one that transcends the limits of the liberal tradition in America—a fact of which Fitzhugh presumably was aware.[17]

More damningly, Harvey Wish, Fitzhugh's biographer, dismisses him as a propagandist—even if he was one worth writing a book about. Genovese refers to the proslavery argument as being, in the view of many (though not necessarily himself), "an elaborate rationale." If the description is applicable to Fitzhugh, one might justly say, "Rest in peace." But consider these lines from an 1855 letter of Lincoln's: "As a nation, we began by declaring that 'all men are created equal.' We now practically read it 'all men are created equal, except negroes.'" Lincoln did not say the new reading was that of one section only—nonslaveholders throughout the nation had acquiesced in the perpetuation of slavery on the grounds that the doctrine of human equality did not include Negroes. Americans had grown averse to facing the consequences for slavery of the doctrine of equality in its original form. They were likewise averse to rejecting the doctrine, so they had agreed to keep it, with this exception. A shrewd propagandist for slavery, then, would have sought to justify the exception, thereby assuring whites that the enslavement of blacks presented no danger to their own equality and freedom. That is to say, such a propagandist would have done just what Lincoln accused Stephen Douglas of doing. Lincoln claimed that Douglas "constantly moulds the public opinion of the North to [southern] ends; and if there are a few things in which he seems to be against you [of the South]—a few things which he says that appear to be against you, and a few that he forbears to say which you would like to have him say—you ought to remember that the saying of the one, or the forbearing to say the other, would loose his hold upon the North, and, by consequence, [he] would lose his capacity to serve you." But Fitzhugh did just the opposite: "The issue is made throughout the world on the general subject of slavery in the abstract. The argument has commenced. One set of ideas will govern and control after awhile the civilized world. Slavery will every where be abolished, or every where be re-instituted." Fitzhugh's endorsement of slavery in the abstract or (which is to say the same thing) "slavery, *black or white*" was unlikely to have been merely a form of southern propaganda, since the South had no more white slaves than the North.[18]

Moreover, the reaction in the North to this doctrine could not have been difficult to foresee. Lincoln certainly recognized the propaganda value of Fitzhugh's doctrine—that is, its value to Lincoln's side. His law partner William Herndon tells the following story: One day he showed Lincoln an editorial in the Richmond *Enquirer*—evidently by Fitzhugh— "endorsing slavery, and arguing that from principle the enslavement of either whites or blacks was justifiable and right." According to Herndon, Lincoln remarked "that it was 'rather rank doctrine for Northern Democrats to endorse. I should like to see,' he said with emphasis, 'some of these Illinois newspapers champion that.'" Herndon replied that he would have the article published in a paper called the *Conservative*, with the editor of which he happened to be on friendly terms. He did so, to the acute embarrassment of the paper's Democratic backers: "The anti-slavery people quoted the article as having been endorsed by a Democratic newspaper in Springfield, and Lincoln himself used it with telling effect. He joined in the popular denunciation, expressing great astonishment that such a sentiment could find lodgment in any paper in Illinois, although he knew full well how the whole thing had been carried through."[19] If Fitzhugh was a propagandist, he was a disastrously inept one.

To see Lincoln's task in regard to slavery as he saw it, it is necessary to grant as he did that the objects for which his opponents stood were genuinely desirable: it was desirable to set the institution of slavery on the course to extinction in the fastest practicable way, but it was also desirable to preserve the widest scope for local self-government consistent with the Constitution. These opponents sought to reduce the tension, which they regarded as unsustainable, between moral and legal considerations bearing on the question of slavery. They compel us to ask whether Lincoln purchased the superior flexibility of his political approach at the price of consistency. The case that is made here for Lincoln's integrity as a politician—for his undividedness—rests on his refusal to see morality and law as excluding each other. Because he refused to do so, Lincoln did not put himself under the obligation of upholding one to the exclusion of the other, and making that one serve in the other's place.

Chapter 2

Stephen A. Douglas

The Missing Constitutional Basis

A reference to Lincoln's opponents naturally calls to mind Stephen A. Douglas. For the better part of a decade, from the passage of the Kansas-Nebraska Act under Douglas's sponsorship in 1854 to the presidential campaign of 1860, the "Little Giant" could no more free himself from Lincoln's scrutiny, it would seem, than he could free himself from his own shadow. Almost without exception, Lincoln's major speeches of the period are framed as responses to Douglas's views.[1]

It is possible, nevertheless, to exaggerate the importance of Lincoln's attention to Douglas. The events of the 1850s in which Douglas figured so prominently, as portentous in Lincoln's estimation as they no doubt were,[2] did not necessarily change Lincoln's view of the broader, longer-term tendencies he had identified in 1852, to which Douglas's career was incidental. That year, in a public tribute to Henry Clay, Lincoln had spoken of two groups—one "increasing," the other presumably keeping pace. One group would sacrifice the Constitution and the Union "rather than slavery should continue a single hour"; the other comprised those "men, who, for the sake of perpetuating slavery, are beginning to assail and ridicule the white man's charter of freedom—the declaration that 'all men are created free and equal.'"[3] What Lincoln could not see in 1852 was what his own task might be.

Lincoln's responses to Douglas reveal their full significance against the background of these broader tendencies. As Don E. Fehrenbacher observes, in Lincoln's judgment "the Republican program offered the only solution to the problems of slavery and sectionalism because it alone recognized the tension between moral conviction and constitutional guarantees, and yielded as much to either as the other would allow."[4] Douglas refused to recognize that such a tension existed, charging instead that Republicans were agitating the slavery issue for partisan ends. As he had done in 1852, Lincoln pointed to widening divisions in Americans' political house as evidence of the seriousness of the crisis.[5] At the same time, he rebutted the accusation that by joining with radicals (some of them open disunionists) in publicly recognizing this tension, Republicans would only further weaken the Union. In Lincoln's estimation more could be yielded to the Constitution than abolitionists were prepared to accept, and more could also be yielded to moral conviction than many southerners believed safe.

Among Lincoln's speeches of 1854–1860 that are exceptional in not taking the form of replies to Douglas, the most revealing are those he gave in support of John C. Frémont, the 1856 Republican presidential candidate. According to Lincoln, the United States government stood in the same relation to slavery in the territories as the British government had stood to slavery in its infant American colonies. The mother country "would not interfere to prevent it, and so individuals were enabled to introduce the institution without opposition." A statesman-like policy would have checked these individuals. Had the British government acted decisively at a time when slavery was not yet firmly established, it would have merited praise instead of condemnation from later generations. In the same way, the Democrats were "placing the nation in the position to authorize the territories to reproach it, for refusing to allow them [not] to hold slaves."[6] In this instance, however, it was Americans themselves who had to act, through their own government.

The charge of shortsightedness is broad enough to apply to both Douglas and the Democratic nominee, James Buchanan, but there is a difference. Lincoln defined "the question between the parties" in terms that leave no room for Douglas: *Shall slavery be allowed to extend into U.S. territories, now legally free?* Buchanan—who, Lincoln said, expected to be elected by southern votes—"says it *shall*; and Fremont says it shall *not*."[7] Douglas's refusal to give a forthright answer to this question, either in 1856 or two years later when Lincoln debated him, points toward a more fundamental difficulty. It was probably as true of Douglas's supporters as it was of Lincoln's that they were overwhelmingly opposed to slavery in principle; but Douglas encouraged them to view Negro slavery as an exception to which the principle did not apply.

Both Lincoln and Douglas rejected the more radical alternatives that at any event were unacceptable to all but an inconsequential minority of Illinoisans. The question is whether their rejection of these alternatives was based on something more than the fact that they were minority views. Lincoln's attention to Douglas between 1854 and 1860 was dictated by political conditions and does not prove that Lincoln had not thought through the more radical alternatives. Lincoln's position relies on two sources of authority: on the Constitution as to slavery in the states and on the natural justice principles of the Declaration of Independence as to slavery in the territories. The twofold character of Lincoln's position required that he take account of the alternatives in a way that Douglas's popular sovereignty did not.

Harry V. Jaffa, whose ultimate vindication of Lincoln does not prevent him from making the case for Douglas with great care, quotes from an 1848 speech in which the latter declared, "I have no sympathy for abolitionism on the one side, or that extreme course on the other which is akin to abolitionism." Jaffa comments,

> Between these upper and nether millstones Douglas sought a formula of compromise and conciliation. . . . If we would understand why Douglas in the last analysis seems to sympathize more with the pro-slavery extreme than with the abolition extreme, we must remember that the pro-slavery party always took its stand upon the Constitution, albeit according to its own interpretation. . . . The abolitionists, on the contrary, appealed to a "higher law," were willing to damn the Constitution, and admitted no premise to which Douglas might appeal in the interest of any compromise.

In a sense, the abolitionists and the proslavery party were addressing each other, not only because "the extremes have a common interest against the mean," but also because their views of the Constitution were qualitatively different from Douglas's.[8] That the abolitionists went outside the Constitution in judging it according to a "higher law" or law of nature is obvious. Somewhat paradoxically, the proslavery writers had to go outside the Constitution in order to justify their remaining within it. In the case of John C. Calhoun, his interpretive study of the Constitution, *A Discourse on the Constitution and Government of the United States,* is preceded by a theoretical work, *A Disquisition on Government.* The *Disquisition* begins with an account of human nature and does not include the word *slave* or *slavery.* Calhoun's view of the Constitution was based on something more fundamental than the Constitution itself—a quality it shared with the abolitionists' view that it did not share with Douglas's. Lincoln's view shared the same quality.

Douglas defended the free institutions of Illinois, but he refused to endorse them as right for the whole Union. By virtue of the Constitution's silence on the moral status of slavery, and in accordance with the provision in his Nebraska bill that left the people of any territory "perfectly free to form and regulate their domestic institutions in their own way, subject only to the Constitution of the United States," Douglas refused to take a public position on the moral question presented by slavery extension.[9] Lincoln's first task, then, was to argue not the wrongfulness of slavery but its gravity as a public question. The introduction of slavery into new territories was not to be left to the self-interested designs of a few enterprising settlers; moreover, the framers of the Constitution could not have been indifferent to the spread of slavery.

Lincoln did not confine himself to invoking the authority of the framers; he sought to demonstrate that their hostility to the principle of slavery was well founded. He did this chiefly by reference to the natural equality of men as set forth in the Declaration of Independence. In countering this argument, Douglas did not adopt the relatively straightforward position taken by Calhoun. Instead of denying the truth of the Declaration, Douglas assumed the same position that Chief Justice Roger Taney did in the Dred Scott case, denying that the signers of the Declaration ever intended the words *all men* to include blacks. The signers "referred to the white race alone, and not to the African, when they declared all men to have been created equal . . . they were speaking of British subjects on this continent being equal to British subjects born

and residing in Great Britain." Jaffa wrote, "the interpretation of Douglas
and Taney certainly does the 'obvious violence' [to the language of the
Declaration] that Lincoln asserts that it does. We may even supplement
Lincoln's indictment by pointing out that Douglas's interpretation
transforms the Declaration from a document of natural law to one of
positive law." It seems unnecessary to regard this point as a supplement
to Lincoln's indictment. The distinction between natural law and positive law, or natural rights and legal rights, is implied in Lincoln's satire
on Douglas's reading of the Declaration—"We hold these truths to be
self-evident that all British subjects who were on this continent eighty-
one years ago, were created equal to all British subjects born and *then*
residing in Great Britain." Lincoln then addressed this appeal to his
audience, "are you really willing that the Declaration shall be thus frit-
tered away?—thus left no more at most, than an interesting memorial
of the dead past . . . without the *germ* or even the *suggestion* of the individual rights of man in it?"[10]

Besides doing violence to the language of the Declaration of Independence, Douglas's substitution of legal for natural rights made the
Declaration almost valueless as a guide to the intentions of the framers
of the Constitution, since the Constitution also is concerned with legal
rights. It was the difference between the "all men" of the Declaration
and the "We, the People" of the Constitution that permitted Lincoln to
view the Constitution from the outside, as it were, in order to better distinguish those provisions that were matters of principle from those that
were the results of compromise or concessions to sectional interests.
Douglas's conflation of the two had the effect of turning interest into a
kind of principle, even one of the "fundamental principles of this government." Americans could both safeguard their present interests and
congratulate themselves on maintaining the Union as their fathers
made it:

The framers of [the] Constitution never conceived the idea that uniformity in the domestic institutions of the different states was either desirable or possible. They well understood that the laws and institutions
which would be well adapted to the granite hills of New Hampshire
would be unfit for the rice plantations of South Carolina; they well
understood that each one of the thirteen states had distinct and separate

interests, and required distinct and separate local laws and local institutions. . . . Mr. Lincoln and myself differ radically and totally on the fundamental principles of this government. . . . He goes for consolidation and
uniformity in our government. I go for maintaining the confederation of
the sovereign states under the Constitution, as our fathers made it, leaving each state at liberty to manage its own affairs and own internal institutions.

The references to "uniformity," as the context makes clear, refer to the
expectation expressed in Lincoln's "House Divided" speech that the
Union would eventually "become all one thing, or all the other"—all
slave or all free. Douglas is calling his auditors' attention to the unques-
tionable fact that in some parts of the Union slavery was enormously
profitable, and he implies that the institution was abolished elsewhere
because it had proved to be unprofitable. The fact that slavery was not
profitable in the North undoubtedly eased the way to its abolition there;
the question was how much weight ought to be given to the fact that it
was profitable in the South. As Lincoln said in 1854, the profitability of
slavery could be the decisive consideration only if "there is no right
principle of action but *self-interest.*" He did not take the contrary view
for granted, but he had little success engaging Douglas in a debate on
human nature. Douglas refused to accept the consequences of his own
defense of the institutions of his state and section.[11]

Illinois was a free state but restricted the privileges of citizenship to
whites. Douglas defended the denial of political rights to blacks in his
state on the grounds of their inferiority. What prevented him from
going further and endorsing their enslavement throughout the Union?
Douglas observed in an early speech, "In the North it is not to be
expected that we should take the position that slavery is a positive
good—a positive blessing. If we did assume such a position, it would be
a very pertinent inquiry, Why do you not adopt this institution? We
have moulded our institutions at the North as we have thought proper."
This "very pertinent inquiry" might be put to Douglas himself. He disagreed with the people of Maine in making blacks the political equals of
whites; but he denied disagreeing with the people of the southern states
in making them slaves, except insofar as his state's different experience
with slavery may be said to constitute a disagreement. "Finding that

[slavery] was not profitable," Douglas asserted, "we abolished it for that reason, and became a free State."[12] Since the fitness of blacks for freedom did not change with their state of residence, the argument for diversity in their status rested on the different interests of the whites.

Douglas's efforts to link his Republican opponent with the abolitionists are evidence of that group's unpopularity with most Illinoisans. At a deeper level Douglas's disdain for the abolitionists reflected their divergent views of government. Where blacks were concerned, Douglas would assimilate natural rights to political ones. To deny blacks some of the privileges of citizenship or to deprive them of their freedom altogether was a mere matter of discretion. Local legislative bodies might decide on either course as their own interests dictated. Behind the abolitionists' critique of the policies of mainstream parties touching slavery was a critique of the conception of government that made it possible for slavery to be treated as a matter of policy. The abolitionists gave voice to a sentiment that was more widely shared than their conviction of the overriding priority of the slavery question—that there is something unworthy of the best in human nature in the devices by which popular government is carried on: the soliciting of votes by appeals to interest that are hardly distinguishable in principle from their outright purchase, and the logrolling and horse-trading that are the legislative equivalent. Thoreau, whose posthumous reputation is a sign of how widely such reservations have been felt, wrote in "Resistance to Civil Government,"

> Statesmen and legislators, standing so completely within the institution, never distinctly and nakedly behold it. They speak of moving society, but have no resting-place without it. They may be men of a certain experience and discrimination, and have no doubt invented ingenious and even useful systems, for which we sincerely thank them; but all their wit and usefulness lie within certain not very wide limits. They are wont to forget that the world is not governed by policy and expediency.[13]

The feeling that democratic politics is a petty thing seems to be based on the perception of a moral world order in the face of which human considerations of policy and expediency appear small indeed. The superiority of nature, even in the more limited sense of the world of living creatures, over human artifice is confirmed by Thoreau in a passage from his essay "Slavery in Massachusetts" that actually contains an allusion to Douglas. Thoreau wrote, "Nature has been partner to no Missouri Compromise. I scent no compromise in the fragrance of the water-lily. It is not a *Nymphœa Douglasii.*" Of course Douglas was associated with the *repeal* of the Missouri Compromise, but the point is evidently that all compromises as such are inherently weak, since they are based on the will of the parties and not on natural justice. As Thoreau said, "whatever the human law may be," a nation will inevitably pay the penalty for its injustice. This is not to imply that Thoreau's critique necessarily leaves Lincoln untouched, but he escapes the judgment that follows the passage from "Resistance to Civil Government" quoted above—that a politician who "never goes behind government . . . cannot speak with authority about it."[14]

Douglas's attempt to limit politics to the foreground activity of adjusting conflicting interests necessitated a certain lack of forthrightness on his part that distinguished him from his rival. What Douglas called the "great principle of popular sovereignty" amounted, Lincoln said, to putting slavery "upon the cotton gin basis"—justifying its expansion and perpetuation on the spurious grounds of economic necessity. The real necessity, in Lincoln's view, was to reduce the difference of opinion about slavery to its most basic elements, namely, "the difference between the men who think slavery a wrong and those who do not think it a wrong." On this point, Douglas was less candid than some southerners. Lincoln went on to say that any Republican who "is impatient of the constitutional guarantees thrown around [slavery], and would act in disregard of these . . . is misplaced standing with us."[15] The fundamental terms of difference were moral, but they were moral in a sense that comprehended the guarantees of law.

Lincoln had begun the senatorial campaign with his "House Divided" speech, in which he rejected the possibility that the Union could continue permanently divided between free and slave states. Douglas, by contrast, had staked his political fortunes on just the possibility that Lincoln rejected. The thrust of Lincoln's attack was directed at the delusive attractiveness of Douglas's position, which did not require coming down on the side either of freedom or of slavery. Douglasism represented an evasion of the question; but since there was really no evading it, his doctrine represented, in fact if not by intent, a concession to the pro-slavery faction. Douglas treated slavery as a matter affecting whites only insofar as their interests might be involved. To do this was to take the same ground tacitly that Alexander H. Stephens would take avowedly when he spoke of the slave as "fitted for that condition which he occupies in our system."[16] Nothing could justify Douglas's complacency about the spread of slavery, except an assumption of this kind about the world beyond politics. But for that it is necessary to look elsewhere.

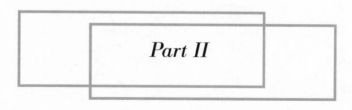

Part II

The Defense of Slavery

Constitutional Justice and Its Limits

Man . . . is, by nature, law-making and law-abiding.

George Fitzhugh, 1856

Chapter 3

Alexander H. Stephens

Slavery, Secession, and the Higher Law

Anyone who studies the career of Alexander H. Stephens of Georgia as it unfolded during the half decade preceding the outbreak of the Civil War is sure to be struck by two things: his defense of slavery and—until the secession of his state was an accomplished fact—his defense of the Union. As to slavery, he expressed, though in an extreme form, an opinion that was evidently widespread in the South; as to the Union, he stood against such an opinion. If Stephens was willing to hazard his political fortunes in the one instance, it seems unreasonable to assume that he was merely seeking to advance them in the other. If Stephens's actions in both instances proceeded from his deeply held convictions, then the question arises as to the connection between these actions. Stephens's defense of slavery was based not on its constitutionality but on its conformity, as he asserted, to natural law. Nor was his defense of the Union dependent on the allegedly proslavery character of the basic law—a view of the Constitution that was common to abolitionists and southern fire-eaters. Stephens, for his own part, did not succeed in establishing a satisfactory connection between the objects he defended; his lack of success indirectly confirms the relation between freedom and law on which Lincoln's Unionism rested.

Stephens defended Negro slavery as naturally just, most notoriously in his "Cornerstone" speech of March 21, 1861, in which he avowed racial equality to be the basis of the new Confederate government. Stephens claimed that the Confederacy, of which he had been elected vice president, was "the first government ever instituted upon the principles in strict conformity to nature, and the ordination of Providence, in furnishing the materials of human society." Harry V. Jaffa wrote of the Cornerstone speech in his study *A New Birth of Freedom* that "no utterance of the time reveals more fully the inner truth about the impending conflict." The authority that Jaffa would ascribe to the speech he calls "the Gettysburg Address of the Confederate South" is rendered doubtful, however, by Stephens's tardiness in embracing the cause of southern independence.[1] According to Stephens, the Confederacy rested on a sounder constitutional basis than the Union did; nevertheless, he had resisted secession until the action of his state had in his judgment left him no choice but to acquiesce. In the Gettysburg Address, Lincoln would draw a connection between the end of slavery and the perpetuation of popular government in the American Union. The weakness of Stephens's Unionism lay in his failure to see slavery and secession as related aspects of a larger question about the durability of popular self-government.

Stephens's Cornerstone speech was devoted to a comparison of the old federal constitution and the new Confederate constitution, to the advantage of the latter insofar as the new constitution, by its basis in natural law, "has put at rest, *forever,* all the agitating questions relating to our peculiar institution." Even before secession, however, Stephens had placed the defense of slavery upon a higher basis than the constitutional rights of the states. In 1859, on the occasion of his retirement from the House of Representatives, Stephens had spoken in similar terms, borrowing the language of William H. Seward's "Higher Law" speech.

> We must stand on the "higher law," as well as upon the constitution. The latter must be subordinate to the former. But as I read the inscriptions upon the canvas of the universe about us and around us, and over us, as well as the teachings of inspiration, "order is nature's first law;" with it, come gradation and subordination; this principle extends from the Throne of the Creator to the utmost limits of his works. We see it in the heavens above . . . we see it in the earth below, in the vegetable and ani-

mal kingdoms . . . we see similar distinctions and gradations in the races of men, from the highest to the lowest type.[2]

The defense of slavery presented in the Cornerstone speech was not new; what was new was the translation of the higher law of racial inequality into the positive, constitutional law of the new Confederate government. Still, the opportunity of translating natural law into positive law had not been sufficient to induce Stephens to abandon the federal constitution.

When Stephens spoke out during the secession crisis in favor of maintaining the Union, it was not the first time he had resisted sectionalism. As a member of Congress he had joined Lincoln in registering opposition to the Mexican War, defying President James Polk, a fellow southerner. Jaffa acknowledges that Stephens's November 1860 Milledgeville speech against secession "seems at first glance to be entirely opposed to what Stephens would say . . . in the Cornerstone speech." Nevertheless, he argues that "analysis will show no real contradiction"; in his Unionist speech, Stephens "still stands upon the Calhounian ground of state equality, which meant the legal equality within the Union of those who affirmed and those who denied the morality of slavery." If Stephens did not shift his theoretical ground, these speeches are surely evidence of a tension within it. Legal equality is a much weaker ground of defense than the ground Stephens had assumed even in his 1859 retirement speech. At best, the old constitution was in conformity with the higher law of racial inequality only by accident. As Stephens admitted in that speech, the "leading public men of the South, in our early history, were almost all against [slavery]." He did not blame them; they had simply been men of their age. Stephens and his contemporaries knew better: "It was a question which they did not, and perhaps could not, thoroughly understand at that time. It was then a new question in the construction of constitutional government. It is still a problem, in process of solution."[3] A southern confederacy would be in a position to solve the problem "forever." The founders' putative error about slavery might have suggested that they were wrong about other matters as well. But Stephens did not welcome the opportunity of a new founding.

According to Stephens biographer Thomas E. Schott, the Georgian "may have questioned the policy of secession but never its constitutionality." Even so, the question provoked by Lincoln's election was to Stephens not simply one of prudent policy. Paraphrasing what he called the core of Stephens's argument in the Milledgeville speech, Schott wrote, "Lincoln's election simply was not sufficient grounds to break up the Union. His election had been constitutional. How could the South, which had always boasted of her devotion to the fundamental law, leave the Union when the Constitution had not been violated?" Indeed, Stephens said, "To make a point of resistance to the government, to withdraw from it because a man has been constitutionally elected, puts us in the wrong."[4] There was a question of constitutional morality involved.

The higher law view of the Constitution would permit an appeal from the positive law whenever a moral principle was felt to be at stake. In Lincoln's more politically minded view, the Constitution is based on principles of natural justice that can be invoked only when the Constitution itself is silent or its interpretation subject to doubt as, for example, in regard to the power of Congress to exclude slavery from the federal territories.[5] Commenting on Seward's "supposed proclamation of a 'higher law,'" Lincoln admitted that he had not read the speech in which this proclamation appears, so that he could not "by its connection, judge of its import and purpose." But he declared that "in so far as it may attempt to foment a disobedience to the constitution, or to the constitutional laws of the country, it has my unqualified condemnation."[6] It seems likely that in speaking of the higher law, Stephens was simply borrowing the term that Seward's speech had made famous, and that his view of constitutional morality actually did not differ very widely from Lincoln's. Stephens's firmness in standing against the "very large majority" of state legislators who "were against remaining longer in the Union" is difficult to explain on any other hypothesis.[7]

That higher law constitutionalism had a southern secessionist analogue is evident from other speeches given in Milledgeville, then the capital of Georgia, during the same week in November that Stephens spoke there. Thomas R. R. Cobb delivered one such speech on November 12, two days before Stephens's speech in defense of the Union. Cobb admitted that the election of Lincoln was valid according to the "forms" of the Constitution but insisted that it violated the spirit. "And am I told this spirit is too indefinite and shadowy a substance to be made the basis of resistance? And can there be a Georgian who will never resist so long as the form and letter of the Constitution is not broken?" Cobb even quoted a Bible verse that was a favorite of the abolitionists, "the letter killeth, but the spirit giveth life" (2 Cor. 3:6).[8]

The use of the term *higher law* by northerners made it possible for Henry L. Benning, another leader of the secessionists in Georgia and a participant in the Milledgeville debate, to argue with plausibility, against Stephens and other Unionists that "as soon as [the Republican party] can acquire the physical power to act, it will act, and will abolish slavery. The Constitution, with that party, is already a dead letter—a thing void, under the operation of the 'higher law.'" Quoting Garrison's famous description of the Constitution, Benning argued that the North "holds slavery to be a sin and a crime, 'a league with hell and covenant with death'; and holding this sentiment, she does not consider herself bound to keep any covenant or agreement favorable to slavery, and the only question with her as to any such agreement or covenant, is as to whether she has the strength to violate it with impunity." Later in the speech, however, Benning would say that Lincoln's election had been unconstitutional because it had been contrary to the intent of the Constitution.[9] Stephens's professed allegiance to the higher law did not diminish his fidelity to the letter of the Constitution.

Jaffa describes the "doctrine of the equality of [slave and other] property as defined by positive law" as "the heart of the justification of secession." Later he writes of the Cornerstone speech, "This remarkable address conveys, more than any other contemporary document . . . the soul of the Confederacy."[10] There is reason for thinking that the previous statement is closer to the truth—that the defense of slavery by natural law was subject to difficulties that were recognized by many southerners, who accordingly placed their defense of southern institutions, in or out of the Union, on a different basis. Stephens's resistance to higher law arguments on the secession question suggests that he, too, may have had doubts.

In a speech at Edwardsville, Illinois, in 1858, Lincoln introduced the following extract from Henry Clay:

> I know there are those who draw an argument in favor of slavery from the alleged intellectual inferiority of the black race. Whether this argument is founded in fact or not, I will not now stop to inquire, but merely

say that if it proves anything at all, it proves too much. It proves that among the white races of the world any one might properly be enslaved by any other which had made greater advances in civilization. And, if this rule applies to nations there is no reason why it should not apply to individuals; and it might easily be proved that the wisest man in the world could rightfully reduce all other men and women to bondage.

Lincoln's own version of this argument, preserved in a fragment, has been cast in the form of a dialogue. The error of the interlocutor is the same as that of Stephens in attempting to justify Negro slavery by reference to the "alleged intellectual inferiority of the black race." The argument is a dishonest one, inasmuch as its real aim is to justify an existing state of affairs.

> If A. can prove, however conclusively, that he may, of right, enslave B.—why may not B. snatch the same argument, and prove equally, that he may enslave A.?—
>
> You say A. is white, and B. is black. It is *color*, then; the lighter, having the right to enslave the darker? Take care. By this rule, you are to be slave to the first man you meet, with a fairer skin than your own.
>
> You do not mean *color* exactly? You mean the whites are *intellectually* the superiors of the blacks; and, therefore have the right to enslave them? Take care again. By this rule, you are to be slave to the first man you meet, with an intellect superior to your own.
>
> But, say you, it is a question of *interest*; and, if you can make it your interest, you have the right to enslave another. Very well. And if he can make it his interest, he has the right to enslave you.[11]

The opening question made no reference to race; the interlocutor simply assumes that A is white and B is black. Accordingly, he readily agrees with the suggestion that A's color gives him the right to enslave B. Of course, the interlocutor is thinking of all the characteristics that, to his mind, distinguish blacks and whites—color standing for all the rest. He evidently thinks that a difference in intellect is among these. By agreeing to make intelligence the distinguishing criterion, however, he is forced back to the racially unspecified ground of the opening question and made to face the consequences, slavery "to the first man you meet, with an intellect superior to your own."

Having been driven from the high ground of right, the interlocutor makes his stand upon the morally dubious ground of interest. If it is in the interest of whites that blacks should be their slaves, the reverse is also true. The maintenance of Negro slavery thus depends in the last analysis upon the possession of superior might by the class of white masters, rather than upon any natural differences. The interlocutor begins with a false but, in a sense, morally attractive view, namely that his color entitles him to make a slave of another of the opposite color. He is brought to a truer but far less attractive view—that slavery is justifiable, if at all, solely by reference to the master's interest.

Such a view would have been especially unattractive to Stephens, who was repelled by the utilitarian argument exemplified by Preston Brooks's "cotton gin basis." In the same speech in which he had avowed his belief in the higher law, Stephens explained his objection. "One hundred men have no right to have happiness at the expense of ninety-nine, or a less number. If slavery, as it exists with us, is not the best for the African, constituted as he is—if it does not best promote his welfare and happiness, socially, morally, and politically, as well as that of his master, it ought to be abolished."[12] Did Stephens permit himself to doubt the beneficence of African slavery? He can hardly have been unaware of the difficulty Lincoln points to in his dialogue.

There is a curious reference in the Cornerstone speech to the Constitution of 1787 that Stephens had defended publicly in his home state less than five months before. For a moment he reverts to a defense of the Constitution against the antislavery interpretation. Stephens admits that the assumption that slavery would pass away "though not incorporated into the constitution, was the prevailing idea at that time." "The constitution, it is true, secured every essential guarantee to the institution while it should last, and hence no argument can justly be urged against the constitutional guarantees thus secured, because of the common sentiment of the day." Lincoln did urge such an argument—though not against guarantees plainly written in the Constitution, as proponents of the higher law did. As president-elect, he told Stephens that the South would be in no more danger from interference with its slaves under a Republican administration than it had been "in the days of Washington." By implication, Lincoln's administration would not be less antislavery than the first president's.[13]

The comparison of the Lincoln and Washington administrations is from one of the letters that Lincoln and Stephens exchanged while the question of Georgia's secession was still pending. In rejecting this comparison, Stephens relied upon a reading of the Constitution according to which the federal government had no lawful power over slavery, any more than it did over religion. The guarantees for slavery written into the Constitution put the institution beyond any need for justification. In his last letter to Lincoln, dated December 30, 1860, Stephens responded to Lincoln's question whether "the people of the South really entertain fears that a Republican administration would, *directly,* or *indirectly,* interfere with their slaves, or with them, about their slaves." Stephens wrote,

> Their apprehension and disquietude do not spring from that source. They do not arise from the fact of the known anti-slavery opinions of the President elect. Washington, Jefferson, and other Presidents are generally admitted to have been anti-slavery in sentiment. But in those days anti-slavery did not enter as an element into party organizations.
>
> Questions of other kinds, relating to the foreign and domestic policy—commerce, finance, and other legitimate objects of the general government—were the basis of such associations in their day. The private opinions of individuals upon the subject of African slavery, or the *status* of the negro with us, were not looked to in the choice of Federal officers, any more than their views upon matters of religion, or any other subject over which the government under the constitution had no control.

At the end of his letter, Lincoln had commented, "You [of the South] think slavery is *right* and ought to be extended; while we [of the North] think it is *wrong* and ought to be restricted. That I suppose is the rub. It certainly is the only substantial difference between us." Stephens's response suggests that southerners were more intent on seeing differences over the interpretation of the Constitution—over what was or was not among the "legitimate objects of the general government."[14]

Lincoln was prepared to accept disagreement about slavery even among the members of his cabinet, but he could not tolerate disagreement concerning the constitutional duty of the South. His public silence during the months between his election and his inauguration amounted to a declaration of his intention to assume the presidency on the same terms as all his predecessors: there would be no bargaining for the office. Lincoln did seek in private letters to southern Unionists to allay fears that his administration would interpret the Constitution in a willfully partisan manner. At the same time, Lincoln insisted that the fundamental disagreement between his party and the South *was* about slavery, not about the Constitution. In writing to John Gilmer, a North Carolinian whom Lincoln considered for a place in his cabinet, he used the same language that he would later use in the letter to Stephens and, with minor changes, in his first inaugural address. The "only substantial difference" between the sections, he argued, was over whether slavery was "right and ought to be extended" or "wrong and ought to be restricted."[15] The southern inclination to see constitutional threats in legitimate differences of opinion had diverted attention from the real issue.

The doubts that Stephens raised in his letter about southern reliance on a higher law seem to have been shared by Lincoln. The president-elect had declined to offer fresh public assurances to the South (his letter to Stephens was marked "*For your own eye only*"), because he feared that any statement of his would be misconstrued or misrepresented. Nevertheless, Stephens urged, "as one who would have you do what you can to save our common country," that a "word 'fitly spoken' by you now, would indeed be 'like apples of gold, in pictures of silver.'" Following this quotation from Proverbs, Stephens added, "I entreat you be not deceived as to the nature and extent of the danger, nor as to the remedy." Lincoln's own views of the danger and the remedy are expressed in a famous fragment, apparently composed in response to Stephens, in which Lincoln makes use of the same biblical figure to describe the relation between the Constitution and the Declaration of Independence:

> The assertion of that *principle* [of "Liberty to All"], at *that time* [in the Declaration of Independence], was *the* word, "*fitly spoken*" which has proved an "apple of gold" to us. The *Union*, and the *Constitution*, are the *picture* of *silver*, subsequently framed around it. The picture was made, not to *conceal*, or *destroy* the apple; but to *adorn*, and *preserve* it. The *picture* was made *for* the apple—*not* the apple for the picture.
>
> So let us act, that neither *picture*, or *apple*, shall ever be blurred, or broken.

The fragment ends with a warning: "That we may so act, we must study, and understand the points of danger." These points seem to have been two, in Lincoln's judgment. In the South, the danger arose from the failure to acknowledge that "the *picture* was made *for* the apple—*not* the apple for the picture": that liberty was not a creature of the Constitution, but the other way around. One danger lay in a rootless or misguided constitutionalism, another in the moral extremism or contempt for positive law associated with higher law doctrines. The second danger was to be feared from abolitionists in the North who believed that the Constitution was made "to *conceal,* or *destroy*" the principle of liberty to all, not "to *adorn,* and *preserve* it."[16]

In 1845, in reference to Texas, then a republic outside the Union, Stephens had expressed a view of slavery that was strikingly similar to Lincoln's. "Liberty," he said, "always had charms for me, and I would rejoice to see all the sons of Adam's family, in every land and clime, in the enjoyment of those rights which are set forth in our Declaration of Independence as 'natural and inalienable,' if a stern necessity . . . did not, in some cases, interpose and prevent. Such is the case with the States where slavery now exists. But I have no wish to see it extended to other countries." The desire of Texans to join the Union produced alarm in the North at the prospect of a further spread of slavery from the older states. Years after, in the midst of a similar crisis over the admission of Kansas, Lincoln would criticize Stephen Douglas for assuming that "the public mind is all at once to cease being agitated" by slavery, if Americans will only "quit talking about it." Stephens did not quit talking about slavery after the annexation of Texas, but, as we have seen, his later pronouncements had strangely little connection with American constitutional tradition. For that reason, Stephens's proclamations did nothing to quiet the public mind—even, or especially, in his own section of the Union.[17]

Stephens could not bridge the gap between his moral and constitutional views of slavery. His failure in this respect helps to explain why he was unable to persuade more of his fellow Georgians to join him in standing firm for the Union. At the conclusion of Stephens's Milledgeville speech, Robert Toombs, a personal friend but a political adversary on the secession question, called for three cheers for Stephens, "one of the brightest intellects and purest hearts of Georgia." No doubt this tribute was sincere, but there may have been an element of calculation in it too: Toombs, who had spoken the previous evening in favor of secession, "thus wisely deflected demands for his own response."[18] Nevertheless, in the end it was the fire-eating Toombs and his associates that won the day.

If it were as true in law and politics as it is in philosophy that "the claim of intellectual superiority [is] the only serious argument in favor of slavery,"[19] Lincoln's task would have been simpler than it was. As a constitutional institution, slavery made certain claims upon the residents of the free states. How far did those claims extend? What Lincoln called "the only substantial difference" between the sections—the rightness or wrongness of slavery as bearing on the territorial question—could not be resolved in a peaceful, constitutional manner unless the Union held together. Stopping on his way to Washington in Steubenville, Ohio, just across the Ohio River from Virginia, Lincoln took the occasion to remark,

> We everywhere express devotion to the Constitution. I believe there is no difference in this respect, whether on this or on the other side of this majestic stream. I understand that on the other side, among our dissatisfied brethren, they are satisfied with the Constitution of the United States, if they can have their rights under the Constitution. The question is, as to what the Constitution means—"What are their rights under the Constitution?" That is all.[20]

There was no question of denying rights that were not in dispute between the sections. The majority might be wrong, Lincoln went on to say; if so, there would be an opportunity to rectify the mistake in four years' time. But the judgment of the majority must prevail in the meantime. It was the failure of southern Unionists such as Stephens to rally their wavering comrades on the question of constitutional morality presented by Lincoln's election that prevented a political settlement of the substantive difference that lay behind it.

Chapter 4

John C. Calhoun

The Politics of Interest

If John C. Calhoun knew Lincoln at all—Lincoln served one term in Congress from 1847 to 1849, and Calhoun died in 1850—he would have known him as Lord Charnwood says Lincoln's fellow members of Congress did, as a "pleasant, honest, plain specimen of the rough West." Yet it is justifiable to treat Calhoun as an opponent of Lincoln inasmuch as Lincoln came to define his position on the slavery question in contradistinction to Calhoun's position. Unlike Stephen A. Douglas, Calhoun and "all the politicians of his school" had forthrightly "denied the truth of the Declaration" as to human equality. Years before his debates with Douglas, Lincoln had spoken of these politicians as "a few, but an increasing number of men, who, for the sake of perpetuating slavery, are beginning to assail and to ridicule the white man's charter of freedom—the declaration that 'all men are created free and equal.'"[1] If white Americans could not uphold that charter without calling the enslavement of the blacks into question, could they assail it without endangering their own freedom? This, according to Lincoln, was the problem with which Calhoun and his followers were obliged to contend.

In arriving at this conclusion, Lincoln most likely had Calhoun's Senate speeches in mind; but a more revealing source is Calhoun's theoretical work, *A Disquisition on Government.* One biographer calls the

Disquisition a "summary of the doctrines [Calhoun] progressively advocated throughout his whole political career"; *summary,* however, hardly
does justice to the care with which Calhoun elaborated his argument in
the work. Nevertheless, that careful argument betrays its author into
what must have been, in one respect, an uncongenial conclusion. The con-
stitutionalist and political theorist—of whom Alexander Stephens would
say, "Government he considered a science, and in its study his whole soul
was absorbed"—was compelled by the logic of his own argument to rank
society and its private interests above government and constitution.[2]

Calhoun was the acknowledged leader of the states' rights school.
"Defending slavery was not the touchstone of Calhoun's political
thought," wrote H. Lee Cheek in a recent study.[3] Nor was opposition to
slavery the touchstone of Lincoln's political thought. For both men,
slavery was one aspect of a larger question about the nature of popular
government and its prospects for survival in the United States and the
world. As befits a work of theory, there are few references to specifically
American topics in *A Disquisition on Government,* and no discussion of
slavery as such; but the historical circumstances of the work's composi-
tion, as well as the content of the argument, lend support to Lincoln's
interpretation of Calhoun's career.

In a letter to his daughter, Calhoun described the *Disquisition* as "the
preliminary work, which treats of the elementary principles of the
Science of Government." "Preliminary" is a reminder that the *Disquisition* was followed by a much longer work of constitutional interpretation, *A Discourse on the Constitution and Government of the United States.*
The aim of the *Disquisition,* then, was to set forth the principles in the
light of which the Constitution was to be read. Were they new principles? Cheek's answer is ambiguous: "In articulating the inherited understanding of properly constituted popular rule for his political situation,
Calhoun may be called the last of the Founders." If Calhoun may be
called a founder, then he was not simply articulating an inherited understanding. The key to resolving the ambiguity seems to be the phrase "for
his political situation." What characterized that situation? Cheek wrote,
"The transition [under Andrew Jackson] from a stable, disciplined mode
of popular rule to an undisciplined 'spoils' system convinced Calhoun
that a recovery of the earlier ethos was necessary if the country were to
survive." Some followers of Calhoun have credited him with prescience:

they have cast Lincoln and his party in the role of underminers of the Constitution. In this respect Cheek's interpretation is more reasonable, but in another respect it is less so. A focus on the Jacksonian revolution makes it possible to avoid serious discussion of another aspect of Calhoun's political situation: the growing conviction among his contemporaries that slavery was set to become a permanent feature of the American constitutional order.[4]

Calhoun's self-imposed task, according to Lincoln, was to reinterpret the constitutional order in such a way as to make it consistent with slavery as a permanent feature. If he was right, Calhoun's views represented a falling off from the principles of the generation that framed and ratified the Constitution. Some interpreters, however, have suggested another possibility: they have pointed to influences in Calhoun's thought that predate the liberalism of the framers. August O. Spain, for example, credits Calhoun—whose favorite authors, he says, were Aristotle and Edmund Burke—with having "claimed for American thought the heritage of the modern western world from ancient Greece." Calhoun's and Aristotle's "broad flexible criteria of the legitimate sphere of governmental function were essentially the same," since both understood "the development of the higher qualities of men" as within that sphere.[5] Spain is referring to the passages in *A Disquisition on Government* in which Calhoun speaks of the object of government—to "perfect" as well as to "protect" and "preserve" society. To the extent that Calhoun agrees with Aristotle, one might expect to find that he disagrees with Locke. Indeed, Calhoun rejected the theory of government that would restrict its legitimate sphere to the protection of certain natural rights, understood as having their origin in a "state of nature" anterior to government. More important than who influenced Calhoun is what grounding he offered for his theory.

Calhoun does not refer explicitly to a natural end for human beings, but such an end is implied in his phrase "a full development of [man's] moral and intellectual faculties." This, after bare existence, is the end of the "social state," which "cannot exist without government. The assumption rests on universal experience. In no age or country has any community ever been found, whether enlightened or savage, without government of some description." Although he cites universal experience, Calhoun bases his theory of government not on history but on an analysis of human nature—on "that constitution of our nature, which, while it impels man to associate with his kind, renders it impossible for society to exist without government." This is

> the fact . . . that, while man is created for the social state, and is accord-
> ingly so formed as to feel what affects others, as well as what affects him-
> self, he is, at the same time, so constituted as to feel more intensely what
> affects him directly, than what affects him indirectly through others; or,
> to express it differently, he is so constituted, that his direct or individual
> affections are stronger than his sympathetic or social feelings.

Because of this fact of human nature, each individual "has a greater regard for his own safety or happiness, than for the safety or happiness of others; and, where these come in opposition, is ready to sacrifice the interest of others to his own." Government is the "controlling power" that prevents what otherwise would arise: "a state of universal discord and confusion, destructive of the social state and the ends for which it is ordained" (*Works*, 1:2-3, 4).[6]

Government does not originate in an act of the human will; it is "not permitted to depend on our volition." Government is a thing of "Divine ordination"; Calhoun's concern is with the "contrivance of man" that he calls *constitution*. His analysis of human nature leads him to the further conclusion that government, too, is problematical without a similar controlling power:

> government . . . has itself a strong tendency to disorder and abuse of its
> powers. . . . The cause is to be found in the same constitution of our
> nature which makes government indispensable. The powers which it is
> necessary for government to possess, in order to repress violence and
> preserve order, cannot execute themselves. They must be administered
> by men in whom, like others, the individual are stronger than the social
> feelings. And hence, the powers vested in them to prevent injustice and
> oppression on the part of others, will, if left unguarded, be by them con-
> verted into instruments to oppress the rest of the community.

"Constitution" is the means by which this result is prevented (*Works*, 1:7, 8).

Calhoun's concern, then, is not to distinguish among forms of government—between those based upon consent or the sharing of offices and those based upon hereditary privilege, for example—but to demonstrate that all government is defective without constitution. And constitution is emphatically something contrived by men, a product not of necessity or divinity but of human wisdom. Calhoun seems, then, to leave a wide scope for the exercise of reason in politics. This impression is misleading, however, for two reasons.

First, constitution does not have the exalted status in Calhoun's scheme that the foregoing remarks would suggest. Calhoun neatly summarizes his argument to this point: "Having its origin in the same principle of our nature, *constitution* stands to *government,* as *government* stands to *society;* and, as the end for which society is ordained, would be defeated without government, so that for which government is ordained would, in a great measure, be defeated without constitution." One might think that constitution was correspondingly a thing of greater dignity than government, and government than society. However, Calhoun affirms that just the opposite is true. He maintains that "although society and government are . . . intimately connected with and dependent on each other,—of the two society is the greater. It is first in the order of things, and in the dignity of its object; that of society being primary,—to preserve and perfect our [human] race; and that of government secondary and subordinate, to preserve and perfect society." The conclusion is unavoidable that constitution is yet further subordinate, inasmuch as its object is to preserve and perfect government (*Works,* 1:5, 7).

This strange inversion of the expected hierarchy evidently represents Calhoun's debt to Lockeanism as opposed to the Aristotelian view, notwithstanding his explicit rejection of the state-of-nature doctrine. Calhoun affirms that government with constitution is preferable to government without it, and society with government is preferable to society without it (if such a society were possible); so in Locke's account, civil or political society is preferable to the state of nature. But why? It is preferable because political society protects the freedom of prepolitical man—the freedom that derives from the state of nature. It is doubtful whether political society in Locke's view is superior in dignity to the state of nature, however superior it certainly is in other respects. Similarly, in Calhoun's theory, government, especially constitutional government, protects the interests of society, understood as distinct from and of a higher order of dignity than government.[7] Calhoun has said that each member of society "is ready to sacrifice the interests of others to his own" and that government exists to prevent him from doing so; constitutional government prevents the governors from sacrificing the interests of the governed to their own. These interests are accordingly impervious to reason as exercised through politics. They are sacrosanct. Calhoun's analysis of the problem of parties points to what may be called the classical solution—a relatively small, homogeneous community whose simple way of life offers little incentive for one portion to try to enrich itself at the expense of the rest—but there is no sign that Calhoun has given it any attention. The end of a constitution is not to equalize interests in the community but "to equalize the action of the government, in reference to the various and diversified interests of the community" (*Works*, 1:15).

The second reason that the initial impression of Calhoun's openness to reason in politics is misleading is because of his subsequent emphasis on the role of conflict and accident in the formation of constitutions. Constitutional governments, he maintains,

> have, for the most part, grown out of the struggles between conflicting interests, which, from some fortunate turn, have ended in a compromise, by which both parties have been admitted, in some one way or another, to have a separate and distinct voice in the government. Where this has not been the case, they have been the product of fortunate circumstances, acting in conjunction with some pressing danger, which forced their adoption, as the only means by which it could be avoided.

The first sort of case, in which a constitution comes to be through a struggle of conflicting interests, fits Calhoun's descriptions of the Roman and British constitutions, the two historical examples to which he devotes detailed treatments. The second case is evidently a reference to the United States Constitution.[8] Calhoun's historical research has led him to conclude, "It would seem that it has exceeded human sagacity deliberately to plan and construct constitutional governments, with a full knowledge of the principles on which they were formed; or to reduce them to practice without the pressure of some immediate and urgent necessity" (*Works*, 1:78).

Contrary to what is indicated in the first number of *The Federalist,* then, the distinctiveness of the American Constitution does not lie in the substitution of "reflection and choice" for "accident and force." According to Calhoun, its distinctiveness lies rather in the substitution of "the various natural interests, resulting from diversity of pursuits, condition, situation and character of different portions of the people" for "artificial orders or classes" such as those of Rome or Great Britain (*Works,* 1:80).

Slavery might seem to be an exception to the exclusion of artificial orders or classes from the American constitution. A consideration of slavery awaits an answer to this question: Does Calhoun's assumption of a natural end for man—an end that depends on government for its fulfillment, namely, "a full development of his moral and intellectual faculties"—provide the basis for a standard of justice that might over-come differences of interest? In view of the superiority in dignity of society over government, this standard must be compatible with the protection of interests that are impervious to the public use of man's moral and intellectual faculties.

Calhoun has characterized the end of society as "primary" and that of government as "secondary and subordinate." Government exists nevertheless to "perfect" as well as to "preserve" society, and it would seem impossible for government to fulfill this end without being in some respect more perfect than society—presumably with respect to justice. In introducing the idea of constitution, however, Calhoun seems to forget the higher purpose that he had assigned to govern-ment. He omits for a time any mention of perfecting society, writing only that government is intended "to protect and preserve society" (*Works,* 1:7–10).

Calhoun's first reference to a natural end for man was in these words: "In no other [state than the social], indeed, could he exist, and in no other,—were it possible for him to exist,—could he attain to a full development of his moral and intellectual faculties, or raise himself, in the scale of being, much above the level of the brute creation." The *or* here might indicate that Calhoun means to distinguish "a full develop-ment of [man's] moral and intellectual faculties" from the process of "rais[ing] himself, in the scale of being"—that is, progress. Alternatively, it might indicate that he means to equate moral and intellectual development with social progress. This uncertainty is resolved much later in the *Disquisition*, after Calhoun has introduced his famous doctrine of the concurrent majority as an essential feature of constitutional government. When he does come to speak again of the perfection of society, and with it of a full development of man's faculties, Calhoun reveals that in linking these he has had no definite end in mind. He has been thinking of a process that is apparently open-ended.

> If the two [majorities, numerical and concurrent] be compared, in reference to the ends for which government is ordained, the superiority of the government of the concurrent majority will not be less striking. These, as has been stated, are twofold; to protect, and to perfect society. . . .
> To perfect society, it is necessary to develop the faculties, intellectual and moral, with which man is endowed. But the main spring to their development, and, through this, to progress, improvement and civilization, with all their blessings, is the desire of individuals to better their condition.

Calhoun does not have to distinguish very strictly between the perfection of society and the perfection of the faculties with which man is endowed because he is not, after all, thinking of the perfection of individual men and women. It is sufficient for his purposes that individuals are desirous of bettering their condition; he does not require that they be desirous of bettering themselves. Calhoun reveals how the protection of interests as the end of government can be compatible with the perfection of man's faculties as the end of human life:

> For this purpose, liberty and security are indispensable. Liberty leaves each free to pursue the course he may deem best to promote his interest and happiness, as far as it may be compatible with the primary end for which government is ordained;—while security gives assurance to each, that he shall not be deprived of the fruits of his exertions to better his condition. These combined, give to this desire the strongest impulse of which it is susceptible. (*Works*, 1:51-52)

If human beings do have a natural end, in Calhoun's view, it is a collective one: the perfection of "our [human] race." The precise character of human perfection may be hidden from the present, but we know that progress toward this end results from leaving each individual as free as is consistent with the preservation of society to pursue his interest. By *moral faculties,* Calhoun means the qualities that make a community capable of self-government:

> some communities require a far greater amount of power than others to protect them against anarchy and external dangers; and, of course, the sphere of liberty in such, must be proportionally contracted. The causes calculated to enlarge the one and contract the other, are numerous and various. Some are physical. . . . Others are moral;—such as the different degrees of intelligence, patriotism, and virtue among the mass of the community, and their experience and proficiency in the art of self-government. (*Works,* 1:53-54)

Of course, a community that is moral in the highest degree will find that its interests are best served because it will be entitled to the largest liberty.

The "sphere of liberty" in any community, then, is proportionate to the degree that its members possess certain moral qualities. Calhoun admits that "it may be true, that a people may not have as much liberty as they are fairly entitled to, and are capable of enjoying" (*Works,* 1:54-55). Does "fairly entitled" imply a standard of justice to which slaves could appeal or to which others could appeal on their behalf? For Calhoun, a full development of human faculties is a matter of historical progress. The precise content of this progress must be left indefinite, but it clearly is associated with the growth of liberty. No people will be successful in governing themselves if the development of their intellectual and especially their moral faculties has not already reached a certain level. If not prematurely gained, liberty will, in turn, give a fresh impetus to further development. "The progress of a people rising from a lower to a higher point in the scale of liberty, is necessarily slow;—and by attempting to precipitate, we either retard, or permanently defeat it" (*Works,* 1:56). Presumably it cannot be known in advance, however, how much liberty a people is "fairly entitled to" and "capable of enjoying." What then of a people or portion of a people prevented from rising to a higher point in the scale of liberty? On the basis of his own assumptions, Calhoun would have to agree that to deny them the possibility of a fuller development of their human faculties was naturally unjust.

In his "Speech on the Reception of Abolition Petitions" (February 6, 1837), Calhoun is recorded as having said,

> Never before has the black race of Central Africa, from the dawn of history to the present day, attained a condition so civilized and so improved, not only physically, but morally and intellectually. It came among us in a low, degraded, and savage condition, and in the course of a few generations it has grown up under the fostering care of our institutions, as reviled as they have been, to its present comparatively civilized condition. (*Works*, 2:630)[9]

Calhoun's assertion of blacks' moral and intellectual improvement under slavery implies that he thought they would one day be fit for freedom and hence entitled to claim it. According to Guy Story Brown, Calhoun's principles justify slavery only as a temporary necessity, since "Calhoun never rested his position on slavery on the 'natural' or 'innate' or 'abstract' inferiority of black Africans."[10] But it would not have been in the slaveholders' interest to grant their slaves freedom, whether they were entitled to it or not. The question of fitness is irrelevant unless government has the authority to apply a standard of justice that is superior to considerations of interest. For one portion of a community will deny liberty to another if, as is likely, they find it in their interest to do so and are not prevented from doing so by government. Still, the end that Calhoun has assigned to constitution is to prevent those who administer the government from converting their powers "into instruments to oppress the rest of the community"—to prevent the perversion, by the operation of laws, of government powers "into instruments to aggrandize and enrich one or more interests by oppressing and impoverishing the others" (*Works*, 1:7, 15). Slavery was, of course, an institution protected by laws. Calhoun's analysis suggests that those laws must over time become increasingly oppressive. Was there no constitutional remedy for it?

The end of constitution cannot be secured "by instituting a higher power to control the government, and those who administer it. This would be but to change the seat of authority, and to make this higher power, in reality, the government; with the same tendency, on the part of those who might control its powers, to pervert them into instruments of aggrandizement" (*Works*, 1:8-9). The only remedy lies in "such an organism [that is, "interior structure" of government] as will furnish the ruled with the means of resisting successfully this tendency on the part of the rulers to oppression and abuse." Calhoun adds that it must be such an organism "as will furnish the means by which resistance may be systematically and peaceably made" (*Works*, 1:12). But Calhoun makes it clear that the *establishment* of constitutional governments is by no means systematic or peaceful—or indeed just, except insofar as claims about justice are backed by force.

As has been noted, constitutional governments, according to Calhoun, "have, for the most part, grown out of the struggles between conflicting interests, which, from some fortunate turn, have ended in a compromise, by which both parties have been admitted, in some one way or another, to have a separate and distinct voice in the government" (*Works*, 1:78). The Roman constitution, one of Calhoun's two principal historical examples, came into being when the plebeians rose up in mutiny against the patricians and "refused to continue any longer in service." The tale of injustice done to an old soldier had "roused the indignation of the plebeians to the utmost pitch." But the patricians, in coming to terms with the plebeians, were not moved by the soldier's tale or by any considerations of justice whatever—for they were the very ones who, until that moment, had freely "plundered and oppressed" the plebeians (*Works*, 1:93-94). The plebeians forced the patricians to grant them a voice in the government—this was hardly an example that Calhoun would have wanted the slaves to follow.

It is true that Calhoun has mentioned another path to the adoption of constitutional governments: where they have not grown out of the struggles between conflicting interests, such governments "have been the product of fortunate circumstances, acting in conjunction with some pressing danger, which forced their adoption, as the only means by which it could be avoided." Would the mere danger of a slave insurrection, however pressing, have been sufficient, even in fortunate circumstances, to have produced a fundamental reform in the southern system of labor, elevating the status of the slaves and giving them a voice in the government? It is doubtful whether such an outcome, assuming that it was possible, could be distinguished from the alternative—settlement of an actual insurrection—on any moral grounds, since the effective principle in both cases is force. A reference to Lincoln may not be out of place here. In his 1860 Cooper Institute address, Lincoln responded to the southern charge that "we [Republicans] stir up insurrections among your slaves." Occasional killings of masters or overseers, or even "local revolts extending to a score or so," would, Lincoln said, "continue to occur as the natural results of slavery; but no general insurrection of slaves, as I think, can happen in this country for a long time."[11] Far from serving as the impetus behind Republican opposition to slavery, the possibility of such an insurrection was admitted to be grounds for a legitimate objection to Republicanism.

Calhoun offers a theoretical defense of minorities, but it would be misleading to call him a defender of minority rights. The decisive point, as Harry V. Jaffa has expressed it, is what "entitles a minority to consideration." For Calhoun, a minority is entitled to consideration if it can "compel" consideration; that is, if "the cost of excluding it" to those in a position to give or withhold consideration "is greater than the cost of including it."[12] The rights of minorities rest on no foundation but their determination to assert them.

Calhoun would substitute interest—what each community is inclined to view as justice to itself—for natural justice. This proposal represents an attempt to get around the question stated at the beginning of this chapter—whether denying liberty to some does not endanger liberty for all. Carl L. Becker remarks, "Calhoun identified natural law with the positive law of particular states, the state of nature with the state of political society as history actually gave it rather than as it might be rationally conceived and reconstructed."[13] The argument in the *Disquisition* reveals the limits as to what might be done in the way of political reform along Calhounian lines.

It is tempting to assume that the answer to the slavery question lay simply in extending democracy or democratic liberty. In one sense this is a truism: slaves could not be governed democratically without ceasing to be slaves. In another sense, however, it would be more accurate to say that the problem in the South was an excess of democracy, or rather of democracy of a certain sort. Consider William Peterfield Trent's description of the course taken with regard to slavery by the politicians of the antebellum South, led by Calhoun. According to Trent, instead of telling the planter what they knew or ought to have known to be true, "They told him that slavery was morally justifiable. . . . They told him that slavery was economically and socially a blessing. They told him that the nation which Washington had founded and called a nation was in reality a league of states, from which it would soon be proper to withdraw. They told him, finally, that he was the happiest, the richest, the bravest, the most intelligent man alive." The paradox is that the planter was betrayed by an excessive deference. Calhoun and his followers failed to heed the principle laid down by Burke in his "Speech to the Electors of Bristol": "Your representative owes you, not his industry only, but his judgment; and he betrays, instead of serving you, if he sacrifices it to your opinion."[14]

Trent's criticism of southern politicians is not to be understood as implying that a solution to the slavery problem was easy. Indeed, "it would have needed a statesman with the genius and character of Washington to have seen clearly the South's duty in 1830, and forced her into the right path." If it seems an overstatement to assert that genius was required to discern what the people of the South had to do, it surely would have required character to make them do it; and character in this sense is not a conspicuous virtue of democratic politicians. Of course, Trent does not mean "forced" in a despotic sense, which would have been anathema to Washington, as it was to Calhoun.[15]

It was a fortunate circumstance that Britain's own slavery question did not fully test Burke's principle of representation. It did not do so for the simple reason that the colonies were not represented in Parliament. Tocqueville makes it clear why slavery presented so intractable a problem in the United States—so much more so than in the British West Indian colonies, where slavery was abolished in 1833: "If the English of the West Indies had governed themselves, one can be sure that they would not have accorded the act of emancipation that the mother country has just imposed." Ralph Lerner comments on Tocqueville's remark, "It was precisely because the imperial authorities at home have no great stake in the institution that they can afford to act on larger principles of justice and the national interest and impose a solution."

Slavery in the colonies could be abolished without creating a precedent dangerous to the liberties of Britons at home. While the Parliament in London was bound to take the views of the planters into consideration, it had every right to impose emancipation—it did not have to seek a political resolution to the question of slavery in the colonies.[16]

Calhoun was correct, of course, in maintaining that the states stood in a fundamentally different relation to the government in Washington than the British colonies did to Parliament. In *A Discourse on the Constitution and Government of the United States,* he expressed a fear that the southern states might "sink down from independent and equal sovereignties, into a dependent and colonial condition." Furthermore, they might do so "under circumstances that would revolutionize them *internally,* and put their very existence, as a people, at stake" (*Works,* 1:380). In his interpretation of the Constitution, however, Calhoun goes beyond ruling out an imperial solution to the slavery problem; he effectually rules out a political solution. His rejection of the principle of enlightened representation is consistent with his rejection of the view that the American Congress was a genuine national legislature like the British Parliament. From the national point of view, *congress,* with its diplomatic associations, was an unfortunate choice of name for the body established by the Constitution of 1787. According to Burke, "Parliament is not a *congress* of ambassadors from different and hostile interests; which interests each must maintain, as an agent and advocate, against other agents and advocates; but parliament is a *deliberative* assembly of *one* nation, with *one* interest, that of the whole."[17]

In the *Discourse,* Calhoun presents an elaborate argument on legal-historical grounds for the sovereignty of the states that compose the American Union and, consequently, for the superior authority of state governments over the government of the whole. Nevertheless, by offering a theoretical argument as well, he concedes that the historical argument does not settle the question. The government of the United States "is the government of States united in political union, in contradistinction to a government of individuals socially united" (*Works,* 1:113), as is each of the state governments. Insofar as society is superior in dignity to government, as Calhoun has said in the *Disquisition,* the states are superior to the Union. More practically,

> As to all other purposes [than those which "appertain to the States in their relations with each other, or in their relations with the rest of the world"], the separate governments of the several States were far more competent and safe, than the general government of all the States. Their knowledge of the local interests and domestic institutions of these respectively, must be much more accurate, and the responsibility of each to their respective people much more perfect. (*Works*, 1:215)

The general government was created by the states, according to Calhoun, to do those things that the states could not do, or could not do as well, by themselves. It should do them, however, as nearly as possible in the manner that the states would, if they were able.

The closeness of the state governments to their respective peoples protected against one possible source of injustice, but it did so at the price of vulnerability to another source, as Tocqueville's remark on West Indies emancipation makes clear. On one hand, it is less likely that the state governments will betray the interests of their people, whether through ignorance or deceit. On the other hand, it is less likely that these governments "can afford to act on larger principles of justice and the national interest." The British Parliament had imposed a solution over the heads of the West Indies planters. The question for American statesmen was whether a whole people could "put itself in a way above itself."

> It happens that a man places himself outside the prejudices of religion, country, race—and if this man is a king, he can work surprising revolutions in society: a whole people cannot thus put itself in a way above itself.
>
> A despot coming to intermingle the Americans and their former slaves under the same yoke would perhaps succeed in mixing them: as long as American democracy remains at the head of affairs, no one will dare to attempt such an undertaking.

This is not an endorsement of despotism: elsewhere Tocqueville wrote that the words *despotism* and *benefit* "could never be found united in my thought." And there is another statement by Tocqueville that mitigates the bleakness of his assessment of the slavery problem in the United States. What he suggests in the passage quoted above is impossible for a

whole people to do, is very nearly what he describes the American people as having actually done at the conclusion of the Revolution. When
Americans adopted their constitution, they elevated themselves, if not
above themselves, at least above their "habitual level."

> When great perils threaten the state, one often sees the people fortu-
> nately choose the most appropriate citizens to save it.
> It has been remarked that when danger presses, man rarely remains at
> his habitual level; he elevates himself well above or falls below. So does it
> happen to peoples themselves. . . . I said above that in America statesmen
> of our day seem very inferior to those who appeared at the head of affairs
> fifty years ago. This is due not only to the laws, but to circumstances.[18]

It was to these circumstances that Tocqueville attributed the superiority not only of statesmen like Washington but also of the federal constitution that they brought into being. By the constitutions of the states,
"the members of the legislative body are bound constantly and in the
narrowest manner to the least desires of their constituents." In contrast,
"The legislators of the Union thought that this extreme dependence of
the legislature denatured the principal effects of the representative system by placing in the people themselves not only the origin of powers,
but also the government."[19]

The legislators of the federal government were able, then, to apply a
less narrow and more statesmanlike understanding of their responsibility to their constituents than were their counterparts in the states.
The nearest American analogy with the British West Indian colonies
was not the states, however, but the federal territories. In one respect,
the situation in the territories was more favorable to freedom than the
situation in the British colonies: it was a question not of abolishing
slavery in the territories but merely of preventing its introduction. This
was a question for the whole nation—not an occasion for invoking a
higher law, as William H. Seward seemed to call for, but for consulting
the principles that the nation regarded as peculiarly its own. Lincoln
expressed it this way: "I insist, that if there is ANY THING which it is the
duty of the WHOLE PEOPLE to never entrust to any hands but their own,
that thing is the preservation and perpetuity, of their own liberties, and
institutions."[20]

Many years later, Lincoln would note that one difficulty in arguing the slavery question with men of avowedly liberal principles lay in the fact that "the world has never had a good definition of the word liberty."[21] An even greater difficulty lay in defining what men might do when their liberty seemed to be threatened by other men—as Calhoun asserted the liberty and even the existence of the southern people would be threatened by extending liberty to their slaves. The argument from self-preservation complicated the question of the disposition of slavery in the states where it was already established. Through the 1850s Lincoln referred the question of slavery in the states to a certain "necessity."[22] He made it clear, however, that the argument of necessity could not be invoked to justify slavery as a permanent institution, and, of course, it had no application whatever in the case of the territories. In Lincoln's judgment, Calhoun was to be faulted not for invoking the rule of necessity in reference to the existing institution of slavery but for going beyond that rule to invoke the standard of right.

Calhoun rejected the state-of-nature doctrine in its historical or anthropological sense, that is, as the state in which human beings existed before government and to escape the danger that existed before governments were established. However, he preserves the doctrine (though not the name) in what is arguably a far more important sense: the dangerous state in which the subjects of an absolute ruler stand, relative to that ruler. Calhoun's science of government abets a tendency among men of liberal or Lockean principles, in the words of Herbert J. Storing, "for justice to be reduced to self-preservation, for self-preservation to be defined as self-interest, and for self-interest to be defined as what is convenient and achievable."[23] Storing does not say that these men define justice expressly in such terms. But Locke's teaching discourages self-examination; it focuses attention on possible sources of injustice that lie without rather than within society.

The *Discourse* reveals how far this tendency has insinuated itself into Calhoun's interpretation of the Constitution. The implied powers that Congress may exercise under the "necessary and proper" clause in Article I, section 8 of the Constitution are, according to Calhoun, subject to two rules. First, "they must be so carried into execution as not to injure others"—that is, other powers, such as those the states reserve to themselves; and second, in cases of conflict, "the less important should yield to the more important—the convenient to the useful; and both to health and safety—because it is *proper they should do so*" (*Works,* 1:254-55). These strictures would be unobjectionable if Calhoun presented them as marking off cases of necessity, when justice must yield to considerations of a lower but more urgent nature. But his use of the word *important,* as well as his description of these rules as resting "on the fundamental principles of morals," encourages the suspicion that for him "health and safety," or *collective* self-preservation, are not considerations of a lower order of dignity; they are the foundation of justice itself.[24]

Storing makes his point in reference to slaveholders, but a similar tendency might be noted among northerners whose interest lay in limiting slavery. To them Lincoln could say, "we have an interest in the maintenance of the principles of the Government, and without this interest, it is worth nothing"; but he did not pretend that interest itself could be one of those principles. The difficulties of defining the proper scope of interest and justice must be great in any popular government; they are compounded beyond hope of remedy by Calhoun's assigning to interest a quasi-moral status in his science of government. Certainly Calhoun could not have written the tribute that Lincoln addressed in 1858 to "Our German Fellow-Citizens": "Ever true to *Liberty,* the *Union,* and the Constitution—true to Liberty, not *selfishly,* but upon *principle*—not for special *classes* of men, but for *all* men; true to the Union and the Constitution, as the best means to advance that liberty."[25]

Chapter 5

George Fitzhugh

The Turn to History

George Fitzhugh's antireform writings circulated widely in the 1850s, reaching even the northwestern state of Illinois. They were read with interest by a Springfield lawyer who in later years would preside over the greatest reform in American history since the adoption of the Constitution. Fitzhugh's reputation did not survive the downfall of the society that he had taken up his pen to defend. However, the obscurity into which events have cast him is not necessarily deserved. One sign of Fitzhugh's breadth is the fact that no more than a small fraction of the chapter headings in either of his books, *Sociology of the South* and *Cannibals All!* make reference to slavery. The success or failure of a form of society presents a bigger and more enduring question than the fate of one institution. Lincoln acknowledged that Fitzhugh's doctrine of the failure of free society was not without some justification: to save it Lincoln called on "every one who really believes, and is resolved, that free society is not, *and shall not be,* a failure."[1]

Lincoln and Fitzhugh differed in their judgments about the prospects for free society, and they differed accordingly in their views of the wisest course to follow in the crisis that had come upon the American people. The difference in the character of their judgments had consequences for the firmness with which their views were maintained. In the period between Lincoln's election and the outbreak of war, there was intense pressure put on Republican leaders to support a compromise on the issue of slavery in the territories, in the hope of averting disunion. With the firing on Fort Sumter, northern sentiment quickly turned against measures perceived as conciliatory toward the South, and, by summer's end, many northerners were even prepared to support a policy of forcible emancipation. In view of the pressures to which Lincoln was exposed, it might seem that Fitzhugh's private station would be more favorable to a cool appraisal of the alternatives; but Fitzhugh felt obliged to endorse every new historical dispensation, even at the expense of his own consistency.

Fitzhugh shared Lincoln's disdain for the complacent doctrine that "all men are created equal, except negroes"—or, to use Fitzhugh's own words, for the view of slavery as an "exceptional" institution that did not threaten Americans' "long-cherished political axioms" (*CA*, 7). In Lincoln's view, Americans' acquiescence in Negro slavery meant a retrogression in political principles that was dangerous to the freedom of whites as well as blacks. But Fitzhugh argued that it was the freedom of the whites in accordance with these axioms, not the enslavement of the blacks in defiance of them, that was really exceptional. From a broad historical perspective, this was undoubtedly true. Was free society, this "something new under the sun" (*SS*, 8), an unqualified success? The abolitionists evidently did not think so; their efforts at reform typically went beyond the abolition of slavery to embrace such causes as temperance—prohibition of liquor in the service of moral freedom—and woman's rights. This was true of both Garrison and Frederick Douglass, for example. If free society in the northern United States and western Europe was agreed to be, in some measure, a failure, then two paths were open: to push ahead with the reforms advocated by the abolitionists and their allies, or to readopt the "normal and natural" institution of slavery. The difficulty with these reforms was that they seemed to promise a cure for the ills of free society in even greater freedom.[2]

Fitzhugh perceived that for Calhoun slavery was still an exceptional institution. He mentions the South Carolinian infrequently in his work and usually not in terms of praise. In *Sociology for the South*, Calhoun is portrayed as the archdefender of free trade (*SS*, 73). Fitzhugh saw the contradiction in what Lincoln's secretary John G. Nicolay would characterize, many years later, as the southern dream of "an unholy league between perpetual bondage and free trade." In the same work, Fitzhugh includes a disparaging reference to the "abstract doctrines of nullification and secession" (*SS*, 188); and in an 1860 essay entitled "Small Nations," he contrasts his own theory of "State nationality" with the state sovereignty of the "Calhoun school."[3] Fitzhugh's work may be read as a protest against Calhoun's reliance on interest—as an effort to recover the moral high ground. Nevertheless, the result was in considerable measure the same. Friedrich Nietzsche's criticism of "the mighty historical orientation of the age" applies as much to Fitzhugh's work as it does to Calhoun's: "admiration for the 'power of history' . . . turns into naked admiration for success and leads to the idolatry of the factual."[4]

In *Cannibals All!* Fitzhugh forthrightly pointed out the error into which other defenders of slavery had fallen.

> Until the lands of America are appropriated by a few, population becomes dense, competition among laborers active, employment uncertain, and wages low, the personal liberty of all the whites will continue to be a blessing. . . . But the negro has neither energy nor enterprise, and, even in our sparser population, finds, with his improvident habits, that his liberty is a curse to himself, and a greater curse to the society around him. These considerations, and others equally obvious, have induced the South to attempt to defend negro slavery as an exceptional institution, admitting, nay asserting, that slavery, in the general or in the abstract, is morally wrong, and against common right. With singular inconsistency, after making this admission, which admits away the authority of the Bible, of profane history, and of the almost universal practice of mankind—they turn round and attempt to bolster up the cause of negro slavery by these very exploded authorities. (*CA*, 199)

This passage expands upon a remark in *Sociology for the South:* "Ham, a son of Noah, was condemned to slavery and his posterity after him. We do not adopt the theory that he was the ancestor of the negro race. The Jewish slaves were not negroes, and to confine the justification of slavery to that race would be to weaken its scriptural authority, and to lose the whole weight of profane authority, for we read of no negro slavery in ancient times" (*SS*, 98).[5] Fitzhugh concluded the passage from

Cannibals All! "If we mean not to repudiate all divine, and almost all human authority in favor of slavery, we must vindicate that institution in the abstract."

Although Fitzhugh could say, "We deem this peculiar question of negro slavery of very little importance" (*SS*, 93), he could not avoid saying something in favor of the South's peculiar form of slavery. Granting for the sake of argument that his vindication of slavery in the abstract is adequate, one might still ask: why this form of slavery and not another? Fitzhugh has little to say that does not put him in the same position as those whose "singular inconsistency" he arraigns. He admits that "as a general and abstract question, negro slavery has no other claims over other forms of slavery, except that from inferiority, or rather peculiarity, of race, almost all negroes require masters, whilst only the children, the women, the very weak, poor, and ignorant, &c., among the whites, need some protective and governing relation of this kind" (*CA*, 201). The condition of slavery offered few incentives to enterprise and forethought on the slaves' part, so a fair trial of their abilities would have been impossible under conditions prevailing in the South; nevertheless, Fitzhugh is not concerned with distinguishing between natural abilities and habits acquired in slavery. His chapter entitled "Negro Slavery" in *Sociology for the South* concludes simply, "We need never have white slaves in the South, because we have black ones" (*SS*, 93).

It might seem that Fitzhugh failed to take his own premises seriously—if it is possible to vindicate slavery in the abstract, it should be possible to show that a particular form of slavery is best of all. Of course, that best form might bear little resemblance to the form of slavery actually existing in the South. Fitzhugh's apparent indifference to the possibility of a reformed southern society is, however, consistent with the authorities that he cites in *Cannibals All!* Setting aside the Bible, which was subject to conflicting interpretations, one is left with "profane history" and "the almost universal practice of mankind." In Fitzhugh's view, the success of slave society is proved by the fact that slavery in one form or another has been almost universal; it was a short step from here to the conclusion that slavery is natural. To Fitzhugh, "it seems that 'first causes,' 'fundamental principles,' and the 'higher law' mean one and the same thing: an *ignis fatuus* that it is dangerous to pursue, and hopeless to overtake" (*CA*, 134). His rejection of such standards of right made it difficult for him to distinguish between a necessity to which human beings must submit and a genuine good. If the "little experiment of universal liberty that has been tried for a little while in a little corner of Europe" (*SS*, 70-71) had indeed failed, and was showing signs of failure even in America, Fitzhugh's historical orientation practically ruled out the search for an alternative that might preserve some of its benefits; he admitted that a governmental policy based on free competition "would stimulate energy, excite invention and industry, and bring into livelier action, genius, skill and talent" (*SS*, 11–12).

From Fitzhugh's vantage point in slave society, he claimed to view with equanimity the growth of "the multitudinous Isms of the North" that revealed the "state of public opinion, or, to speak more accurately, the absence of any public opinion, or common faith and conviction about anything" in that section (*CA*, 9). But it is clear that the South could not altogether escape the consequences of the failure of free society. The southern public, too, had had to face Fitzhugh's assault on its "long-cherished political axioms," since those axioms were the same as the North's. Many southern and northern states still lived under Revolutionary-era constitutions, and, of course, those states were joined by the Constitution of 1787. Fitzhugh admitted the errors of the would-be "legislating philosophers" who framed these laws, but he denied the necessity of radical changes in the institutions they were credited with having set up. He was compelled to draw a distinction between what these legislators did and what they evidently thought they were doing.

> Our Revolution . . . was the mere assertion by adults of the rights of adults, and had nothing more to do with philosophy than the weaning of a calf. . . .
>
> But the philosophers seized upon it . . . and made it the unwilling and unnatural parent of the largest brood of ills that had ever appeared at one birth since the opening of the box of Pandora. Bills of Rights, Acts of Religious Freedom, and Constitutions, besprinkled with doctrines directly at war with all stable government, seem to be the basis on which our institutions rest. But only seem to be; for, in truth, our laws and government are either old Anglo-Saxon prescriptive arrangements, or else the gradual accretions of time, circumstance, and necessity. (*CA*, 133)

Constitutions, in fact, are not made but "discovered," Fitzhugh claimed, and consequently the framers' task was no more than to modify the institutions taken over from their English ancestors. "When society has worked long enough, under the hand of God and nature, man observing its operations, may discover its laws and constitution. The common law of England and the constitution of England, were discoveries of this kind. Fortunately for us, we adopted, with little change, that common law and that constitution. Our institutions and ancestry were English. Those institutions were the growth and accretions of many ages, not the work of legislating philosophers" (SS, 176).

As for the principles of the Declaration of Independence, Fitzhugh conceded to them a certain validity so far as they had served a useful purpose at a particular historical moment, but no further:

> Those axioms have outlived their day. . . . All men begin very clearly to perceive that the state of revolution is politically and socially abnormal and exceptional, and that the principles that would justify it are true in the particular, false in the general. . . . When, in time of revolution, society is partially disbanded, disintegrated, and dissolved, the doctrine of Human Equality may have a hearing, and may be useful in stimulating rebellion; but it is practically impossible, and directly conflicts with all government, all separate property, and all social existence. (CA, 7-8)

Fitzhugh had Jefferson and his contemporaries in mind when he said, in the same paragraph, that "the wisest and best of men are sure to deduce, as general principles, what is only true as to themselves and their peculiar circumstances." For all his conservatism, then, Fitzhugh could not avoid claiming to understand the framers and other founders better than they understood themselves. Lincoln ascribed, and claimed the founders' warrant for ascribing, a superior dignity to the principles of the Declaration of Independence over the provisions of the Constitution: "The *picture* was made *for* the apple—*not* the apple for the picture."[6] For Fitzhugh, the hierarchy is reversed. The Constitution, or rather the unwritten "discovered" constitution that it imperfectly reflects, acquires dignity by virtue of its deep historical roots, while the principles of the Declaration are mistaken generalizations from the circumstances of a moment.

The most striking sign of Fitzhugh's historical orientation, however, is that while he says slavery is "natural, normal, and necessary" (*CA*, 199, for example), he does not say that it is just. At best, slave society is just in the negative sense of minimizing "unjust exaction" from its laborers (*CA*, 35). In a more exalted sense, free society is more just. Its higher classes are the victors in the war of wits that such society engenders, while their counterparts in slave society form a "privileged class."

> Our citizens, like those of Rome and Athens, are a privileged class. We should train and educate them to deserve the privileges and to perform the duties which society confers on them. Instead of, by a low demagoguism, depressing their self-respect by discourses on the equality of man, we had better excite their pride by reminding them that they do not fulfil the menial offices which white men do in other countries. (*SS*, 93)

To say that southern whites should be trained and educated to deserve their privileges is to admit that they are not naturally deserving of them. The matter is not so simple, however, since southern society is presented by Fitzhugh as an example of "that natural and historical society, which has usually existed in the world, with its gradations of rank and power, its families, and its slaves" (*CA*, 72). Fitzhugh maintains that it is natural for societies to confer privileges and duties unequally upon their respective classes because this is how societies have developed historically. Government cannot say otherwise because government "is the creature of society," and society "does not owe its sovereign power to the separate consent, volition or agreement of its members. Like the hive, it is as much the work of nature as the individuals who compose it" (*SS*, 26).

Human societies are, of course, not supplied ready-made by nature, for otherwise Fitzhugh's defense of slavery would be pointless. The North could reinstitute slavery; the South could abolish it and establish a new kind of society. If "man struggles in vain against nature" (*SS*, 71), one might still raise a doubt as to whether it is possible to know in advance that a proposed reform is against nature and hence in vain; for Fitzhugh did not deny that certain historical reforms had been beneficial. Indeed, since he rejects "first causes," "fundamental principles," and the "higher law," he can hardly fail to affirm that "frequent reforms are

required . . . to adapt [institutions] to the gradually changing circumstances of mankind" (SS, 208). The American Revolution is an example
of such a reform—Fitzhugh denies that it was a revolution in the strict
sense. "Total changes, which revolutions propose, are never wise or
practicable, because most of the institutions of every country are
adapted to the manners, morals, and sentiments of the people. Indeed,
the people have been moulded in character by those institutions, and
they cannot be torn asunder and others substituted, for none others will
fit. . . . Our separation from England was a great and salutary reform,
not a revolution" (SS, 208-9).

Fitzhugh is obliged to reconcile the assertion that human society is a
work of nature like the hive with the fact that such societies change over
time, not only "gradually" but sometimes with dramatic suddenness. In
speaking of the Reformation—another great and mostly salutary
reform, in Fitzhugh's view—he could just as well have been speaking of
the American Revolution:

> The Reformation was but an effort of Nature—the *vis medicatrix
> naturæ* [healing power of nature]—throwing off what was false, vicious,
> or superfluous, and retaining what was good.
>
> The great men of the day but show larger portions of the common
> thought. Men, and all other social and gregarious animals, have a com-
> munity of thought, of motions, instincts, and intuitions. The social body
> is of itself a thinking, acting, sentient being. This is eminently observable
> with the lower animals. Bees and herds perform their evolutions with too
> much rapidity and precision to leave any doubt but that one mind and
> one feeling, either from within or without, directs their movements. (*CA*,
> 132)

In the same chapter, Fitzhugh praises the ancient lawgivers Moses,
Lycurgus, Solon, and Numa, who "built their institutions to last,
enjoined it on the people never to change them, and threw around them
the sanctity of religion to ward off the sacrilegious hand of future inno-
vation" (*CA*, 134). What connects these cases of extreme aversion to
change with the extreme openness to change that Fitzhugh recom-
mends in the preceding paragraph in *Cannibals All!*—where he writes
that "all legislation should be repealable," including "platforms, resolu-

tions, bills of rights, and constitutions"—is the reliance on discretionary authority.

When Fitzhugh maintains, "More of despotic discretion, and less of Law, is what the world wants," he is identifying law with moral suasion, which he rejects (*CA*, 248). But when he observes elsewhere in the book, "Man . . . is a social and gregarious animal . . . like all animals of that kind . . . by nature, law-making and law-abiding" (*CA*, 101), he is identifying law, that is unwritten law, with necessity. "Throw our paper platforms, preambles and resolutions, guaranties and constitutions, into the fire, and we [Americans] should be none the worse off, provided we retained our institutions—and the necessities that begot, and have, so far, continued them" (*CA*, 133). But Fitzhugh is unable to reconcile his sociological view of law with the political judgment that he praises in men such as Washington, the "wise, good, and practical men" by whom the American Revolution was "originated and conducted to successful issue" (*CA*, 130).

Fitzhugh's historical orientation has the effect of interposing a barrier between himself and the men of the Revolutionary era, making impossible a return to their principles as they understood them. Fitzhugh admits that the reforming legislators of the Revolutionary era viewed themselves as establishing new institutions of government, on the basis of universally valid principles—they did not view themselves as expressing a "common thought" bearing no necessary relation to justice. They might have been ignorant of their own motives, but it seems doubtful that the Revolutionaries could have done as they did if they had shared Fitzhugh's historical orientation. Such would-be reformers are likely to have waited, perhaps forever, for the historical winds to shift, instead of boldly staking their lives, fortunes, and sacred honor on the success of a difficult and uncertain enterprise. Lincoln refers to this problem in his speech in Independence Hall and offers his own conclusion:

> I have often pondered over the dangers which were incurred by the men who assembled here and adopted that Declaration of Independence—I have pondered over the toils that were endured by the officers and soldiers of the army, who achieved that Independence. I have often inquired of myself what great principle or idea it was that kept this Confederacy so long together. It was not the mere matter of the separation of the

colonies from the mother land; but something in that Declaration giving liberty, not alone to the people of this country, but hope to the world for all future time.[7]

Fitzhugh shared Lincoln's desire to save the country. In *Cannibals All!* he warns that the abolitionists, in their mistaken philanthropy, "will probably succeed in dissolving the Union, [and] in involving us in civil and fratricidal war" (*CA*, 232). Garrison and his followers, not Fitzhugh, "propose disunion" (*CA*, 95). But to Lincoln's question to his audience in Independence Hall, "Now, my friends, can this country be saved upon that basis?"—upon the basis of a "principle or idea" of timeless validity—Fitzhugh must have answered no. The suggestion of a universal principle similar to Lincoln's in Fitzhugh's assertion that "slavery will every where be abolished, or every where be re-instituted" proves to have been deceptive.

It would be unfair to Fitzhugh, by the terms of his historical orientation, to say that he had failed to draw the correct conclusion from his study of English statesmen, who "have for centuries past anticipated and prevented revolutions, by granting timely reforms" (*SS*, 208-9). As long as the "common thought" in the South remained one of defiance, it must be judged an idle question whether timely reforms could have prevented what Fitzhugh would come to call the "Revolution of '61."

Fitzhugh's substitution of historical rights for natural rights was milder than Calhoun's substitution of interest for justice—milder in spirit if not in effect. Fitzhugh found it impossible to maintain his moderate stance in the rising tide of prosecession feeling in the South. Harvey Wish notes, "As a good Southerner, Fitzhugh followed the secessionists to war, although with reluctance at first. . . . He had hoped that Buchanan and the Northern conservatives would save the Union. As these hopes ebbed, his essays for De Bow began to assume an increasingly intransigent tone, in keeping with the new militant sentiments of his section." Fitzhugh's reversals of position during this period include his endorsement of a revival of the African slave trade and his conversion to the doctrine of Negro inferiority. These reversals may indicate something questionable in Fitzhugh himself, as Wish seems to have supposed; but it is just as likely that they indicate the questionableness of history as a constitutional basis. James Fitzjames Stephen's satire on the Tory school of English historians captures the futility of Fitzhugh's position: "The best institutions for a nation are those which suit it—in other words, those which it has already got, for if they did not suit it they would not be there. Theories are of no value unless they are supported by facts. Therefore, all theories which condemn existing facts go for nothing, and none are true except those which justify what exists."[8]

Fitzhugh privately acknowledged the weakness of his public stance. In an 1855 letter to George Frederick Holmes (the "Professor H." of the preface to *Cannibals All!*), Fitzhugh had written, "I assure you, Sir, I see great evils in Slavery, but in a controversial work I ought not to admit them." C. Vann Woodward calls this a "damaging admission," but other readers may find that Fitzhugh's credibility gains with the disclosure that his view of slavery was more equivocal than might appear from his published writings.[9] More interesting than the question of Fitzhugh's character is why he thought he had to write a "controversial work"— why he could not be more candid. No doubt the intellectual and political circumstances of the United States in the 1850s had much to do with why, but that does not excuse Fitzhugh. Should he not have tried to rise above the circumstances of his time? But to have him do so on the basis of history is to ask an impossibility.

Because of his tendency to identify the natural with the historical or actual, Fitzhugh found it all but impossible to make a judgment about the justice or injustice of actual social or political institutions. At best, he was able to distinguish between a form of society that is in a sense natural because it has developed out of the family and another that is in the same sense unnatural because it rests for support on a theoretical foundation: slave society and free society, respectively. Henry Maine might have had Fitzhugh in mind when he wrote in his book *Ancient Law*, "Much industry and some learning have been bestowed in the United States of America on the question whether the Slave was in the early stages of society a recognised member of the Family." Maine admits that the slave most likely was such a member, but he denies what "seems . . . to be assumed in the American arguments on the subject," namely "that, if we allow Slavery to have been a primitive Family institution, the acknowledgment is pregnant with an admission of the moral defensibility of Negro-servitude at the present moment." He is inclined to Lincoln's view of the subject rather than to Fitzhugh's: "The simple wish to use the bodily powers of another person as a means of ministering to one's own ease or pleasure is doubtless the foundation of Slavery, and as old as human nature."[10]

The possibility of denying the historical distinctiveness of American slavery gave Fitzhugh an opening to claim that his concern was with slavery "in the abstract" and to cite ancient authorities as well as modern ones in defense of the institution. Because Fitzhugh's thought was not bounded by the horizon of the American political tradition, he could counter Locke with Aristotle, without arguing that the men of the Revolutionary era were Aristotelians. Lincoln's claim that the Republicans "stick to, contend for, the identical old policy on [slavery] which was adopted by 'our fathers who framed the Government under which we live'" made it possible for him to argue that the members of his party, not the Democrats, were the true conservatives.[11] To Fitzhugh, however, it was those "fathers" who deviated, in thought and word if not necessarily in deed, from the older, sounder view, namely "the theory of Aristotle, promulged more than two thousand years ago, generally considered true for two thousand years, and destined, we hope, soon again to be accepted as the only true theory of government and society" (*CA*, 71). But Fitzhugh also presented himself as a defender of the family, and by doing so he invited the question whether Aristotle, too, was such a defender.

Fitzhugh paraphrases Aristotle's theory of government and society, contrasting it with Locke's:

> Man is naturally a social and gregarious animal, subject, not by contract or agreement, as Locke and his followers assume, but by birth and nature, to those restrictions of liberty which are expedient or necessary to secure the good of the human hive, to which he may belong. There is no such thing as *natural human* liberty, because it is unnatural for man to live alone and without the pale and government of society. Birds and beasts of prey, who are not gregarious, are naturally free. Bees and herds are naturally subjects or slaves of society. Such is the theory of Aristotle. (*CA*, 71)

Strictly speaking, however, Fitzhugh was not a student of Aristotle; he claimed to have arrived independently at the same theory. It was not until after Fitzhugh had written *Sociology for the South* that he discovered the identity between his theory and Aristotle's.

> Returning from the North [from New Haven, where Fitzhugh had been invited to lecture[12]], we procured in New York a copy of Aristotle's *Politics and Economics*. To our surprise, we found that our theory of the origin of society was identical with his, and that we had employed not only the same illustrations but the very same words. We saw at once that the true vindication of slavery must be founded on his theory of man's social nature, as opposed to Locke's theory of the Social Contract, on which latter Free Society rests for support. (*CA*, 12–13)

While Fitzhugh claims to agree with Aristotle on "the origin of society" and "man's social nature," he does not claim to agree, except in a qualified way, with Aristotle's argument that some men are fitted by nature to be masters or to be slaves. Fitzhugh does not belong with those modern commentators who "have tended to treat [the] defense [of natural slavery] as though Aristotle considered it to be an adequate defense of actual slavery as well."[13] The nearest Fitzhugh comes in *Cannibals All!* to endorsing Aristotle's theory of natural slavery is when he presents a long extract from an article in the *Edinburgh Review* in which the writer concedes that there is "a certain degree of force" in Aristotle's argument, "if it is limited to the economical relations of the two parties." Fitzhugh asserts, "We would be willing, if necessary, to rest the complete justification of negro slavery on this single extract" (*CA*, 159-60)—not the justification of slavery in the abstract. The writer for the *Edinburgh Review* has the European working classes in mind, but Fitzhugh thinks that his reasoning applies with even greater force to Negroes.

> The moral and domestic feelings of the slave are sacrificed, and his intellect is stunted; but in respect of his physical condition he may be a gainer. "It is necessary," says Aristotle, in his celebrated justification of slavery, "that those who cannot exist separately should live together. He who is capable of foreseeing by his intellect, is naturally a master; he who is able to execute with his body what another contrives, is naturally a slave: wherefore the interest of the master and slave is one." There is a certain degree of force in this argument, if it is limited to the economical

relations of the two parties. It is the interest of the master to maintain his slave in good working order. In general, therefore, he is comparatively well fed, clothed, and lodged; his physical wants are provided for; his food descends into his mouth like manna in the wilderness; he is clothed like the lilies of the field; he has no thought or care for the morrow. (*CA*, 160)

The writer goes on to contrast the condition of the freedman, who "in becoming a free moral agent . . . accepts the responsibilities of that condition; his path is open to virtue, but he is answerable for his acts and their consequences if he deviates into other ways; he can, by foresight, determine his own lot, but he must, in compensation, suffer the penalties of his own improvidence" (*CA*, 163). Accordingly, "it began to be seen that the theory of personal freedom could not be carried consistently into practical effect for the entire community. A man might, in the eye of the law, be presumed able and bound to maintain himself and his family; but want of industry, or intelligence, or providence, or the rapine of the strong, might reduce him to destitution and helplessness" (*CA*, 164).

Fitzhugh's professed willingness to rest his justification of Negro slavery, "if necessary," on the extract from the *Edinburgh Review* is somewhat misleading, since he and the writer have set out from opposite points of departure. The writer would reenslave those members of the newly emancipated European working classes who had shown themselves, by "want of industry, or intelligence, or providence," to be natural slaves. Fitzhugh would keep all the South's slaves in bondage, on the assumption that they would prove unequal to the responsibilities of their new condition if emancipated. Fitzhugh did think more blacks than whites were natural slaves in the economical sense adapted from Aristotle by the writer for the *Edinburgh Review*. Although he admits not all but "almost all negroes require masters" (*CA*, 201), he says nothing about the rest. By quoting with approval the writer for the *Edinburgh Review*, Fitzhugh appears to endorse a version of Aristotle's natural-slave argument, but his disregard of the distinction between natural and legal slavery as applicable to the slaves of the South confirms that this argument is not the deepest stratum of his defense of slavery. To apply a natural standard of fitness in the case of legal slaves would involve Fitzhugh in difficulties that his historical orientation is designed to avoid.

Fitzhugh understood Aristotle as offering a further argument in justification of slavery, based upon the naturalness of the family association and the inclusion of slaves within it. Aristotle "assumes that social life is as natural to man as to bees and herds; and that the family, including husband, wife, children, and slaves, is the first and most natural development of that social nature" (*CA*, 193). Whether Fitzhugh can thus avoid the question of the justice of slavery is another matter. Aristotle introduces the question of justice along with his account of society's origin in the family, understood as including slaves.

Fitzhugh's primary concern is one Aristotle could not have shared. Fitzhugh sought to establish the superiority of "that natural and historical society" that has its origin in the family, over both free society and the forms of society envisaged by progressive critics of free society, the "modern social reformers" whose doctrines had been winning adherents in the northern United States and in western Europe. These reformers, according to Fitzhugh, concurred in regarding free society as an irredeemable failure and in proposing socialism in one form or another in its place. The weakness of the modern socialists lay in their dependence, of which they were presumably unaware, upon "the theory of Locke" that supports free society. The socialists wanted to have it both ways: they condemned the moral effects of free society but approved the liberal measures that inevitably bring about these effects.

The socialists, then, did not offer a genuine alternative to free society. By dissolving natural society, the socialists, too, "place men in positions of equality, rivalry, and antagonism." What distinguishes the socialists from the political economists, who defended laissez-faire capitalism, is that the socialists "promise that when society is wholly disintegrated and dissolved, by inculcating good principles . . . all men will co-operate, love, and help one another." Fitzhugh's quasi-Aristotelian account of society is intended to combine the tough-minded reasoning of the political economists with the humane ends of the socialists. The humane side of slavery is represented by the writer for the *Edinburgh Review* as the exchange of freedom for security, and Fitzhugh confirms this. The political economists offered the prospect that "the eating up the weaker members of society, the killing them out by capital and competition, will improve the breed of men and benefit society" (*CA*, 215). Fitzhugh offers an alternative in the natural ties that bind families together, which are characterized by sternness as well as benevolence.

> Modern social reformers . . . proceeding upon the theory of Locke, which is the opposite of Aristotle, propose to dissolve and disintegrate society, falsely supposing that they thereby follow nature. . . . 'Tis true, after their work of destruction is finished, they see the necessity of society; but instead of that natural and historical society, which has usually existed in the world, with its gradations of rank and power, its families, and its slaves, they propose wholly to disregard the natural relations of mankind, and profanely to build up states . . . where religion shall be banished and in which property, wife and children shall be held somewhat in common. (*CA*, 71-72)

Fitzhugh counts among these reformers the Mormons, along with the followers of Fourier (including Horace Greeley) and the founders of the Oneida community in New York State. Elsewhere, Fitzhugh defines Mormonism as "Socialism—plus the overseer" (*CA*, 228). Here the overseer is revealed to be a patriarch.

> These social establishments, under a self-elected despotism like that of Joe Smith, or Brigham Young, become patriarchal, and succeed so long as such despotism lasts. That is, when the association loses the character intended by its founders, and acquires a despotic head like other family associations, it works well, because it works naturally. But this success can only be temporary; for nothing but the strong rule of a Cromwell or Joe Smith can keep a society together that wants the elements of cohesion in the natural ties that bind man to man. . . .
> 'Tis an historical fact that this family association, this patriarchal government, for purposes of defence against enemies from without, gradually merges into larger associations of men under a common government or ruler. This latter is the almost universal and, we may thence infer, natural and normal condition of civilized man. In this state of society there is no liberty for the masses. Liberty has been exchanged by nature for security. (*CA*, 72)

Fitzhugh's characterization of socialist society as one that "wants the elements of cohesion in the natural ties that bind man to man" applies with almost equal aptness to free society. The difference is the relative integrity of the family association in the latter, temporary as this success, too, may prove to be. For "the natural ties that bind man to man" do not bind men in free society in their extrafamilial relations, which have a contractual basis; and it is questionable whether the family can remain indefinitely as an exception. As Fitzhugh puts it in *Cannibals All!* in his chapter "The Family," the "horrid abuses" of the socialists are but "the approved and practiced outgrowth of free society"; as such, they afford "good proofs of the naturalness and necessity of slavery" (*CA*, 191).

Fitzhugh's account of the origin of society in the family association resembles Aristotle's in the *Politics*, but a closer comparison reveals its incompleteness. Aristotle distinguishes three societies in order of time: the family, the village, and the *polis*. In Aristotle's account, the village is an extension of the family, but the polis is different in kind from the family and the village.[14] Fitzhugh refers to the "historical fact" that the family association "gradually merges into larger associations of men." What is missing from his account is a description of the difference, except in size, between the family and these larger associations.

Fitzhugh maintains that "Aristotle understood this subject [of the family] thoroughly; and it seems to have been generally so well comprehended in his day, that he takes little trouble to explain and expound it" (*CA*, 193). In saying so, Fitzhugh is implying that his contemporaries do stand in need of having the subject explained and expounded to them, presumably because of the changes brought about through the influence of Locke and his followers. According to Alexis de Tocqueville, these changes have tended above all toward lessening the authority of the father and of the eldest son as his heir. The permanent inequality between parent and offspring, and between the firstborn son and his younger siblings, has tended to be de-emphasized in favor of the temporary inequality between adult and child; and the difference between male and female members of the family has tended to be understood as a difference in role rather than in rank.[15]

Tocqueville and Fitzhugh agree that the older "aristocratic" or "patriarchal" family is characterized by the rank-ordering of its members as well as by ties of kinship. What is most characteristic of the family as opposed to the political association is that its gradations of rank are marked by unmistakable natural differences. There is at least a semblance of justice in this, which militates against the impression that these gradations are simply conventional; although of course there is no necessity that they accurately reflect degrees of fitness to rule. If the rank-ordering of family members contributes to harmony, as Fitzhugh asserts, it does so by discouraging reliance on those natural marks of rulership, such as capacity for foresight, that Aristotle cites in his natural-slave argument. Tocqueville says that an American woman submits to her husband's authority self-consciously, in a manly spirit as it were, for the sake of good domestic order. He notes this as something novel— the usual effect of the natural differences that distinguish family members has been to make this kind of self-consciousness unnecessary.

The presence of the slave in the family is anomalous, in that he or she is not bound by ties of kinship with the other members. Aristotle accounts for the slave's having come to be included in the family association by the natural-slave argument. What best shows the anomaly of the slave's status is that some justification is felt to be necessary. But in a society where slavery is a recognized institution and the authority of the master is upheld by law, considerations of natural justice are usually insufficient to counter the pressure of established custom.

Fitzhugh obscures the distinction between the conjectural origin of slavery, in which a kind of natural justice or reciprocity may have played a part, and the conventionality of the established institution. He also obscures the conventional features of traditional family life and, by doing so, the difference between family life and the life of a political community. For Fitzhugh the American states, as products of a continuous historical development, retain something of the naturalness of families; but the Union is artificial, "an attempt at a *paper consent* government." In defending the Union, Fitzhugh relied on an appeal to the "great advantages of friendly and mutual intercourse, trade and exchanges" among the states.

> Considered and treated as a league or treaty between *separate States* or *Nations,* [the Union] may yet have a long and useful existence; for then these *Nations* or *States,* seeing that she has no means of self-enforcement, self-support, or self-conservation, may, for their mutual interests, combine to sustain and defend her. Heretofore, domestic weakness and danger from foreign foes has combined the States in sustaining the Union.

Hereafter, the great advantages of friendly and mutual intercourse, trade and exchanges may continue to produce a like result. (*CA*, 248)

Fitzhugh's actions as well as his words confirm Aristotle's observation that the members of a league or alliance, which as such does not rise to the dignity of a genuine political community, are concerned with justice only in a very limited sense—namely, with preventing injustice to themselves. The bond of such unions is less a concern with justice than it is a concern with interest.[16] The advantages that Fitzhugh refers to did not prevent Virginians from abandoning their allegiance to the Union. Fitzhugh himself did not desert the Union without regret, but he did so without compunction.

Political society thus comes to light as the natural home of justice in the fullest sense. The historical prevalence of despotism in all its forms, including slavery, does not prove that political rule is not natural in the most authoritative sense. Fitzhugh knew that applying a natural standard of fitness—whether Aristotle's standard or Lincoln's—to those who are already slaves by law would put their legal status in question. Fitzhugh saves the naturalness of slavery only by losing sight of, or concealing from view, the distinction between nature and history.

Chapter 6

The Attack on Locke

Notwithstanding his implicit criticism of Locke in the *Disquisition on Government,* Calhoun shared Locke's suspicion of government, a suspicion rooted in the liberal distinction between state and society. If the framers of the Constitution were to be faulted, in Calhoun's judgment, it was for drawing the line with insufficient distinctness. The efforts of Fitzhugh, by contrast, were directed toward *diminishing* the distance between state and society. Traditional societies, he pointed out, do not regard government as something artificial, and, accordingly, they do not share liberals' concern with marking the limits of legitimate government action. Traditional societies do not feel the need to distinguish strictly between submitting to government and consenting to it.

In his Peoria speech, given the same year that *Sociology for the South* was published, Lincoln said, "no man is good enough to govern another man, *without that other's consent"*—a claim about human nature he held to be implicit in American institutions of government as well as explicit in the Declaration of Independence. In his attack on the Declaration, Fitzhugh did not focus on its assertion of human equality, because to do so would have implied that he was defending natural slavery. Fitzhugh knew better: "that natural slavery of the weak to the strong, the foolish to the wise and cunning" was what existed in the North, where "liberty and free competition invite and encourage the attempt of the strong to master the weak; and insure their success."[1] Instead, Fitzhugh reserved his strongest criticism for the next passage in the Declaration: "to secure [their] rights, governments are instituted among men . . . [and] whenever any Form of Government becomes destructive of these ends, it is the Right of the People to alter or abolish it, and to institute new Government, laying its foundation on such principles, and organizing its powers in such form, as to them shall seem most likely to effect their Safety and Happiness." Fitzhugh commented,

> Nothing can be found in all history more unphilosophical, more presumptuous, more characteristic of the infidel philosophy of the 18th century. . . . How any observant man, however unread, should have come to the conclusion, that society and government were such plastic, man-created things, that starting on certain general principles, he might frame them successfully as he pleased, we are at a loss to conceive. But infidelity is blind and foolish, and infidelity then prevailed.[2]

Fitzhugh would replace contractual relations, based on consent, with familial relations, based on submission. The former he associated with Locke, the latter with Aristotle. Yet the family is not in all respects a natural institution, and Fitzhugh's claim to Aristotle's authority cannot be accepted without qualification. With regard to Locke, Fitzhugh is on firmer ground—though not as firm as he would have us think.

A fuller treatment of the contrast between these philosophers is found in Fitzhugh's wartime essay "Revolutions of '76 and '61 Contrasted."

> Human equality, and the origination and entire construction of society and government, by man, are the distinguishing features of the would-be political philosophy of Locke. He teaches the doctrine of the social contract, or compact, and distinctly explains it to mean, that men are not by nature social animals, but originally lived, each adult, separate, to himself, independent and self-governing. That society is an institution that in process of time grew out of positive agreement or compact, and that only those who entered into this agreement were bound by it. . . . He adds, that not only originally did men become members of society by

positive agreement, but that even now, no one becomes a subject of government or member of society except by express agreement.[3]

Fitzhugh exaggerates somewhat for rhetorical effect—Locke's account of the historical origin of government is more complex than he suggests—but Fitzhugh's summary is consonant with the passage he cites from chapter 8 of Locke's *Second Treatise of Government*.

> Men being, as has been said, by Nature, all free, equal, and independent, no one can be put out of this Estate, and subjected to the Political Power of another, without his own *Consent*. The only way whereby anyone devests himself of his Natural Liberty, and *puts on the bonds of Civil Society* is by agreeing with other Men to joyn and unite into a Community, for their comfortable, safe, and peaceable living one amongst another, in a secure Enjoyment of their Properties, and a greater Security against any that are not of it.

Fitzhugh claims that this passage was "almost literally copied into the first two sentences of the Declaration of Independence." He adds that "Locke's doctrine of human equality . . . was . . . put into active force in the Chicago Platform, on which Mr. Lincoln was nominated."[4]

In the course of chapter 8, Locke introduces two objections to his view of consent as the legitimate basis of government (*Second Treatise*, §100). The first is an objection that could have been made by Fitzhugh, "*That there are no Instances to be found in Story of a Company of Men independent and equal one amongst another, that met together, and in this way began and set up a Government.*" Fitzhugh would likely have stated the objection in a form more difficult to answer: that there are *few* instances to be found in history of men that set up a government in this way, and, consequently, that these instances are to be regarded as the exception that proves the rule. For Fitzhugh, the first objection already implies what Locke states as a second objection: "'*Tis impossible of right that Men should do so, because all Men being born under Government, they are to submit to that, and are not at liberty to begin a new one.*" It is easy for Locke to supply a number of examples to meet the first objection, as he stated it; and he is quick to conclude "that Men are naturally free, and the Examples of History [show], that the *Governments* of the

World, that were begun in Peace, had their beginning laid on that foundation, and were *made by the Consent of the People*" (*Second Treatise*, §104).

But there is less to Locke's conclusion than first meets the eye. The next paragraph in the *Second Treatise* begins a passage that introduces, or rather "repeats and extends," what Peter Laslett calls the philosopher's "concessions to patriarchalism," beginning in chapter 6. In chapter 8 Locke says,

> I will not deny, that if we look back as far as History will direct us, towards the *Original of Common-wealths*, we shall generally find them under the Government and Administration of one Man. And I am also apt to believe, that where a Family was numerous enough to subsist by it self, and continued entire together, without mixing with others, as it often happens, where there is much Land and few People, the Government commonly began in the Father. (*Second Treatise*, §105)

In the earlier paragraph to which Laslett refers (*Second Treatise*, §74), Locke had made a similar concession: "'tis obvious to conceive how easie it was in the first Ages of the World, and in places still, where the thinness of People gives Families leave to separate into unpossessed Quarters, and they have room to remove and plant themselves in yet vacant Habitations, for the *Father of the Family* to become the Prince of it." According to Laslett, these concessions "represent the direct influence on Locke of Filmer and traditional attitudes"—although Fitzhugh would say they do no more than acknowledge the evidence of history.[5]

Locke's worry is that history has "given occasion to Men to mistake, and think, that by Nature Government was Monarchical, and belong'd to the Father" (*Second Treatise*, §106). Locke must somehow account for the historical prevalence of patriarchal government without discrediting his own view. He attempts to reconcile patriarchy with consent in several ways, even arguing that consent *was* given to the political power of the father, or that his rule was "elective."

When Locke first takes up the question of patriarchy and consent, he refers to "the express or tacit Consent of the Children, when they were grown up," that government should be in the father, "where it seemed without any change barely to continue" (*Second Treatise*, §74).

The problem for Locke is that if government continued in the father, it was not inaugurated by consent. Locke confirms this supposition in the next section of the *Second Treatise,* in which he speaks of "a tacit, and scarce avoidable consent" to the father's government, adding that the children "made no distinction betwixt Minority, and full Age; nor looked after one and Twenty, or any other Age, that might make them the free Disposers of themselves and Fortunes" (*Second Treatise,* §75). If the children did not distinguish between minority and full age, then they did not distinguish between the "*Freedom of a Man at years of discretion,* and the *Subjection* of a Child *to* his *Parents,* whilst yet short of that Age," which Locke had asserted earlier in the chapter, "are so consistent, and so distinguishable, that the most blinded Contenders for Monarchy, *by Right of Fatherhood,* cannot miss this *difference,* the most obstinate cannot but allow their consistency" (*Second Treatise,* §61). In the absence of such a distinction of ages, there could have been no time at which consent was required to be given, even tacitly. Accordingly, Locke speaks of an "insensible change" by which fathers became the "*politick Monarchs*" of families (*Second Treatise,* §76)— not of consent.

Having conceded this much, Locke reintroduces the criterion of consent in chapter 7, when he speaks again of the "first Ages" (*Second Treatise,* §94). Now, however, the ruler is spoken of not as a father but as "some one good and excellent Man," who, "having got a Preheminency amongst the rest, had this Deference paid to his Goodness and Vertue, as to a kind of Natural Authority, that the chief Rule, with Arbitration of their differences, by a tacit Consent devolved into his hands."

It would take us too far out of our way to follow the twists and turns of Locke's argument as he recovers the principle of consent after having all but conceded it away. He succeeds in making a plausible case for consent in the beginnings of governments in two cases: first, where the father dies without a successor of suitable age, or either the father or his successor has shown himself to be unfit to exercise authority; and second, where a number of families, or members of different families, join together and elect a common head, especially for the purpose of leading them in battle. But as to the crucial case to which these exceptions do not apply, of a family that remains intact without a break in succession, Locke blurs the distinction between consent and submission as he proceeds. This distinction disappears altogether in the conclusion of his reply to the objection that history does not support his claim that governments have their origin in consent:

> Thus we may see how probable it is, that People that were naturally free, and by their own consent either submitted to the Government of their Father, or united together, out of different Families to make a Government, should generally put the *Rule into one Man's hands,* and chuse to be under the Conduct of a *single Person,* without so much as by express Conditions limiting or regulating his Power, which they thought safe enough in his Honesty and Prudence. . . . And thus much may suffice to shew, that as far as we have any light from History, we have reason to conclude, that all peaceful beginnings of *Government* have been *laid in the Consent of the People.* (*Second Treatise,* §112)

Fitzhugh is correct, then, when he accuses Locke of failing to distinguish strictly between submission and consent. "All creatures subject to government, *submit* to be governed, but do not *consent* to be governed," Fitzhugh argues, "a consent government is no government, for it implies that all shall think alike, *consentio.* But to constitute a government at all, the rulers must think for those who are ruled. . . . He alone is governed whose will is subjected and controlled by the will of another. He submits but does not consent."[6] Fitzhugh takes the passage he quotes from chapter 8 of the *Second Treatise* to be an adequate statement of Locke's view, and although Locke surely invites this conclusion by the prominence he gives to the passage, there are reasons for doubting its adequacy, as we have seen. Locke's equivocation about consent represents a concession to the complexity of the phenomenon.

Fitzhugh's claim that "a consent government is no government" derives some support from Locke's failure to reconcile government by consent with what he concedes to be the historical origin of political society. However, Fitzhugh disregards the likelihood that the notion of "consent government" he attributes to Locke simplifies and hence distorts what most of Fitzhugh's contemporaries who were followers of Locke actually stood for—those followers usually drawing as heavily from Locke's famous chapter 5, "Of Property," as from his account of the origin of governments in chapter 8.

One such follower, Frederick Douglass, offers what the editors of his *Papers* call a paraphrase of Locke's theory of property: "that a man has a right to as much soil as is necessary for his existence; and when a human being has incorporated a portion of his own strength and that which belongs to his personality into that soil he therefore has a right to that soil against the universe."[7] Locke would add that a human being has such a right *in the state of nature.* The state of civil society introduces complications; in it "the Laws regulate the right of property, and the possession of land is determined by positive constitutions" (*Second Treatise,* §50). One of Locke's examples of how, even in the state of civil society, the "*labour* that was mine . . . hath *fixed* my *Property*" is "the Turfs my Servant has cut" (*Second Treatise,* §28). Still, Locke speaks of man as having "*Property* in his own *Person.* This no Body has any Right to but himself" (*Second Treatise,* §27). There is evidently a moral distinction in this respect between servants and slaves, which Fitzhugh overlooks or ignores.[8]

Consider the following illustration from Frederick Law Olmsted, whose dispatches from the South in the 1850s represent an invaluable firsthand account of the peculiar institution by a northern nonabolitionist. In the words of his editor at the *New York Times,* Olmsted's pieces "constitute the best report that has ever been made, of the industrial condition and prospects of the Southern section of the Union." He conceded, however, that they had been attacked in abolitionist journals for discussing the subject of slavery "upon a false basis." Although not an abolitionist, Olmsted, like Lincoln, was by no means insensitive to the moral questions involved in weighing the merits and defects of rival systems of labor. Slaves, Olmsted observes,

> cannot be driven by fear of punishment to do that which the labourers in free communities do cheerfully from their sense of duty, self-respect, or regard for their reputation and standing with their employer. A gentleman who had some free men in his employment in Virginia, that he had procured in New York, told me that he had been astonished, when a dam that he had been building began to give way in a freshet, to see how much more readily than negroes they would obey his orders, and do their best without orders, running into the water waist-deep, in midwinter, without any hesitation or grumbling.[9]

We are not told the terms of the free men's employment, but presumably the terms did not include running into water up to their waists in the coldest season of the year. Yet these men did so readily, even cheerfully, when the need arose; while the slaves hesitated, probably asking themselves if a whipping would not be less painful. Nevertheless, Fitzhugh would deny that there was an essential difference between the motives at work in these cases.

> Physical force, not moral suasion, governs the world. The negro sees the driver's lash, becomes accustomed to obedient cheerful industry, and is not aware that the lash is the force that impels him. The free citizen fulfils *con amore,* his round of social, political, and domestic duties, and never dreams that the Law, with its fines and jails, penitentiaries and halters, and Public Opinion, with its ostracism, its mobs, and its tar and feathers, help to keep him revolving in his orbit.[10]

The means of coercion in the free citizen's case are more subtle and manifold, Fitzhugh argues, but the same harsh necessity lies at the bottom. Who can doubt, however, that in this instance Olmsted was the superior psychologist? Fitzhugh *is* correct in suggesting that consent understood in the strictest sense does not capture the difference between the cases. The position that Fitzhugh attacked was much more characteristic of radical reformers such as Thoreau, who faulted society for falling short of "a true respect for the individual,"[11] than it was of more politically minded proponents of reform such as Olmsted or Douglass—or indeed Lincoln.

Free society understands itself as natural inasmuch as it recognizes rights derived from a "state of nature" in which human beings are free. The issue between slave society and free society, then, is between rival theories of society and government, based upon rival theories of human nature. For Fitzhugh, the question is whether a theory of human nature can be correct that denies the naturalness of what he calls in *Cannibals All!* "that natural and historical society, which has usually existed in the world, with its gradations of rank and power, its families and its slaves"—which society he identifies with "patriarchal government" and the "larger associations" that have developed from it. Fitzhugh charges the "modern social reformers" who are Locke's witting or unwitting fol-

lowers with proposing to "dissolve and disintegrate society, falsely supposing that they thereby follow nature"; "the doctrines so prevalent
with Abolitionists and Socialists . . . are legitimate deductions, if not
obvious corollaries from the leading and distinctive axiom of political
economy—Laissez Faire, or Let Alone." In their zeal to abolish even the
"quasi-slavery" of the family and "all existing religious, legal, social and
governmental institutions," these reformers "place men in positions of
equality, rivalry, and antagonism"; accordingly, their reforms can have
no effect but to exacerbate the existing vices of free society. Such positions relative to other men are incompatible with the health or even the
survival of society: "We deny that there is a society in free countries.
They who act each for himself, who are hostile, antagonistic and com-
petitive, are not social and do not constitute a society."[12]

No one is likely to deny that there is an element of truth in Fitzhugh's
picture of free society, however overdrawn it might be. But the question
concerns not only the nature of the disease but also the appropriateness
of the cure. If Locke was a utopian, as Fitzhugh claims,[13] it is nevertheless clear that the United States had advanced a considerable distance
along the path of this kind of utopianism, and the South scarcely less far
than the North.

Although there are indications even in the autobiographies of
Frederick Douglass that Fitzhugh's description of slaves as sustaining a
familial relation to their masters was not completely fanciful,[14] most of
the evidence in these accounts points to the slave as a mere instrument
of his master's profit. Certainly, a familial relation was impossible on
the larger farms, such as the one where Douglass spent his early boyhood. Harvey Wish writes that "Fitzhugh ignored the true capitalistic
economics of the plantation system," but Eugene Genovese is closer to
the mark when he says that Fitzhugh "saw the necessary last step in the
[proslavery] argument, which was that slavery could not survive without the utter destruction of capitalism as a world economic system."[15]

Henry Maine traced the history of law in terms of a movement from
"Status" to "Contract": "from a condition of society in which all the
relations of Persons are summed up in the relations of Family," including slaves, "towards a phase of social order in which all these relations
arise from the free agreement of Individuals."[16] Douglass experienced
both conditions firsthand, along with an intermediate phase in which

he entered into a contract with his own master. Douglass's account shows the force of Fitzhugh's insight into the tension between slavery and capitalism—and why the slaveholders' Lockean economics had incidental advantages for the slave.

As a skilled shipyard worker in Baltimore, Douglass was granted at his request the "much-coveted privilege" of hiring his time from his master at a fixed weekly rate, an arrangement he reports was "quite common" in that city. He could keep whatever he earned above the amount agreed upon, and he was allowed "to make all bargains for work; to find my own employment, and to collect my own wages." In return, he was obliged "to board and clothe myself, and buy my own . . . tools." While his master "derived all the benefits of slaveholding by the arrangement, without its evils, I endured all the evils of being a slave, and yet suffered all the care and anxiety of a responsible freeman." Yet Douglass welcomed the arrangement as a step in the direction of freedom: "It was something even to be permitted to stagger under the disadvantages of liberty." It was the revocation of this privilege by his master that precipitated Douglass's second—and this time successful—attempt to run away to the North.[17]

In one respect, Douglass's life as an urban wage-earner was less tolerable than his life as a field hand had been—at least it was less tolerable before the agreement to hire his time, when he was still required to turn over to his master all he had earned. "The practice, from week to week, of openly robbing me of all my earnings, kept the nature and character of slavery constantly before me. I could be robbed by *indirection,* but this was *too* open and barefaced to be endured." The fact that his master occasionally let him keep some of his earnings only made the matter worse. "The fact, that he gave me any part of my wages, was proof that he suspected that I had a right *to the whole of them.*" This was a practical admission—by a slaveholder, no less—of the laborer's right, as Lincoln put it, "to eat the bread, without leave of anybody else, which his own hand earns."[18]

According to Fitzhugh, the radical reformers in the North were Lockeans, even if they did not know or would not avow it: they took Locke's criterion of consent to the furthest limit. Lincoln acknowledged consent to be the legitimate basis of economic as well as political relations, but he did so in full awareness of its complex and ambiguous character. He knew the susceptibility of human nature to the influence of fashion, which, he said, "is just as strong on one subject as another." He observed the quickness of party men, in particular, "to see the *wisdom* and *justice*" of a measure they had previously disapproved, once their leader has endorsed it. The action of men under such influence was not likely to meet the requirements for consent laid down by the most exacting reformers, but Lincoln's study of human nature did not cause him to despair. There is a freedom in the contests between parties that one should not expect to find within party ranks.[19]

Locke attached a kind of disclaimer to his account of the role of consent in the origin of government: even if consent has not in fact been the foundation of governments, that is not a sufficient reason that it should not be, because "at best an Argument from what has been, to what should of right be, has no great force" (*Second Treatise*, §103). An argument from what has been will not be sufficient for a philosopher who has concluded, "Reason being plain on our side, that men are naturally free ... There can be little room for doubt ... where the Right is" (*Second Treatise*, §104). Nevertheless, such an argument must carry considerable weight with a statesman, even a Lockean statesman. By proceeding too quickly with reforms, he risks the very consent his reforms have as their aim to establish more broadly.

Lincoln pursued a statesmanlike course in this respect. Slavery was objectionable to him for the same reason that it was objectionable to the abolitionists: "The master not only governs the slave without his consent; but he governs him by a set of rules altogether different from those which he prescribes for himself." Still, Lincoln's disagreement with the abolitionists went deeper than (to quote Richard Hofstadter's phrase) a mere matter of "the pace of historical change."[20] Through the course of his patient engagement with conditions as he found them, Lincoln was sustained by a view of the human capability for self-government that was at once more sober and more generous than the view held by either Fitzhugh or the reformers he criticizes.

Part III

Abolitionism

Natural Justice and Its Limits

What is wanted is men, not of policy, but of probity—who recognize a higher law than the Constitution, or the decision of the majority.

Henry David Thoreau, 1854

Chapter 7

Henry David Thoreau

The Question of Political Engagement

In a democracy it is not enough to be right in order to be effectual; you must persuade a sufficient number of your fellow citizens that you are right. Indeed, it may not even be enough even to do that, if you cannot also persuade them that it is in, or at least not against, their interest to sustain you. Democracy imposes limits on political action that some would-be reformers have found very difficult to accept. The abolitionists failed to persuade sufficiently many Americans that they were right, to save their cause from consignment to the political margins; or they failed to persuade sufficiently many to put the rightfulness of that cause ahead of their own interests. One or two days before the execution of John Brown, Lincoln said, in reference to Brown's raid on Harpers Ferry, "We have a means provided for the expression of our belief in regard to Slavery—it is through the ballot box—the peaceful method provided by the Constitution."[1] But if no more than an inconsequential minority of Americans could be found who neither denied the wrong of slavery nor were willing to express their belief in regard to it through the ballot box, above all in the states where it existed, what remedy could there be for slavery short of the overthrow of majoritarian democracy—short of the activism of a John Brown? No one among Lincoln's opponents subjected democracy to a more radical critique in view of the indifference of the majority to a great moral wrong than did Brown's admirer Henry David Thoreau.

Critique, however, implies a degree of political engagement that Thoreau proved unable to sustain. His engagement, such as it was, was propelled by anger. Thoreau was outraged by the federal government's inhumane policies concerning slavery; but his belief in humanity was continually challenged by his experience of mankind. In the angriest of his lecture-essays, "Slavery in Massachusetts," which was provoked by news of the recapture in Boston of a fugitive slave, Thoreau finds fault with judges and lawyers for their narrow view of the case—because they "persist in being the servants of the worst of men, and not the servants of humanity." It is hard to avoid the impression, nevertheless, that for Thoreau the "worst of men" included just about everyone. In the same essay he asks, "Will mankind never learn that policy is not morality?"

Wendell Glick has written, "Thoreau's chief purpose in 'Civil Disobedience' was to wean men away from their adherence to an insidious relativism and to persuade them to return again to the superior standard of absolute truth."[2] Thoreau endorsed the "absolute truth" of the wrongfulness of slavery; what he could not accept was that, in Lincoln's words, "our government rests in public opinion. Whoever can change public opinion, can change the government, practically just so much." A durable element of public opinion in the United States, as Thoreau knew well, was support for the Constitution—or at least for an interpretation of it that Thoreau did not share. Bob Pepperman Taylor cites a passage from Thoreau's lecture-essay "A Plea for Captain John Brown" in which "Brown is praised as 'an old-fashioned man in his respect for the Constitution, and his faith in the permanence of this Union.'" Taylor comments, "The clear implication is that Thoreau holds the general principles of the Constitution to be perfectly adequate for informing our understanding of the nature of just government; his defense of Brown is, in fact, a sort of defense of that government." In a note he adds, "There are higher laws than the Constitution, of course, but Thoreau appears to hold the view that, properly understood, the principles of the Constitution conform to these higher laws." The Constitution, then, was properly understood by Brown, Thoreau, and like-minded abolitionists—not by the majority of citizens or the legislators and other officials that represent them. Even if Thoreau's constitutional interpretation was in some sense the correct one, there remained the problem of adverse public opinion. Frederick Douglass faced the same problem, but he evidently thought there was some possibility of changing people's minds about the meaning of the Constitution, at least in the North. Thoreau was far less confident. He did speak of himself as "doing my part to educate my fellow-countrymen," but he believed above all in teaching by example, and his example, perhaps even more clearly than his words, reveals Thoreau's deep skepticism about politics.[3]

The question of political engagement provoked a split in the abolitionist movement between the moral suasionists, whose acknowledged leader was William Lloyd Garrison, and the political or voting abolitionists, who would eventually gain a convert in Douglass. But Thoreau associated with neither group—does he offer an alternative? Before addressing this question we must dispose of a smaller but more basic one: Was Thoreau an abolitionist at all? His biographer Henry Seidel Canby denies that he was; certainly Thoreau was not one in the formal sense: he was never a member of an abolition society. But as Nick Aaron Ford points out in his rejoinder to Canby, the same criterion would have excluded John Brown. Nevertheless, Canby's point is well taken: Thoreau "made no sharp distinction between African slavery and other kinds less frequently condemned by his neighbors."[4] I accept the label of abolitionist for Thoreau but with one reservation. Thoreau's lack of formal abolitionist credentials suggests a lack of confidence in the efficacy of abolition as a popular reform movement—a movement that depends for success on winning numbers to its cause. Indeed, these points are related. If the legal enslavement of people of African descent was not amenable to reform in this manner, there would seem to be little hope for relief from subtler forms of bondage.

Seen from the point of view of numbers, the connection between reform and democratic politics is unmistakable. In the case of abolition, that connection is doubly significant. Opposition to slavery would seem to be grounded in the assumption that all human beings are naturally capable of governing themselves; and if they are capable of governing themselves, they ought to be capable of reforming themselves. If, therefore, slavery is found to be altogether resistant to reform by peaceful, orderly means, democracy too comes into question—and with it the most evident ground of opposition to slavery, the capability of self-government. Thoreau's skepticism about reform is suggestive, then, of a deeper skepticism about democracy and even of an ambivalence about slavery itself.

Had Thoreau lived in different times, he might have been content to live the sort of apparently apolitical life described in his most famous book, *Walden*. Had he been content to live in obscurity on the shores of Walden Pond, the claim of superiority implicit in his aloofness would have had no political consequences. As it happened, a series of events beginning in the 1840s, all connected with slavery, provoked Thoreau to increasingly bitter denunciation of the course of the nation, his state, and above all his fellow citizens. Slavery cast its shadow even over Thoreau's life in the woods: it was while he was living in his hut (though significantly during a visit to town) that he was arrested and compelled to spend a night in jail because, as he declares in *Walden*, "I did not pay a tax to, or recognize the authority of, the State which buys and sells men, women, and children, like cattle, at the door of its senate-house." But perhaps slavery in the nation's capital was not the real issue after all.[5] In *Walden*, Thoreau also wrote, "I sometimes wonder that we can be so frivolous, I may almost say, as to attend to the gross but somewhat foreign form of servitude called Negro Slavery, there are so many keen and subtle masters that enslave both North and South. It is hard to have a Southern overseer; it is worse to have a Northern one; but worst of all when you are the slave-driver of yourself." One statement points toward political engagement for the sake of a general emancipation, the other toward withdrawal from politics in the name of self-emancipation. "Self-emancipation even in the West Indian provinces of the fancy and imagination,—what Wilberforce is there to bring that about?" There is no Wilberforce; you must bring about your freedom by yourself.[6] That the form of political action in question is nonrecognition of authority does not eliminate all tension between the alternatives of engagement and withdrawal. Thoreau would contend with this difficulty during the remainder of the 1840s and through the 1850s.

Thoreau presented his essay "Resistance to Civil Government," defending nonpayment of his tax, in the form of a lecture early in 1848, less than six months after he left his hut in the woods; he agreed to the essay's publication the following year. When the essay was republished after Thoreau's death, it appeared under the more familiar title "Civil

Disobedience." Whether the new title had Thoreau's authorization cannot be determined, but whether it did or not the difference in titles
reflects the ambiguous character of his apology. In refusing to pay the
tax that the law demanded, was he offering resistance to an unjust law?
Or was he merely declining to obey it—recognizing a duty only to
"wash his hands" of "even the most enormous wrong"? One must be
careful not to read into Thoreau's essay the meaning that civil disobedience has acquired since his lifetime. Thoreau may not have intended his
disobedience to serve as a catalyst for reform. He may not have expected
any considerable number of his fellow citizens to follow his example; he
may have justified his disobedience by reference to circumstances peculiar to himself. The interpretation of Thoreau as a reformer is attended
by this difficulty: if he had believed that he could persuade any considerable number of people to do as he did, why did he not pursue reform
by the ordinary means available to citizens of a democracy? By his own
account, Thoreau had stopped paying the poll tax six years before
"Resistance to Civil Government," but he did not call attention to the
fact until after his night in jail.[7]

Thoreau concludes the first paragraph of "Resistance to Civil Government" with a reflection gratifying to democrats, namely that the
Mexican War, which he elsewhere in the essay couples with slavery,[8] is
"the work of comparatively a few individuals using the standing government as their tool; for, in the outset, the people would not have consented to this measure." In the next to last paragraph of the essay,
Thoreau praises "the seasonable experience and the effectual com-
plaints of the people," without which, left to the guidance of Congress
alone, "America would not long retain her rank among the nations"
(*Reform Papers*, 63, 89).[9] These passages would lead one to suppose
that, in Thoreau's view, the American government is insufficiently
democratic—that the problem lies not with the people but with the
politicians. Taken a step further, Thoreau's view seems to be that government itself, not solely undemocratic government, is the problem.
Hence the essay's opening: "I heartily accept the motto,—'That government is best which governs least;' and I should like to see it acted up
to more rapidly and systematically. Carried out, it finally amounts to
this, which I also believe,—'That government is best which governs not

at all.'" Thoreau, however, immediately adds: "and when men are pre-pared for it, that will be the kind of government which they will have" (*Reform Papers*, 63). Thoreau plainly does not think men are now pre-pared for such a government, and it is not evident whether he thinks they are likely ever to be: "The people must have some complicated machinery or other, and hear its din, to satisfy that idea of government which they have. Governments show thus how successfully men can be imposed on, even impose on themselves, for their own advantage" (*Reform Papers*, 63-64).

If the problem lies ultimately with the people's mistaken idea of gov-ernment, then it is wrong to blame Congress for its faults, or even to blame some individuals who use the government as their tool. Thoreau has said that the people would not have consented to the war in the out-set, admitting that they sustained the work of these individuals in the end, as the individuals themselves must have calculated that they would.

From this point of view, it begins to appear that the American democracy works too well, that the government is too democratic—that it allows the people to impose too successfully on themselves, even for their own, presumably material, advantage. Near the end of "Resistance to Civil Government," Thoreau wrote, "The authority of gov-ernment, even such as I am willing to submit to . . . is still an impure one: to be strictly just, it must have the sanction and consent of the gov-erned" (*Reform Papers*, 89). If the American government does not have his consent, it does have the consent of a majority of the governed—that is exactly the difficulty.

The fact that men are not prepared for the best government, and that the government they do have is the kind they deserve to have, since it satisfies, all too well, their mistaken or self-serving idea—all of this does not cause Thoreau at once to give up the cause of reform. Lower-ing his sights somewhat, Thoreau begins again: "But, to speak practi-cally and as a citizen, unlike those who call themselves no-government men, I ask for, not at once no government, but *at once* a better govern-ment" (*Reform Papers*, 64). The difficulty, however, remains: to the extent that reform by democratic or majoritarian means may succeed, it does so only by defeating the purpose of reform in the deep sense, namely self-reformation. On the problem of slavery in particular, Thoreau wrote:

There is but little virtue in the action of masses of men. When the majority shall at length vote for the abolition of slavery, it will be because they are indifferent to slavery, or because there is but little slavery left to be abolished by their vote. *They* will then be the only slaves. Only *his* vote can hasten the abolition of slavery who asserts his own freedom by his vote. (*Reform Papers,* 70)

Thoreau is unable to foresee any conditions under which a majority of men could assert their own freedom by their votes. The solution to the problem of reform lies, therefore, with the minority, if it lies with anyone at all. "We are accustomed to say"—Thoreau has said it himself—"that the mass of men are unprepared; but improvement is slow, because the few are not materially wiser or better than the many." To be precise, the few *are* wiser and better, but their superiority in wisdom and goodness is immaterial because it is ineffectual. "There are thousands who are *in opinion* opposed to slavery and to the war, who yet in effect do nothing to put an end to them. . . . They hesitate, and they regret, and sometimes they petition; but they do nothing in earnest and with effect. . . . At most, they give only a cheap vote, and a feeble countenance and God-speed, to the right, as it goes by them" (*Reform Papers,* 68-69).

What would it mean to do something in earnest and with effect, to put an end to slavery and the war? Thoreau gives two apparently quite different answers, first holding out hope of a peaceful reformation and then casting doubt on it. A few might follow Thoreau's example and refuse to recognize the authority of the state. "It is not so important that many should be as good as you, as that there be some absolute goodness somewhere; for that will leaven the whole lump." In practical terms: "Some are petitioning the State to dissolve the Union, to disregard the requisitions of the President. Why do they not dissolve it themselves,— the union between themselves and the State,—and refuse to pay their quota into its treasury?" Thoreau argues, "If a thousand men were not to pay their tax-bills this year, that would not be a violent and bloody measure, as it would be to pay them, and enable the State to commit violence and shed innocent blood" (*Reform Papers,* 69, 72). But Thoreau himself voices a doubt as to the effectuality of such a course: "This is, in fact, the definition of a peaceable revolution, if any such is possible." If it is not possible, one should not shrink from the consequences. "But even suppose blood should flow. Is there not a sort of blood shed when the conscience is wounded? . . . I see this blood flowing now" (*Reform Papers*, 76-77).

The peaceful withdrawal of support to the state may precipitate a bloody revolution. The ambiguous nature of Thoreau's recommendation of peaceful reform is captured in a memorable pair of sentences: "Cast your whole vote, not a strip of paper merely, but your whole influence. A minority is powerless while it conforms to the majority; it is not even a minority then; but it is irresistible when it clogs by its whole weight" (*Reform Papers*, 76). His assurance of irresistibility notwithstanding, Thoreau appears to concede that the majority will resist the substitution of a minority's judgment for its own; what then?

The prospective consequences of what Thoreau proposes are indeed fearful—not least to Thoreau himself, as one who would claim the attention of a democratic public. His indignation at the denial to the slave of his rights as a man stands in contrast with his estimation of his fellow men generally. To put it most plainly, Thoreau regards the mass of men as slavish. If they are so, Thoreau's skepticism about the possibility of reform by democratic means is certainly justified. To be true to himself, he should have endorsed government by the few; but that was too radical a step. At most, Thoreau wishes for a government that would "cherish its wise minority." Thoreau seems reluctant to admit to himself how closely recent political events have touched him; his denial in this context is bizarre: "the government does not concern me much, and I shall bestow the fewest possible thoughts on it" (*Reform Papers*, 86). His call for withdrawal from the state by "those who call themselves abolitionists" leaves it an open question whether he counts himself among their number.

> I do not hesitate to say, that those who call themselves abolitionists should at once effectually withdraw their support, both in person and property, from the government of Massachusetts, and not wait till they constitute a majority of one, before they suffer the right to prevail through them. I think that it is enough if they have God on their side, without waiting for that other one. Moreover, any man more right than his neighbors constitutes a majority of one already. (*Reform Papers*, 74)

Thoreau's call, if heeded, will precipitate a revolution, peaceable or otherwise, in which he seems to project no further role for himself. How confident is he of its success? It would not, after all, be a popular revolution—not at the outset, perhaps not ever. (Its resemblance to the Mexican War as "the work of comparatively a few individuals" is closer than Thoreau would like to admit.) When Thoreau comes to speak of his own act of withdrawing support to the state in the form of taxes, this ostensibly political act appears rather as the act of an archindividualist. Thoreau speaks of himself in this connection as a neighbor and as a subject but not (as he had done in calling for "*at once* a better government") as a citizen, which would show his withdrawal in a less favorable light.

> I have never declined paying the highway tax, because I am as desirous of being a good neighbor as I am of being a bad subject; and as for supporting schools, I am doing my part to educate my fellow-countrymen now. It is for no particular item in the tax-bill that I refuse to pay it. I simply wish to refuse allegiance to the State, to withdraw and stand aloof from it effectually. (*Reform Papers*, 84)

Thoreau is in an awkward position: on one hand, he regards the "millions" of his fellow citizens who demand his tax as "not wholly a brute force, but partly a human force"; on the other hand, he suspects that they do so "without the possibility, such is their constitution, of retracting or altering their present demand" (*Reform Papers*, 85).

At the conclusion of "Resistance to Civil Government," Thoreau all but concedes the impossibility of reconciling his position with "a democracy, such as we know it." His political hopes still lie in reform, inasmuch as democracy is on the way toward "a true respect for the individual." In the meantime, Thoreau will conduct himself as if the state he has imagined were already actual; the rest of mankind will have to rely on itself.

> The progress from an absolute to a limited monarchy, from a limited monarchy to a democracy, is a progress toward a true respect for the individual. Is a democracy, such as we know it, the last improvement possible in government? . . . I please myself with imagining a State at last which can afford to be just to all men, and to treat the individual with

respect as a neighbor; which even would not think it inconsistent with its own repose, if a few were to live aloof from it, not meddling with it, nor embraced by it, who fulfilled all the duties of neighbors and fellow-men. A State which bore this kind of fruit, and suffered it to drop off as fast as it ripened, would prepare the way for a still more perfect and glorious State, which also I have imagined, but not yet anywhere seen. (*Reform Papers*, 89-90)

Self-emancipation is consistent with the sort of life Thoreau led at Walden Pond, a life spent aloof from politics. In Thoreau's judgment, self-emancipation may even demand such a life. Yet even in his hut Thoreau's aloofness was not perfect. A more consistently antipolitical writer, Epicurus, reveals why: "If parents are rightfully angry with their children, it is, of course, useless for the children to resist and not beg their forgiveness; but if parents have no just or logical reason for their anger, it is foolish for the child to inflame their unreason further by nursing his own anger and not to seek, by being considerate, to turn aside their wrath through other means."[10] If governments are as much like unreasoning parents as Epicurus was inclined to think, there can be no sense in provoking them by acts of disobedience. But Thoreau could not bring himself to follow Epicurus's advice. Even the passive form of resistance that Thoreau practiced exposed him to the risk of arrest and imprisonment. He was evidently willing to assume that risk (at least for a time), but he was not willing to assume the leadership of a political or revolutionary movement. Thoreau, however, could not be wholly satisfied with his choice. His dissatisfaction is reflected in his reaction to news of the attempted rescue of the fugitive slave Anthony Burns from the Boston Courthouse and, later, to news of John Brown's raid on Harpers Ferry.

Thoreau finally could not be satisfied waiting for a government that would either "cherish its wise minority" or suffer that minority to live aloof from it. "Slavery in Massachusetts" represents an advance inasmuch as Thoreau rejects the posture of aloofness. "I had never respected the Government near to which I had lived," he maintains, "but I had foolishly thought that I might manage to live here, minding my private affairs, and forget it" (*Reform Papers*, 106). Thoreau rejects aloofness—

but in favor of what? Until this question can be answered, his rejection brings him no closer to a solution but only serves to make the problem more acute.

One possible solution has not yet been taken notice of. Thoreau's criticism in "Slavery in Massachusetts" of the course of action—or rather inaction—of the governor in the Burns case assumes a role within democratic politics for the wise minority. Thoreau criticizes the governor for failing to act as a member of that minority should. "The worst I shall say of [the governor] is, that he proved no better than the majority of his constituents would be likely to prove. In my opinion, he was not equal to the occasion" (*Reform Papers*, 94). To be equal to the occasion, the governor should have been better than those who elected him—as they presumably believed him to be. The same assumption seems to supply the bitterness in Thoreau's reference in the essay to Daniel Webster as the "maker" of the Fugitive Slave Law (*Reform Papers*, 97), and it underlies his much milder criticism in "Resistance to Civil Government": "They who know of no purer sources of truth, who have traced up its stream no higher, stand, and wisely stand, by the Bible and the Constitution" (*Reform Papers*, 88). *They* wisely stand, but Thoreau implies that to do so is blameworthy in someone like Webster. Nevertheless, he seems unable to decide whether the fault lies with politics itself or with a too narrow idea of politics. "Notwithstanding [Webster's] special acuteness and ability, he is unable to take a fact out of its merely political relations, and behold it as it lies absolutely to be disposed of by the intellect,—what, for instance, it behoves a man to do here in America to-day with regard to slavery." Here Thoreau seems to place the blame on politics itself; the problem was not that Webster failed as a politician but that he succeeded all too well. In an earlier remark, however, Thoreau had more clearly left open the possibility of a philosophic politics: "Webster never goes behind government, and so cannot speak with authority about it." Those statesmen, who "standing so completely within the institution, never distinctly and nakedly behold it," are failures even as statesmen; they cannot speak with authority even about government (*Reform Papers*, 86-87). Thoreau, then, was unwilling to rule out a possible political role for the wise minority. This is not to deny that the prevailing tendency in his thought is hostile to this possibility, only that it need be so.

In the same context, Thoreau distinguishes between "those legislators who contemplate no essential reform in the existing government" on one hand; and "thinkers, and those who legislate for all time," on the other (*Reform Papers*, 87). By "existing government" Thoreau evidently means the government established under the existing federal constitution, which Webster defended. "He well deserves to be called, as he has been called, the Defender of the Constitution. There are really no blows to be given by him but defensive ones. He is not a leader but a follower. His leaders are the men of '87." Those men may not have understood themselves to be legislating "for all time," but they contemplated, and carried through, an essential reform in the then existing government— not essential enough to satisfy Thoreau, but enough to distinguish them from the politicians of his day. Above all they recognized the insufficiency of merely defensive blows. Their success made politicians of Webster's type possible, politicians who do not lead but follow. There is also a favorable reference in "Resistance to Civil Government" to George Washington and Benjamin Franklin, who were delegates to the Constitutional Convention (although Thoreau has them in mind above all in their role as revolutionaries), and disparagement of those who, "esteeming themselves children of Washington and Franklin, sit down with their hands in their pockets, and say they know not what to do, and do nothing" (*Reform Papers*, 69). Thoreau is calling on his contemporaries to see the Constitution as the framers and their contemporaries saw it—before it *was* the Constitution. As for himself, Thoreau rejects the Constitution on just this basis. "The question is not whether you or your grandfather, seventy years ago, did not enter into an agreement to serve the devil, and that service is not accordingly now due; but whether you will not now, for once and at last, serve God,—in spite of your own past recreancy, or that of your ancestor,—by obeying that eternal and only just CONSTITUTION, which He, and not any Jefferson or Adams, has written in your being" (*Reform Papers*, 103).

The barrier to a political role for the wise minority was not only the majoritarian principle of "a democracy, such as we know it," but also, and less remotely, Americans' loyalty to their constitution of seventy years' standing. Having rejected a political role for himself under that constitution, Thoreau has in effect rejected such a role altogether. Accordingly, he makes his appeal to the higher law. "What is wanted is men, not of policy, but of probity—who recognize a higher law than the Constitution, or the decision of the majority" (*Reform Papers*, 104). The question remains, however, what these men of probity are to do. In "Resistance to Civil Government," Thoreau concedes that while "all men recognize the right of revolution; that is, the right to refuse allegiance to and to resist the government, when its tyranny or its inefficiency are great and unendurable," still "almost all say that such is not the case now" (*Reform Papers*, 67). What had changed in the state of northern public opinion by 1854 was alarm at the *extension* of slavery—as Thoreau scornfully says of his Concord townsmen, "It was only the disposition of some wild lands a thousand miles off, which appeared to concern them" (*Reform Papers*, 91). The time for revolution had not yet arrived. At best, one could follow the example of those "champions of liberty" who had attacked the Boston Courthouse; but such a course of action depends on someone being locked up inside to rescue. Having rejected aloofness, Thoreau's challenge is to rise above a merely reactive stance, and in this he clearly fails.

Thoreau had by all appearances gone back to minding his private affairs when, some five years after the Burns case and "Slavery in Massachusetts," news of John Brown's raid on Harpers Ferry reached Concord. The troubles in Kansas had not proved merely a distraction to New Englanders after all: it was, according to Thoreau, "through [Brown's] agency, far more than any other's, that Kansas was made free" in the interval—this Brown who "was by descent and birth a New England farmer, a man of great common sense, deliberate and practical as that class is, and tenfold more so" (*Reform Papers*, 112–13).

But Brown's putative success in Kansas stood in contrast with his violent "recent failure" in Virginia. Thoreau's primary concern in the lecture-essay "A Plea for Captain John Brown" is to save Brown from the consequences to his reputation of the perception that the Harpers Ferry raid was "a wild and desperate attempt" that met its just end (*Reform Papers*, 116). One is given the impression, however, that much more is at stake in the defense of Brown than his reputation, or the reputation of his cause. It is striking that Thoreau has so little to say in "A Plea for Captain John Brown" about slavery, and nothing unambiguously in favor of Brown's course as to its effectuality in ending slavery. When

Thoreau maintains, "I shall not be forward to think him mistaken in his method who quickest succeeds to liberate the slave," he means the individual slave, rescued by force. When he further declares, "I speak for the slave when I say, that I prefer the philanthropy of Captain Brown to that philanthropy which neither shoots me nor liberates me," he is evidently contrasting Brown with an abolitionist of the Garrison type, and he does not say which outcome, being liberated or shot, he deems more likely (*Reform Papers*, 133). The possibility that the Garrison type of reformer may in fact be more efficacious does not prevent Thoreau from ranking him below the Brown type. Taylor notes that Thoreau's extravagant rhetoric in defense of Brown was matched by African American writers, notably Frederick Douglass. He quotes from an editorial by Douglass entitled "Captain John Brown Not Insane" but omits the words after the semicolon: "This age is too gross and sensual to appreciate his deeds, and so calls him mad; but the future will write his epitaph upon the hearts of a people freed from slavery, because he struck the first effectual blow." As we have seen, Thoreau ventures no such prediction.[11]

Thoreau's defense of Brown is too passionate to be accounted for solely by his admiration of Brown's qualities or his endorsement of Brown's cause. Brown must have represented a solution to the problem with which Thoreau had been contending: the role of the "wise minority" or the "men of probity." It is instructive to compare "A Plea for Captain John Brown" with an early lecture-essay of Thoreau's, "Reform and the Reformers," which is his most sustained treatment of the theme of reform. "The Reformer who comes recommending any institution or system to the adoption of men, must not rely solely on logic and argument, or on eloquence and oratory for his success, but see that he represents one pretty perfect institution in himself, the center and circumference of all others, an erect man" (*Reform Papers*, 184). Thoreau may well have thought of himself as such a man or "institution," but it would be difficult for anyone to think of him as an example of the type of reformer he praises in this passage: "We rarely see the Reformer who is fairly launched in his enterprise, bringing about the right state of things with hearty and effective tugs, and not rather preparing and grading the way through the minds of the people. To the man of industry and work it is not quite essential that I should *think* with him" (*Reform*

Papers, 185, 186). Was not Brown, however, an example of a reformer "fairly launched in his enterprise," a man who went to work straightaway and did not wait until others agreed with him? And if someone should question the effectiveness of his "tugs," at least those given at Harpers Ferry, Thoreau could reply, "What the prophets even have said is forgotten, and the oracles are decayed, but what heroes and saints have done is still remembered, and posterity will tell it again and again" (*Reform Papers*, 185). Certainly to Thoreau neither Brown's heroism nor his saintliness was in doubt. Brown was superior even to "ordinary heroes"; and as for his saintly qualities, Thoreau says, "No man has appeared in America as yet who loved his fellow man so well, and treated him so tenderly. He lived for him. He took up his life and he laid it down for him" (*Reform Papers*, 131, 133).

The contrast between the two types of reformer runs through Thoreau's antislavery essays, but until "A Plea for Captain John Brown," the type of which he could approve lacked an exemplar. In "Resistance to Civil Government," Thoreau rates the words even of Webster more highly than "the cheap professions of most reformers"; and he says scathingly, "Reform keeps many scores of newspapers in its service, but not one man" (*Reform Papers*, 75, 87). But in the same essay he also speaks of "reformers in the great sense," who "serve the State with their consciences also, and so necessarily resist it for the most part" (*Reform Papers*, 66). In "Slavery in Massachusetts," he speaks of "a righteous reform" and of "the weapons of the reformer" (*Reform Papers*, 101, 104)—the weapon in this instance being not to keep newspapers but to throw them away, or better still "to refrain from purchasing and reading these sheets."[12] In "A Plea for Captain John Brown" Thoreau says of his subject, "It was no abolition lecturer that converted him"; and "If he had had any journal advocating '*his cause*,' any organ as the phrase is, monotonously and wearisomely playing the same old tune, and then passing around the hat, it would have been fatal to his efficiency" (*Reform Papers*, 113, 132). Brown was an "efficient" reformer because he was free to disregard others' views.

In the antislavery essays we see movement toward a kind of engagement, at least in rhetoric. Thoreau refrains from criticizing the Constitution (except by implication) in "A Plea for Captain John Brown." Thoreau does not assert that *he* is similarly old-fashioned "in his respect for the Constitution," but he knows this quality will register with his more conservative auditors as a point in Brown's favor, and he is not unwilling to conciliate them (*Reform Papers*, 112). He concludes his defense of Brown, whom he calls a Puritan and "the most American of us all" (*Reform Papers*, 113, 125), with something new in his rhetoric, namely a reference to the Declaration of Independence. Thoreau implies that Brown's career represents the fulfillment of the American political tradition, or rather that the rightful public appreciation of his career will represent such a fulfillment.

> I foresee the time when the painter will paint the scene, no longer going to Rome for a subject; the poet will sing it; the historian record it; and, with the Landing of the Pilgrims and the Declaration of Independence, it will be the ornament of some future national gallery, when at least the present form of Slavery shall be no more here. We shall then be at liberty to weep for Captain Brown. Then, and not till then, we will take our revenge. (*Reform Papers*, 138)

But there is a discordant note in Thoreau's description of Brown's future triumph: his reference to the *present* form of slavery. It recalls to mind the reference in *Walden* to "the gross but somewhat foreign form of servitude called Negro Slavery." Is there no abolishing slavery after all, only a changing of its form? In how much better a state is the North than the South, in this respect?

When the Civil War began, Thoreau was already ill with tuberculosis; he would die of the disease in May 1862. There is conflicting evidence concerning his views on the war. Leo Stoller writes, "Thoreau at forty-four [that is, at the time of his death] supported the government and armies of Lincoln." "The direct assault on slavery which he had praised in John Brown as an individual he now welcomed in the government and the nation." Stoller's characterization of the war as a direct assault on slavery owes more to the views of Frederick Douglass than to those of Lincoln. Joseph Wood Krutch conjectures more plausibly that Brown's raid, "being the act of an individual," was more acceptable to Thoreau than "government-sponsored mass action"; he could only have approved the war by a "readjustment of his principles."[13]

Stoller's conclusion is based on the reports of friends who visited Thoreau during his final months. He admits, however, "The definition of Thoreau's attitude to the Civil War is made difficult by a serious lack of evidence." More telling than these reports is a letter Thoreau wrote two days before the firing on Fort Sumter. Referring to a friend of a friend who had expressed an interest in his work, Thoreau wrote, "As for my prospective reader, I hope that he *ignores* Fort Sumpter, & Old Abe, & all that, for that is just the most fatal and indeed the only fatal, weapon you can direct against evil ever; for as long as you *know of* it, you are *particeps criminis* [a partner in the crime]. . . . I do not so much regret the present condition of things in this country (provided I regret it at all) as I do that I ever heard of it." Stoller argues that Thoreau retired to his hut by Walden Pond because "American society as it stood in the mid-forties gave no hint of ever becoming better." His refusal to pay the poll tax was "an act of desperation, chosen because political circumstances had not yet allowed him a more effective one." In time, however, "the nation did grow better," and the northern response to the southern rebellion proved it. Hence Thoreau's slow turn, beginning in the late 1840s, away from the "utopian" and toward the political, ending finally in support for Lincoln and the Union.[14] This description of Thoreau's career fails, however, to account for the fitfulness of his engagement with politics.

Stoller is obviously referring to improvement or progress in a far more humble sense than Thoreau himself does at the conclusion of "Resistance to Civil Government," where he speaks of "progress toward a true respect for the individual." Nevertheless, the same consideration applies. Thoreau seems to have had the thought that those in the vanguard of historical change are always a minority, but time eventually proves them to have been right and the majority wrong. This is a plausible argument—if one is assured that the expectation of progress is reasonable. A perfect assurance would have removed the incentive for political action, but Thoreau's problem lay elsewhere. A more generous estimate of the capabilities of his fellow citizens would have sustained Thoreau in the unpopular positions he felt compelled to take, but he seems to have been unable to overcome the suspicion that they were after all incurably slavish. His affirmation of a higher law binding human beings did not elevate but rather diminished their stature in his

eyes, since they so seldom lived up to it.[15] Thoreau obscures the difficulty when he lays the sins of society at the door of "the State," as if these
were altogether distinct. But his rejection of politics presupposes a more
radical separation of state from society than he himself could be satisfied with; he was simply deceiving himself when he wrote "the government does not concern me much." As a consequence, Thoreau's strong
sense of justice spent itself in feckless indignation.

Lincoln offered this advice to reformers: "If you would win a man to
your cause, *first* convince him that you are his sincere friend"; having
gained his heart, "you will find but little trouble in convincing his judgment of the justice of your cause, if indeed that cause really be a just
one." Thoreau could not deny that politicians, as dubious as their
motives must at times appear, had succeeded better than higher law
men at winning adherents to their causes, for precisely the reason that
Lincoln's remarks suggest. Thoreau remained ambivalent about reform
because he recognized the force of this unwelcome truth: human beings
are political animals as well as moral ones. To confine the scope of his
critique to "the injustice of *our* politics" or "specific corruptions in
American society" is to do him a disservice. Thoreau questioned politics as such, and politics is questionable in some respects. He is clear
about the shortcomings, but he is unable to offer an alternative that is
not more questionable still. Lincoln's point applies with even greater
force to abolitionists than to the temperance reformers he was addressing. Those reformers whose cause is grounded on the principle of
human equality ought least of all to "assume to dictate to [another
man's] judgment, or to command his action, or to mark him as one to
be shunned and despised." This is why, as Lincoln said on another occasion, "the promulgation of abolition doctrines tends rather to increase
than to abate [slavery's] evils."[16]

Chapter 8

William Lloyd Garrison

From Disunionist to Lincoln Emancipationist

It was the Emancipation Proclamation that solved the problem in regard to which Lincoln had said less than ten years before, "if all earthly power were given me, I should not know what to do"—the problem of the existing institution of slavery. The Emancipation Proclamation marked a convergence of views on the part of abolitionists and Republicans that culminated in an exuberant tribute by William Lloyd Garrison, the most famous abolitionist of all, to "that noble man, Abraham Lincoln," offered in Charleston, South Carolina, on April 14, 1865, the very day Lincoln would be shot. "Of one thing I feel sure," Garrison declared, "either he has become a Garrisonian Abolitionist or I have become a Lincoln Emancipationist, for I know that we blend together, like kindred drops, into one, and his brave heart beats for human freedom everywhere." Lincoln himself is reported to have made the following reply, eight days earlier, to a comment about "the country's gratitude for his great deliverance of the slaves": "I have been only an instrument. The logic and moral power of Garrison, and the anti-slavery people of the country and the army, have done all." The abolitionist whose motto was "No Union with Slaveholders!" and the president who had written, "What I do about slavery, and the colored race, I do because I believe it helps to save the Union; and what I forebear, I forebear because I do *not* believe it would help to save the Union," made common cause at last.[1]

Nevertheless, the extraordinary character of the Civil War years makes it dangerous to generalize from them. Holding the views that he did about the scope of executive authority under the Constitution, Lincoln could not have freed the slaves if the Union had remained whole. The fact that Lincoln issued the Emancipation Proclamation "upon military necessity" does not justify the conclusion that he had abandoned those views. Garrison's case is different. Orestes Brownson once remarked that a man who "proposes to abolish slavery . . . by abolishing law," as he believed the abolitionists were inclined to do, "is always a tyrant in his heart."[2] There are points in Garrison's career that would tend to confirm this judgment; but Lincoln's presidency showed Garrison something about the relation of freedom to law that he had not seen before.

In view of their eventual convergence, it is tempting to see the earlier differences between Lincoln and Garrison as having their origin solely in the president's purpose to preserve northern unanimity in the unprecedented crisis of the Union. Even before the issuance of the Emancipation Proclamation, Garrison said, "I do not know that some margin of allowance may not be made even for the Administration." He imagined Lincoln replying to his abolitionist critics, who urged him to issue such a proclamation without delay: "Gentlemen, I understand this matter quite as well as you do. I do not know that I differ in opinion from you; but will you insure me the support of a united North if I do as you bid me?" Garrison acknowledged that "there is some ground for hesitancy, as a mere matter of political expediency," but he does not seem to have thought that there might be a matter of principle involved.[3] Lincoln himself thought otherwise.

In spite of Garrison's assumption that the differences between Lincoln and the abolitionists were largely tactical rather than substantive, writers on the period have naturally taken sides. Garrison biographer Henry Mayer, for example, writes that by the spring of 1864 the abolitionist "had virtually declared himself to be a Republican"; but Mayer ascribes the shift to "the moral progress that Lincoln had demonstrably made" or "the way he had grown in office," and he points to the "contrast between the president's December 1863 message in which he reiterated his unequivocal commitment to emancipation and the grad-

ualist, colonizationist statement of the year before." Historians who follow in the line of the abolitionists have tended to show, in the words of
Don E. Fehrenbacher, "scorn for the devious ways of statecraft and
admiration for the clean, straight tracks of radical reform." J. G. Randall
offers a different view: "It is the part of statesmen to prevent an emo-
tionally dangerous question from getting out of hand and to deal with
problems on the level of adjustment." Such a view of the statesman's
task may not be sufficient to distinguish Lincoln from Stephen Douglas,
but it is sufficient to distinguish Republicans from abolitionists. The
sort of adjustment Randall speaks of is not likely to follow "clean,
straight tracks."

The postwar description by Garrison's coadjutor Oliver Johnson of
Lincoln as having "by a single stroke of his pen, lift[ed] four millions of
human beings from the condition of chattels to that of men," reflects
the grounds for action that Johnson himself could most heartily
approve; it more clearly expresses the wish of the radical reformer than
the reality of the statesman. Jefferson Davis offers his own version of
this description in his memoirs. Davis wrote, "at a single dash of the
pen, four hundred millions of our property was to be annihilated, the
whole social fabric of the Southern States disrupted, all branches of
industry to be disarranged, good order to be destroyed, and a flood of
evils many times greater than the loss of property to be inflicted upon
the people of the South." Johnson and Davis agree as to the autocratic
character of Lincoln's action in issuing his proclamation, differing only
in their expression of approval or disapproval of its effects. Neither
gives political considerations as much weight as Lincoln gave them.[4]

As late as the summer of 1862, when Lincoln wrote, "What I do about
slavery, and the colored race, I do because I believe it helps to save the
Union" in a public letter to the influential New York editor Horace
Greeley, he seemed to hold out hope of a restoration of the Union, if not
precisely "as it was," then the nearest possible thing. Lincoln wrote, "The
sooner the national authority can be restored; the nearer the Union will
be 'the Union as it was.' . . . My paramount object in this struggle *is* to
save the Union, and is *not* either to save or to destroy slavery. If I could
save the Union without freeing *any* slave I would do it, and if I could
save it by freeing *all* the slaves I would do it; and if I could save it by freeing some and leaving others alone I would also do that." Lincoln did not

say that he would save the Union if it meant keeping the slaves in slavery forever. He had consistently denied that it was possible to save the Union—any Union "worthy of the saving"—by accepting the permanence of slavery; that was the very point on which he had differed with Stephen Douglas. Restoration of the Union as it was would have meant contending against slavery by political means; with allowance for the extraordinary circumstances of the war, Lincoln's handling of the border states suggests something of the course he would likely have taken. But in the same letter Lincoln had written, then struck out, this sentence, following his reference to "the Union as it was": "Broken eggs can never be mended, and the longer the breaking proceeds the more will be broken." The breaking had proceeded for more than a year already—too long, perhaps, for the old Union to be restored. In another letter from that summer Lincoln was more blunt, declaring that "this government cannot much longer play a game in which it stakes all, and its enemies stake nothing. Those enemies must understand that they cannot experiment for ten years trying to destroy the government, and if they fail still come back into the Union unhurt."[5] In fact, when these letters were written, Lincoln had already decided on a proclamation freeing the slaves in states that persisted in rebellion; he had read a draft to his cabinet and was only waiting for the right moment to issue it.[6] In view of Lincoln's decision, it is reasonable to assume that the letter to Greeley was intended, in part, to prepare the public mind to accept the proclamation as a Union-saving measure—hence within the implied scope of the president's constitutional authority. The Union might yet be saved, but, for better or worse, it would not be the Union exactly as it was.

Although guilty of overstatement, Garrison was correct to see Lincoln as issuing the proclamation with considerable reluctance. In the same issue of the *Liberator* that carried the text of the preliminary emancipation proclamation, Garrison wrote, "We admit that President Lincoln has been hoping and trying to restore the old state of things, with as little damage to slavery as possible; but, surely, nothing can be more preposterous than such an expectation—an expectation happily no longer indulged in, even by himself, as witness his recent Emancipation Proclamation." It was the issuance of the final proclamation on January 1, 1863, that marked the decisive turn in Garrison's estimation of Lincoln. Until the last moment he doubted the president's resolve, especially in view of Lincoln's endorsement of gradualism in his December 1862 message to Congress. "A man so manifestly without moral vision, so unsettled in his policy, so incompetent to lead, so destitute of hearty abhorrence of slavery, cannot be safely relied on in any emergency," Garrison wrote in the *Liberator*'s final issue of 1862. In September, Garrison had declared himself "not so jubilant . . . as many others" over the preliminary proclamation, because of his belief that "this Proclamation is not all that the exigency of the times and the consequent duty of the government require." But when he printed the text of the final emancipation proclamation in the first issue of 1863, he appended this comment: "It is a great historic event, sublime in its magnitude, momentous and beneficent in its far-reaching consequences, and eminently just and right alike to the oppressor and the oppressed, as well as imperatively called for by the fearfully imperiled state of the country." Garrison further predicted, "THE PEOPLE will sustain it—the army will receive fresh inspiration—and all Rebeldom be filled with consternation in view of their inevitable doom."[7]

Although Garrison pronounced the doom of the Confederacy inevitable following Lincoln's proclamation, his reference to the hoped-for reactions of the people and the army suggests he harbored a prudent doubt. In his response to the preliminary proclamation, Garrison wrote that "it emancipates more than three-fourths of the entire slave population, as fast as they shall become accessible." He might have written, *if* they should become accessible, for that was by no means certain. Whether they became accessible or not depended on the fortunes of the army—hence Garrison's hope that it would "receive fresh inspiration."

Lincoln is reported to have told a party of abolitionists that visited the White House in January 1863, a party that included Wendell Phillips but not Garrison, "most of us here present have been all our lives working in minorities, and have got into a habit of being dissatisfied." Garrison succeeded better than other abolitionists in freeing himself from this habit, in part because he had come to understand better than they did the importance of military success. Phillips opened the conference by thanking the president for his proclamation and asking him "how it was working," to which Lincoln replied "that he had not expected much from it at first, and consequently had not been disappointed; he had hoped and still hoped that something would come of it after a while." Moncure Conway, the member of the party who recorded this exchange, reported, "This remark made us all feel uneasy; it was plain from [the president's] manner, even more than his words, that it had not occurred to him that our interest was in anything but the *military* aspects of his proclamation."[8] Conway was almost certainly mistaken in thinking that Lincoln failed to understand his visitors' interest; more likely, he wanted them to understand his interest—which Garrison now shared.

But Garrison had also expressed his hope that "the people will sustain [the Proclamation]," and toward this end he, as a famous and increasingly respected editor and public speaker, was in a position to do something more than just hope. What he did justified Lincoln's commending to the country's gratitude the "moral power" of the abolitionist as well as the material power of the army, for having "done all."

Notwithstanding his mistrust of Lincoln before 1863, Garrison had in fact been occupying ground fairly close to Lincoln's since the beginning of the war. Before 1861, Garrison had dismissed the relevance of natural law for the interpretation of the Constitution, in order to make the distinction between legality and morality unmistakably clear. The Constitution was nothing more than a compact entered into by the states—that is, by the white people of the states—to serve their interests. Garrison looked at the Union in much the same light as did John C. Calhoun—a fact that did not go altogether unnoticed in the South.[9] Until the firing on Fort Sumter, Garrison had been willing to "Let the line be drawn between us where free institutions end and slave institutions begin!" With the beginning of the war, however, Garrison was forced to distinguish between his own "disunionism" (which he never expressly repudiated) and southern "secessionism." According to Garrison's sons, "Neither he nor the American Anti-Slavery Society had ever advocated the right of a State to secede from the Union *ad libitum,* without reason; and only a revolutionary right, for the causes set forth in the Declaration of Independence, could justify the South in its course." If they are right, Garrison's defense of the Union, such as it was, was not altogether new; but the war compelled him to make it explicit.[10]

Similarly, Garrison's criticism of the preliminary proclamation for failing to be "all that the exigency of the times and the consequent duty of the government require" implies that it fell short politically as well as morally in his eyes in not calling for universal emancipation. This position is made explicit in the editorial by Garrison that accompanied his criticism, "Drafting—What is the Duty of the Abolitionists?" In that editorial, Garrison reminds his readers that "since the organization of the Southern Confederacy, we have ceased to make any distinctive issue with the Constitution of the United States," and he quotes from a lecture he gave in January of that year, "When I said I would not sustain the Constitution, because it was a covenant with death and an agreement with hell, I had no idea that I would live to see death and hell secede. Hence it is that I am now with the government." Garrison explains that his earlier rejection of the Constitution had, paradoxically, been necessitated by respect for its terms, and hence was not inconsistent with his present position.

> Before the rebellion, the Abolitionists scrupulously abstained, through a thirty years' struggle, from asking Congress or the President to emancipate a single slave in all the slave States; because they recognized the conditions upon which the Union was formed, and were too conscientious to ask for any exercise of power, even to break the chains of the oppressed, which could not be legitimately used. . . . They have been careful from the beginning till now to do nothing wrong, and to ask nothing of the government but what it has a right CONSTITUTIONALLY to enact. If they now invoke it to exercise extraordinary powers, it is because the revolt and secession of the South render resort to those powers not only legitimate, but indispensable.

To say that this government should now assume extraordinary powers was not to claim for it powers that were despotic or dictatorial.

> To say that [the war power] is a despotic power, or that it supersedes the Constitution for the time being, is to forget the radical distinction which exists between an hereditary and a popular government. As claimed and used by European dynasties, it is ever without reference to the popular will, and therefore despotic; but what THE PEOPLE have expressly provided for, in their organic law, to be used whenever the emergency arises, according to the imminence of the peril that threatens the public safety and the stability of the government, is neither despotic nor outside of the Constitution.

Garrison thus connects, as Lincoln did most memorably in the Gettysburg Address, the question of slavery with the larger question of the fate of popular government. Astonishingly, in this context he even gives a qualified endorsement to compensation for loyal slaveholders who would lose their property under a decree of universal emancipation: "exceptional cases are to be provided for, not to baffle the necessary measures of the government for its own preservation," and one way these cases may be provided for is "by making good whatever pecuniary loss may be sustained." Garrison concludes, "Thus, every obstacle to CONSTITUTIONAL EMANCIPATION is taken out of the way, and the government is, and must be, if true to itself, wholly on the side of liberty. *Such a government can receive the sanction and support of every Abolitionist, whether in a moral or military point of view.*"[11]

That the government did prove true to the terms of the proclamation of September 22 did not, of course, mean that the end of slavery was certain, even in the states and parts of states still in rebellion the following January 1—even assuming an eventual northern victory, which no one had any right to assume. As Mayer puts it,

> The link between military necessity and emancipation, though crucial in persuading Lincoln and the public opinion he represented to act, remained . . . an uncertain foundation for social transformation. Emancipation depended not simply upon winning the war, which in January 1863 itself seemed doubtful, but making a devastating conquest of the slaveholding states that would enormously complicate postwar settlement of the labor and racial issues and the eventual transition from military occupation to civilian government. Universal and lasting freedom, moreover, required further action not only to end slavery in the "loyal" states, but to establish a firmer constitutional foundation for abolition than an executive wartime edict, which might be overturned by a lenient successor or a hostile court or set aside in a negotiated truce.[12]

"Universal and lasting freedom" depended, then, on the progress not only of northern arms but also of northern opinion, especially as registered in the choice of Lincoln's successor—which would be either Lincoln himself in a second term or one more "lenient," more willing to make the disposition of slavery a matter for negotiation in the interest of bringing the war to an early conclusion. Garrison, mindful of what was at stake, took the controversial step of supporting the renomination of Lincoln over the more radical sort of candidate favored by many other abolitionists, including Wendell Phillips. Like others far from the battle lines, Garrison could do nothing to affect the military situation directly; but he could perform a valuable service in helping to shape public opinion in favor of Lincoln's war policy. For the first time in his career, Garrison's views began to converge with those of a considerable segment of the public, and this fact could not but reinforce his growing moderation. In May 1864 Garrison pronounced this very sober judgment on Lincoln's antislavery record in office:

> Grant that there are many sad things to look in the face; grant that the whole of justice has not yet been done to the negro ... still, looking at the question broadly, comprehensively, and philosophically, I think the people will ask another question—whether they themselves have been one hair's breadth in advance of Abraham Lincoln? Whether they are not conscious that he has not only been fully up with them, but, on the whole, a little beyond them? As the stream cannot rise higher than the fountain, so the President of the United States, amenable to public sentiment, could not, if he wished to do it, far transcend public sentiment in any direction. For my own part, when I remember the trials through which he has passed, and the perils which have surrounded him—perils and trials unknown to any man, in any age of the world, in official station—[here follows a recitation of the antislavery and pro-Negro acts of Lincoln's administration, and the difficulties attending them]; when I remember that we have now nearly reached the culmination of our great struggle for the suppression of the rebellion and its cause, I do not feel disposed, for one, to take this occasion, or any occasion, to say anything harshly against Abraham Lincoln.[13]

In the extraordinary and rapidly changing circumstances of the war, with unlooked-for prospects, such as wholesale emancipation, opening to view, Garrison could invite the people to look at the question of justice for the Negro "broadly, comprehensively, and philosophically"—to reflect on the role of public opinion in the continuance of slavery—with new confidence that he would be heard. But these words seem to be directed as much at his fellow abolitionists: in a similar sense, they, too, lacked a "philosophical" breadth of vision. One of the acts Garrison mentions is that Lincoln "has implored the Border States to get rid of [slavery]." That was not a novel act; Lincoln had done so in May 1862, in this striking language:

> I do not argue. I beseech you to make the arguments for yourselves. You can not if you would, be blind to the signs of the times. I beg of you a calm and enlarged consideration of them, ranging, if it may be, far above personal and partisan politics. . . . So much good has not been done, by one effort, in all past time, as, in the providence of God, it is now your high privilege to do. May the vast future not have to lament that you have neglected it.[14]

For the border states to voluntarily emancipate their slaves required "a calm and enlarged consideration" of "the signs of the times." Something much like this was also required for the abolitionists to recognize that the cherished goals of their movement were now subsumed in what Garrison called "our great struggle for the suppression of the rebellion and its cause." That cause, in Lincoln's view as well as in Garrison's, was slavery.

But Garrison must have been amazed that Lincoln's appeal to the border states to give up slavery was contained in a proclamation *revoking* the order of General David Hunter that would have freed all slaves in the states of Florida, Georgia, and South Carolina. When Lincoln issued his own proclamation four months later, Garrison reacted coolly. Publicly, he welcomed it as "an important step in the right direction"; privately he complained that Lincoln "can do nothing for *freedom* in a direct manner, but only by circumlocution and delay. How prompt was his action against Frémont [who had issued a similar proclamation in Missouri] and Hunter!"[15] Lincoln's "circumlocution and delay" were connected with his constitutional scruples as well as with his reading of public opinion. Garrison's preference for "a direct manner" indicates the distance between his views and Lincoln's in September 1862.

According to John Jay Chapman, the most eloquent of latter-day admirers of Garrison, his distinction lay in his having so far freed himself from the influence of the Constitution that he was able to declare himself wholeheartedly for natural justice ("human feelings") where the Constitution departed from this.

The metaphysical question was always the same, namely: "How far legal argument is valid when it contravenes human feelings?" . . . The unfortunate American statesmen who were obliged to formulate a philosophy upon the matter seem to me like that procession of hypocrites in Dante's Purgatory, robed in mantles of lead. They emerge, each bent down with his weight of logic, blinded by his view of the inherited curse—nursing his critique of the constitution; they file across the pages of our history from Jefferson to Lincoln—sad, perplexed men.

The solution given by Garrison to the puzzle was that the law must give way, that the Constitution was of no importance, after all. This is what any American would have answered had the question concerned the Constitution of Switzerland or of Patagonia. But, for some reason, our own Constitution was regarded differently.

Garrison, then, was able to regard the Constitution with a detachment of which his compatriots were incapable ("Our Country is the World, our Countrymen are all Mankind" was another of his mottoes). Of Americans in the antebellum period generally, however, Chapman writes, "The Constitution was so inwoven with our social life that the conflict between the letter and the spirit was ubiquitous. The restless probings went forward at the fireside, in the club, in the shop."[16] These Americans—"for some reason"—could not look upon their own constitution as they would have that of a foreign country.

It is notorious, however, that Garrison was unable to regard the politics of the antislavery movement with similar detachment—most notably in the case of his dispute with Frederick Douglass.[17] Garrison's lack of detachment in this respect may simply be the price he paid for his detachment in respect to the politics of the Constitution: having denied himself engagement in larger matters, he went to excess in smaller ones. Chapman offers a different explanation. He maintains that the problem was not any distortion in the character of Garrison's political engagement but the fact that he engaged in politics at all; politics is inherently distorting. Without mentioning Thoreau, Chapman assumes the high moral ground of Thoreau's critique of politics. What saves Chapman from Thoreau's contempt for politics is his acceptance of what he calls the "logic of natural law," the "great law of influence." It was by the operation of this law that abolitionists were in time succeeded by Liberty men, Liberty men by Free-Soilers, and Free-Soilers by Republicans. Chapman attributes to Wendell Phillips the view that was also Thoreau's: the preference of antislavery men for political organizations was "merely evidence of human perversity." Garrison, by contrast, "especially during the war," "became reconciled to that law." Chapman's acceptance of this law is consistent, however, with his view that Garrison's own political activity, such as it was, was a mistake:

> It is apparent that a man who assumes Garrison's grounds as to the importance of the spirit, and the unimportance of everything else, can never turn aside and adopt any institution, without doing violence to his own principles. To disparage all government because it is "the letter that killeth," and thereafter to swear fealty to some party, or adopt a symbol, or advise a friend to vote with the Whigs is inconsistent. . . . Garrison had not the mental training to perceive this. . . . From time to time his nature drew a veil over his theories, and so obscured them that he was able to support the Constitution of the United States, to rejoice in bloodshed, to take active part in political contests,—both in the great occasional National elections (as when he came out for Lincoln or Frémont), and in the continuous petty politics of the Anti-slavery cause.
>
>   . . . Garrison took up the propagation of the Anti-slavery cause by means of Democratic societies—a means which ties up any cause into tight knots as it goes along. . . . He is obliged, at intervals, to throw himself into the intrigue of Anti-slavery government, with the words of Moses on his lips and some vote-getting, hall-packing device in his mind. . . .
>
>   In adopting a formal organization he was adopting part of the very element that his thought rejected: he was fighting the cause of no-government by means of a "machine"; he was supporting the spirit by votes.
>
>   Hence Garrison's share in all the wearisome, little, and at times, degraded bickering between Anti-slavery societies; hence much personal vilification and heated talk over trifles.[18]

In interpreting Garrison as a kind of Thoreauvian, Chapman commits a mistake similar to one committed by Mayer, who, as an admirer of Thoreau as well as of Garrison, tends to assume that the two men always agreed with each other. Mayer offers this quotation from Thoreau's "Slavery in Massachusetts" as "the epitome of Garrisonian skepticism toward party politics": "The fate of the country . . . does not depend on what kind of paper you drop into the ballot-box once a year, but on what kind of man you drop from your chamber into the street every morning." He also cites these words of Garrison from 1839 "that anticipated Thoreau's": "It has never been a difficult matter to induce men to go to the ballot-box; but the grand difficulty ever has been, and still is, to persuade them to carry a good conscience thither, and act as free moral agents, not as the tools of party."[19]

But if Garrison was skeptical about party politics, he did not hesitate to make use of the devices of the party politician. The abolitionist organizations already had many of the characteristics of political parties, which is why Thoreau would have nothing to do with them. As Chapman notes with regret, "Garrison took up the propagation of the Anti-slavery cause by means of Democratic societies." Mayer expresses astonishment that Garrison "took no printed notice" of Thoreau's most famous political essay, "Resistance to Civil Government," in spite of strong circumstantial evidence that he knew of it. It seems not to have occurred to him that Garrison may have ignored the essay because of its implied criticism of him. Thoreau wrote, "to speak practically and as a citizen, unlike those who call themselves no-government men, I ask for, not at once no government, but *at once* a better government." However, Thoreau's promise to speak "practically and as a citizen" is not borne out; Garrison the "no-government man" proved more citizenly.[20]

Chapman's language most resembles Thoreau's where it touches on the object of the war. "The misguided and half-minded man of America had been trained to believe that Slavery was sacred; but *for the Union* he will die. So long as you call it Union he is ready to die for humanity." Chapman could not take seriously the possibility that the man of America understood something that the "educated foreigner," who viewed the North's war as one to extinguish slavery, did not. He would have agreed with the editorialist for the English paper the *Spectator,* who wrote of the Emancipation Proclamation, "The principle asserted is not that a human being cannot justly own another, but that he cannot own him unless he is loyal to the United States." This writer expressed, in an ungracious way, an important truth about the Emancipation Proclamation; but he did not see that loyalty to the Constitution had a bearing on the disposition of slavery. Garrison, as we have seen, endorsed the Proclamation despite reservations about it. Lincoln, too, had doubts, but they were of a different kind from Garrison's. At the time of the issuance of the preliminary emancipation proclamation, Garrison wrote that "every obstacle to constitutional emancipation is taken out of the way, and the government is, and must be, if true to itself, wholly on the side of liberty." Narrowly construed, Garrison's disagreement with Lincoln was over the extent of the president's constitutional powers; more broadly, the disagreement concerned what it meant for the government to be "true to itself."[21]

In September 1861 Lincoln revoked the emancipation edict of Frémont—who reportedly had been influenced by a Garrisonian abolitionist on his staff—and he would revoke the similar edict of Hunter in May of the following year. Mayer writes of Lincoln's action in Frémont's case that the president was "deeply concerned that the [Missouri] edict would alienate public opinion in another crucial border state, Kentucky." That is what Lincoln wrote in his first letter to Frémont on the matter, when he had to exercise a degree of tact with his subordinate. Lincoln could be more candid in writing to Orville H. Browning, a close political associate from his Springfield days. Public opinion was just one aspect of the emancipation question in Lincoln's mind. It was prudent for Lincoln to be concerned about a possibility that would have weakened the Union cause, perhaps fatally, and Garrison understood this. However, Lincoln suggests in the letter to Browning that he would have acted the same way even if he had not had the Kentuckians to worry about. He distinguishes between "policy" as to Kentucky, and what he calls the "principle" at issue: the difference between a matter that is "*purely political*" and one that falls "within the range of *military* law, or necessity."

If the General needs [slaves], he can seize them, and use them; but when the need is past, it is not for him to fix their permanent future condition. That must be settled according to laws made by law-makers, and not by military proclamations. The proclamation in the point in question, is simply "dictatorship." It assumes that the general may do *anything* he pleases—confiscate the lands and free the slaves of *loyal* people, as well as of disloyal ones. And going the whole figure I have no doubt would be more popular with some thoughtless people, than that which has been done! But I cannot assume this reckless position; nor allow others to assume it on my responsibility.[22]

It cannot be doubted that the abolitionists were foremost among the "thoughtless people" Lincoln had in mind. They had not thought through the implications of their own position: to wish for "the whole figure" represented an abandonment of the very ground on which they could, with plausibility, claim to go deeper than the politicians, namely (in Garrison's words) their attention to the "grand difficulty . . . to persuade [men] to carry a good conscience [to the ballot-box], and act as free moral agents." A "dictator," such as Frémont threatened to become, may set aside unjust laws at will, but by the same token he has no use for free moral agents. With the powers at his disposal, he has no need to persuade a refractory people that his course of action is just: he can force that people to comply.

Of course, the question in Frémont's (and later Hunter's) case concerned not only what a general did but also what a president might do. When Lincoln issued his own proclamation, conservative critics were quick to point out the apparent inconsistency. There was little difference, the editorialist for the Washington newspaper *National Intelligencer* wrote, between Hunter's proclamation and Lincoln's, except "in the signatures respectively attached to them." Not that this difference was unimportant to Lincoln: in revoking Hunter's proclamation, he wrote that the questions it raised "are questions which, under my responsibility, I reserve to myself, and which I can not feel justified in leaving to the decision of commanders in the field." If any person possessed the constitutional competence to issue such a proclamation, that person was the commander in chief. Nevertheless, Lincoln would have agreed that the technical constitutionality of a proclamation with his own signature attached to it was a feeble justification.[23]

Writing from the abolitionist side, Chapman similarly criticizes what he understands to be the "technical nature" of Lincoln's thinking. He finds Lincoln inconsistent—not in issuing the Emancipation Proclamation, but in exempting the border states from it.

> Lincoln . . . during the years of his leadership was obliged to stoop to the complex, peculiar, and inferior character of the contemporary mind. He was one of the greatest political geniuses and one of the most beautiful characters that ever lived; and he managed somehow to be intellectually honest and very nearly frank while fulfilling his mission. Yet I can

never read his debates with Douglas or consider his Border-State policy without being struck by the technical nature of all our history. One of Lincoln's chief interests in life, from early manhood onward, lay in emancipation. This he could not say and remain in politics; nay, he could not think it and remain in politics. He could not quite know himself and yet remain in politics. The awful weight of a creed that was never quite true—the creed of the Constitution—pressed down upon the intellects of our public men.

Chapman thought that only a doubt about its technical constitutionality prevented Lincoln from doing what natural justice required: issuing a proclamation of universal emancipation. But Lincoln did not think that even the less doubtful constitutionality of a proclamation freeing only slaves in states or parts of states in rebellion was necessarily a sufficient justification. Frémont's transgression was clear: the general had substituted his own judgment for that of the legislative authorities in a state that was not in rebellion. In the letter to Browning, Lincoln wrote, "Can it be pretended that it is any longer the government of the U.S.— any government of Constitution and laws—wherein a General, or a President, may make permanent rules of property by proclamation?" As a matter of military law, Hunter was on firmer ground in issuing his proclamation. Any executive proclamation, however, is of questionable validity in a "government of Constitution and laws."

> I do not say Congress might not with propriety pass a law, on the point, just such as General Fremont proclaimed. I do not say I might not, as a member of Congress, vote for it. What I object to, is, that I as President, shall expressly or impliedly seize and exercise the permanent legislative functions of the government.[24]

During the summer of 1862, Lincoln further aired his reservations about issuing a proclamation of emancipation in his meetings with groups that urged him to take this step without delay. He told a delegation of Quakers that visited the White House in June, headed by Oliver Johnson and bearing a memorial reportedly drafted by Garrison, "If a decree of emancipation could abolish Slavery, John Brown would have done the work effectually. Such a decree surely could not be more binding upon the South than the Constitution, and that cannot be enforced in that part of the country now."[25] A decree of emancipation might be technically constitutional, and the Constitution might remain technically valid in the South, but only force could make either one of them effectual. Lincoln did not doubt that force was justified, but he had to be careful to distinguish his use of it from Brown's.

The memorial quoted from Lincoln's "House Divided" speech, leaving off at the point where Lincoln had predicted that the Union would "become *all* one thing, or *all* the other," and urged him to seize the "golden opportunity" presented by the war to fulfill the prediction he had made in favor of freedom. But the president rejected this reasoning. Lincoln "agreed with the memorialists, that Slavery was wrong, but in regard to the ways and means of its removal, his views probably differed from theirs. The quotation in the memorial, from his Springfield speech, was incomplete. It should have embraced another sentence, in which he indicated his views as to the effect upon Slavery itself of the resistance to its extension." In the sentence that was omitted, Lincoln had written, "Either the *opponents* of slavery, will arrest the further spread of it, and place it where the public mind shall rest in the belief that it is in course of ultimate extinction; or its *advocates* will push it forward, till it shall become alike lawful in *all* the States, *old* as well as *new*—*North* as well as *South*." The opponents of slavery had prevailed in this manner in the election that had elevated Lincoln to the presidency, and the advocates of slavery had evidently viewed the result in this light. Lincoln's task was to compel recognition of the binding legality of his election: "when ballots have fairly, and constitutionally, decided, there can be no successful appeal . . . except to ballots themselves, at succeeding elections," as he expressed it in his first message to Congress as president. Almost two months after Johnson's visit—and less than ten days before issuing the preliminary emancipation proclamation—Lincoln would tell a similar delegation from Chicago, "I think you should admit that we already have an important principle to rally and unite the people in the fact that constitutional government is at stake. This is a fundamental idea, going down about as deep as any thing." A proclamation of emancipation would contribute to the accomplishment of Lincoln's task insofar as it contributed to victory in the war, but it would carry the risk of further weakening the government of Constitution and laws that Lincoln was pledged to save.[26]

Accordingly, Lincoln issued his decree only when he had arrived at the judgment that circumstances demanded it, and he incorporated into it sections from two recent acts of Congress, the latter of which had already made "forever free of their servitude" all slaves deemed in very broad terms to be captives of war. In his draft, Lincoln had even reminded the American people that they could, if they wished, cancel the decree by voting him out of office: the government, he wrote, would recognize and maintain the freedom of the former slaves "during the continuance in office of the present incumbent." In 1863 Lincoln would use the same reasoning by which he had justified limiting Frémont's powers to justify limiting his own powers as president. Responding to the "great anxiety" of Treasury Secretary Chase, the Radical in his cabinet, "that the emancipation proclamation shall now be applied to certain parts of Virginia and Louisiana which were exempted from it last January," Lincoln stated "what appear to me to be difficulties in the way of such a step."

> If I take the step must I not do so, without the argument of military necessity, and so, without any argument, except the one that I think the measure politically expedient, and morally right? Would I not thus give up all footing upon constitution or law? Would I not thus be in the boundless field of absolutism? . . . Could it fail to be perceived that without any further stretch, I might do the same in Delaware, Maryland, Kentucky, Tennessee, and Missouri; and even change any law in any state?[27]

Lincoln needed the support of public opinion in ending slavery, as a military commander would not have. In the end he received it—with help from Garrison. The abolitionist aided Lincoln's reelection, and he did more: Garrison prepared Americans for the end of slavery by constitutional amendment and for the eventual recognition of Negro citizenship. The difficulty with the Emancipation Proclamation lay in the fact that according to the theory on which it was based, the authority of the federal government continued to extend to all parts of the Union, secession notwithstanding—but Lincoln could not have had much hope that it would be sustained by *southern* opinion, at least not before a long time had passed.

Mayer writes, "With his gift for aphorism Thoreau distilled a dozen years of Garrisonian criticism into a single sentence—'The law will never make men free; it is men who have got to make the law free.'" In this respect a proclamation or decree is the most questionable kind of law: it is the kind least able to make men free, inasmuch as it fails to treat them as free. Mayer also writes that years after the war "Garrison explained the shift in public opinion [away from concern with issues of racial justice] as the 'melancholy' consequence of having emancipated the slaves as a response to military necessity rather than as 'an act of general repentance.'"[28] Repentance can never be compelled; but the melancholy consequence Garrison spoke of would only have been made worse by the precipitate action he had favored. In spite of his reputedly superior insight into the importance of molding public opinion, Garrison was prepared to hazard the loss of public confidence in Lincoln's administration when first Frémont and then Hunter rashly issued edicts of emancipation. Certainly Lincoln's praise of Garrison's "logic and moral power" did not refer to this.

In an 1860 speech Frederick Douglass compared the powers of an American president to those of a king: "Our king is armed with mighty powers. . . . He is Commander-in-Chief of the army and navy.—During his reign he can exercise his power as rigorously as any of the crowned heads of Europe, and do so with greater impunity."[29] The paradox is that these almost kingly powers made it possible for Lincoln to issue the Emancipation Proclamation. Nevertheless, there were limits to what was possible or proper for Lincoln to do. After Lincoln's reelection Garrison wrote to Francis Newman in London, a "sympathizer with the utter distrust of Mr. Lincoln shown by [Wendell] Phillips and his followers," that the president's "primary and all-comprehensive duty is to maintain the Union and execute the Constitution, in good faith, according to the best of his ability, without reference to the views of any clique or party in the land, and for the general welfare. And herein lies the injustice of your criticism upon him. You seem to regard him as occupying a position and wielding powers virtually autocratic."[30] A European observer once compared Lincoln unfavorably with Czar Alexander II, who had emancipated Russia's serfs, on the ground that "while Lincoln only freed the slaves of his enemies the Czar freed the slaves of his friends." Exaggerating to make a point, Lincoln had said Americans were once "the political slaves of King George." The Czar could free even the slaves of his friends, because those friends, too, were his "political slaves."[31]

By the end of the war, Garrison the "Lincoln emancipationist" had come to appreciate the difference between a president and a czar. What he did not fully appreciate—certainly before 1863, perhaps even afterward—is the resemblance between an autocrat and a slave master. His endorsement of even the relatively benevolent despotism of an antislavery general undermined the ground of his own opposition to slavery.

Chapter 9

Frederick Douglass

Antislavery Constitutionalism and the Problem of Consent

Since the 1950s, when Philip S. Foner prepared the first collected edition of Douglass's works and found that "no commercial publisher or even university press displayed the slightest interest in making available the letters, editorials, and speeches of this man of towering dimensions," there has been a striking revival of interest in Frederick Douglass. Little of this new attention has been directed toward Douglass's constitutional views; yet they formed a most important difference between Douglass and Lincoln. In 1876, at the unveiling of the Freedman's Monument in Washington, D.C., Douglass said, "To protect, defend, and perpetuate slavery in the states where it existed Abraham Lincoln was not less ready than any other President to draw the sword of the nation. He was ready to execute all the supposed guarantees of the United States Constitution in favor of the slave system anywhere inside the slave states."[1] Lincoln, of course, regarded these "supposed" constitutional guarantees as binding.

In June 1861, Douglass noted "with moderate exultation, the change which has taken place recently in the attitude of Mr. Garrison and his friends, in respect to the American Union." With the outbreak of war, Douglass's onetime mentor came to see virtues in the Constitution and the Union that he had not seen, or at least had not stressed, before—

virtues Douglass himself recognized ten years earlier. Douglass's transfer of allegiances from Garrison to the political abolitionists would have decisive consequences for the course of his career. Herbert Storing wrote, "The break [with the Garrisonians] was ostensibly over the interpretation of the Constitution. . . . More fundamentally, Douglass revised his opinion about the duty of the Negro reformer in the face of legally sanctioned injustice."[2] Storing defended the revision, but his distinction between the interpretation of the Constitution as the ostensible matter at issue and the duty of the reformer as the more fundamental or presumably genuine one seems to represent a tacit admission of the problematical character of Douglass's newly adopted constitutional views.

Like Garrison, Douglass had long been an opponent of colonization. "We live here," he declared in 1849, "have lived here—have a right to live here, and mean to live here."[3] By the 1850s, Douglass had arrived at the conclusion that his people's place in their country's future was not to be secured by destroying the existing constitutional order, as Garrison proposed, but by extending its acknowledged benefits more widely. Douglass's change of opinion brought him closer to antislavery politicians such as Lincoln. Still, his rejection of the Garrisonian view meant a return to the Constitution of 1787 only in a qualified sense. Douglass's constitution was not one that most Americans would have recognized as their own.

David E. Schrader defends Douglass's constitutional views more robustly than Storing does, but he underestimates the problems that Douglass and other political abolitionists faced in trying to gain support for their views among nonabolitionists. Schrader summarizes the political abolitionists' use of the natural-law tradition against the Garrisonians:

If there is a way of interpreting the text of the law so as to make it consistent with the idea of law, with principles of natural justice and the natural rights of human beings, then the law must be interpreted in that manner. . . . Applied to the Constitution, this meant that if there was a way of interpreting the Constitution that did not commit the Constitution to the support of slavery, which even most of the supporters of the legality of slavery agreed was contrary to the demands of natural justice, then the anti-union and anti-political commitments of the Garrisonians would not follow.[4]

One meaning of *natural* is "innate." Accordingly, one test of the natural-ness of any principle of justice is whether it harmonizes with sympa-thies that are arguably innate because they are shared by people in widely different forms of society. Lincoln pointed to signs of "sympa-thies in the bosoms of the southern people" that "manifest in many ways, their sense of the wrong of slavery." However, in the face of the express denial by southerners—and many northerners—that slavery "was contrary to the demands of natural justice," the signs that Lincoln noted, important as they were, cannot have carried much political weight. His party did not claim the right to exclude slavery from the ter-ritories on the basis of natural justice alone: they sought an electoral mandate for their interpretation of the Constitution as granting Congress this power. In his first inaugural address, Lincoln framed the question this way:

> *May* Congress prohibit slavery in the territories? The Constitution does not expressly say. *Must* Congress protect slavery in the territories? The Constitution does not expressly say.
> From questions of this class spring all our constitutional controversies, and we divide upon them into majorities and minorities. If the minority will not acquiesce, the majority must, or the government must cease.

Republicans could not expect the South to accept a popular judgment in favor of their party's interpretation on a doubtful point of the Constitution, if they could not assure it of their willingness to abide by the customary interpretation on points that were less doubtful, even when those points conflicted with their sense of natural justice.[5]

Schrader suggests that one reason for the relative neglect of Douglass's constitutionalism is that its basis in natural law may strike many in our time as "too dogmatic." From Lincoln's point of view, the difficulty with natural-law interpretations of the Constitution was that the avowal of them made any assurance to the minority of the safety of its constitutional rights less credible. The difficulty was all the greater in view of the absence of any explicit mention of slavery in the text of the Constitution—an absence to which Douglass, like Lincoln, frequently called attention. Lincoln would not oppose the customary interpreta-tion as to the constitutionality of slavery by a novel, if theoretically defensible, reading of the text. This was what he meant when he said in the first inaugural address, "I take the official oath to-day . . . with no purpose to construe the Constitution or laws, by any hypercritical rules." Howard Brotz has written that Douglass was "able to avoid doctrinairism" because his "theoretical reflections emerge from [his] practical concerns"; his position "relat[es] both consideration of power and considerations of principle to the tasks of the political situation."[6] "Hypercritical," however, is close to "doctrinaire." If Douglass's constitutionalism emerged from his practical concerns as dictated by his understanding of the tasks of the political situation, then we must see how his understanding differed from Lincoln's.

Like some members of the Constitutional Convention, the abolitionists "thought the term *legal* equivocal, and favoring the idea that slavery was legal in a moral view."[7] This was more than a problem of language: it provoked the abolitionists to intense debate about the nature of law. The response of Garrison and his followers was to stress the distinction between legality and morality. They did so, however, in a manner that remained equivocal: they condemned the Constitution for failing to measure up to their moral standard, and they readily gave up their hostility to the compact when the outbreak of war opened new possibilities for reforming its objectionable features. The political abolitionists took a different tack. They stressed the *connection* between legality and morality, which led them to the paradoxical conclusion that slavery was, in fact, unconstitutional. Douglass acknowledged that the view of the Constitution he had come to reject was "supported by the united and entire history of every department of the government."[8] He was willing to swallow the paradox, nevertheless, because it gave him the freedom to pursue abolition by political means.

One of the first fruits of Douglass's newly political orientation was the second, much expanded, version of his autobiography, entitled *My Bondage and My Freedom,* which appeared in 1855; the topics covered in its final chapter include "Disciple of Mr. Garrison—Change of Opinion—Causes Leading to It—The Consequences of the Change." The first version of his autobiography, *Narrative of the Life of Frederick Douglass,* was published in 1845, but it ends with Douglass's introduction to the abolitionists in the summer of 1841. *My Bondage and My Freedom* is more than three times as long, in part because it carries the story of his life up to the mid–1850s, but mostly because of its greater detail about his years in slavery. The period that followed the first months of Douglass's "new life" as an abolition speaker (when his role was limited to a simple recitation of the facts of his case) was a time when, Douglass said, "I was now reading and thinking. New views of the subject were presented to my mind" (*MBMF*, 361). The influence of these new views is evident in the altered treatment Douglass gives to his life as a slave in *My Bondage and My Freedom*.

My Bondage and My Freedom includes, for example, this un-Garrisonian observation about Douglass's "old master" from his boyhood in slavery on Maryland's Eastern Shore:

> He could, when it suited him, appear to be literally insensible to the claims of humanity, when appealed to by the helpless against an aggressor, and he could himself commit outrages, deep, dark and nameless. Yet he was not by nature worse than other men. Had he been brought up in a free state, surrounded by the just restraints of free society—restraints which are necessary to the freedom of all its members, alike and equally—Capt. Anthony might have been as humane a man, and every way as respectable, as many who now oppose the slave system; certainly as humane and respectable as are members of society generally. (*MBMF*, 79-80)

The "just restraints of free society" take the form of laws as well as public opinion. An example is given later in the same chapter when Douglass introduces the topic of marriage in connection with his treatment of the relationship between his old master and a slave, Esther, whom he describes as possessing "that which is ever a curse to the slave-girl; namely,—personal beauty." The absence of laws to protect a slave woman in her married or unmarried state left her "at the mercy of the power, caprice and passion of her owner." Douglass's language suggests, however, that he thought the absence of such laws also left the slaves at the mercy of their own caprice and passion: "Slavery provides no means for the honorable continuation of the race. Marriage—as imposing obligations on the parties to it—has no existence here, except in such hearts as are purer and higher than the standard morality around them" (*MBMF*, 85-86).

As for public opinion, Douglass notes that its value as a restraint depends on exposure to wholesome laws and institutions. He gives this description of the plantation where he grew up, the home plantation of the Lloyd family, who employed his old master:

> Its whole public is made up of, and divided into, three classes—SLAVE-HOLDERS, SLAVES, and OVERSEERS. Its blacksmiths, wheelwrights, shoe-makers, weavers, and coopers, are slaves. . . . Every leaf and grain of the produce of this plantation, and those of the neighboring farms belonging to Col. Lloyd, are transported to Baltimore in Col. Lloyd's own vessels; every man and boy on board of which—except the captain—are owned by him. In return, everything brought to the plantation, comes through the same channel. (*MBMF,* 62-63)

Such a public was closed off by its situation from salutary influences:

> Public opinion in such a quarter . . . is not likely to be very efficient in protecting the slave from cruelty. On the contrary, it must increase and intensify his wrongs. Public opinion seldom differs very widely from public practice. To be a restraint upon cruelty and vice, public opinion must emanate from a humane and virtuous community. To no such humane and virtuous community, is Col. Lloyd's plantation exposed. That plantation is a little nation of its own, having its own language, its own rules, regulations and customs. The laws and institutions of the state, apparently touch it nowhere. (*MBMF,* 63-64)

Before the spring of 1861, when the prospect of a war to end slavery appeared before his mind's eye, Garrison had trusted in a "political reformation [that] is to be effected solely by a change in the moral vision of the people." "By converting electors to the doctrine that slavery ought to be immediately abolished," Garrison argued, "a rectified political action is the natural consequence; for where this doctrine is received into the soul, the soul-carrier may be trusted any where, that he will not betray the cause of bleeding humanity."[9] But if Douglass is right that "public opinion seldom differs very widely from public practice," the moral suasionists have apparently been going at the matter backward. The highest task for the opponents of slavery was not to convert individual electors to the doctrine of immediatism, but to foster a humane and virtuous *community.*

Douglass seems to have arrived independently at Alexis de Tocqueville's insight about the power of public opinion in democratic America: not only that this power could be tyrannical, but that it tyrannized over the very people who were supposed to be the source of it.[10] For precisely this reason, however, one is justified in doubting whether public opinion is really as strong as it seems. Is an opinion strong because it is widely held, or is it widely held because it seems to be so strong? Such an insight into the ambiguous character of democratic public opinion naturally raised a doubt about its value as the target of abolitionists' efforts.

In *My Bondage and My Freedom*, Douglass comments on his state of mind after the failure of his first attempt to escape from slavery—he was of course guilty of plotting with his friends to run away, but he could not agree that running away with themselves was a crime: "Such is the power of public opinion, that it is hard, even for the innocent, to feel the happy consolations of innocence, when they fall under the maledictions of this power. How could we regard ourselves as in the right, when all around us denounced us as criminals, and had the power and the disposition to treat us as such" (*MBMF,* 298). The terrible power of democratic public opinion had a less threatening, even hopeful aspect also: it suggested that prejudice against people of African descent might be as weak in fact as it was strong in appearance. Near the end of *My Bondage and My Freedom,* Douglass relates a pair of incidents that lend credence to this view. His experience, "both serious and mirthful, combats [the] conclusion," which many blacks had drawn from their experience, "that there is a natural, an inherent, and an invincible repugnance in the breast of the white race toward dark-colored people." In introducing these incidents, however, Douglass speaks not of whites generally but of Americans: "Leaving out of sight, for a moment, grave facts, to this point, I will state one or two, which illustrate a very interesting feature of American character as well as American prejudice." In each incident, passengers on a train on which Douglass was riding quickly overcame their aversion to his presence when they saw him receive a friendly greeting from an eminent person— a present or future state governor. Douglass concludes, "With such facts as these before me—and I have many of them—I am inclined to think that pride and fashion have much to do with the treatment commonly extended to colored people in the United States" (*MBMF,* 402-5).

Douglass found a strength of character in certain politicians, by no means necessarily antislavery in their views, that enabled them to resist the tyranny of public opinion, at least in private life; and he found this strength in a form that he knew was far more acceptable to most Americans than the form exhibited by his fellow abolitionists. To the "facts" presented in *My Bondage and My Freedom*, two similar incidents must be added that occurred in the same period, 1841–1855, but were recorded in print only after the Civil War. Both involved Democratic members of Congress: Moses Norris of New Hampshire and, more remarkably, Edward Marshall of California, a native of Kentucky (and nephew of the long-serving chief justice of the Supreme Court, John Marshall). Norris offered Douglass accommodation in his home, and Marshall intervened when two of the crewmen of a steamship on which he and Douglass were traveling tried to remove Douglass from his seat in the dining cabin.[11] In the light of these incidents, the problem of slavery in the United States began to assume a new shape in Douglass's mind.

In spite of the greater detail in *My Bondage and My Freedom*, one of the clearest signs of Douglass's new thinking is not something that he adds to this work but something that he leaves out of it. The only overt political commentary in the *Narrative* is excised from the later account of his life. In the earlier work, Douglass wrote,

> Few privileges were esteemed higher, by the slaves of the out-farms, than that of being selected to do errands at the Great House Farm [that is, the home plantation]. It was associated in their minds with greatness. A representative could not be prouder of his election to a seat in the American Congress, than a slave on one of the out-farms would be of his election to do errands at the Great House Farm. . . . The competitors for this office sought as diligently to please their overseers, as the office-seekers in the political parties seek to please and deceive the people. The same traits of character might be seen in Colonel Lloyd's slaves, as are seen in the slaves of the political parties.[12]

In the meantime Douglass had discovered in some politicians the opposite of slavish traits; this gratuitous comparison is dropped from his second autobiography. Douglass's new openness to politics extended even to party organizations.

It is instructive also to compare the reference to Patrick Henry in the *Narrative* with the longer corresponding passage in *My Bondage and My Freedom*. Commenting on his first attempt to escape from slavery, in the company of a few friends, Douglass wrote in the earlier account, "In coming to a fixed determination to run away, we did more than Patrick Henry, when he resolved upon liberty or death. With us it was a doubtful liberty at most, and almost certain death if we failed."[13] Douglass leaves the reader in doubt about whether he thinks the honor customarily given to Henry, and by implication to Henry's contemporaries, is fully deserved. In the second version of his autobiography, Douglass removes this doubt.

> Patrick Henry, to a listening senate, thrilled by his magic eloquence and ready to stand by him in his boldest flights, could say, "Give me Liberty or give me Death," and this saying was a sublime one, even for a freeman; but, incomparably more sublime, was the same sentiment, when *practically* asserted by men accustomed to the lash and chain— men whose sensibilities must have become more or less deadened by their bondage. With us it was a *doubtful* liberty, at best, that we sought; and a certain, lingering death in the rice swamps and sugar fields, if we failed. (*MBMF*, 284)

The point in *My Bondage and My Freedom* was not to withdraw admiration from Henry but to extend it to the fugitive slave.

Years later Douglass would write of the political abolitionists and the Garrisonians that the former group "looked at slavery as a creature of law," while the latter "regarded it as a creature of public opinion."[14] Douglass's conversion to the view of slavery as a creature of law, or rather of one interpretation of the law, did not lead him to devalue persuasion, but he came to recognize the complexity of the psychology behind it. In *My Bondage and My Freedom,* he observes that even slavery, which, as he has often said, is based on the superior physical force of the slaveholders, cannot do without arguments in its justification. The slave "must be able to detect no inconsistencies in slavery. The man that takes his earnings, must be able to convince him that he has a perfect right to do so. It must not depend upon mere force; the slave must know no Higher Law than his master's will. The whole relationship must not only demonstrate, to his mind, its necessity, but its absolute rightfulness" (*MBMF*, 320). It goes without saying that the rightfulness of slavery could never have been made to seem convincing in the absence of force. Law, which brings force to bear even on freemen, must be made to address the reason even of slaves.

Douglass's study of human nature brought within the compass of his understanding motives that would have remained inaccessible to a simple moralist. In the summer of 1862, Douglass argued that a proclamation of emancipation was necessary not solely for moral reasons, but also because the failure of the Union had been a failure of interest. Interest is more humane a motive principle than force, but it has more affinity with force than do ideas.

> It is plain that there can never be any union between the north and the south, while the south values slavery more than nationality. A union of interest is essential to a union of ideas, and without this union of ideas, the outward form of the union will be but as a rope of sand. Now it is quite clear that while slavery lasts at the south, it will remain hereafter as heretofore, the great dominating interest, overtopping all others, and shaping the sentiments and opinions of the people in accordance with itself. (*SSW*, 507)

A union of interests is necessary to the higher achievement of a union of ideas; in a similar way, law combines force with "moral force":

> But a proclamation of Emancipation, says one, would only be a paper order. I answer, so is any order emanating from our Government. . . . All laws, all written rules for the Government of the army and navy and people, are "paper orders," and would remain only such were they not backed up by force, still we do not object to them as useless, but admit their wisdom and necessity. Then these paper orders carry with them a certain moral force which makes them in a large measure self-executing. (*SSW*, 507-8)

Douglass showed a subtler and more generous understanding of the relation of morals, interest, and force than was evinced by the moral suasionists. Although he criticized Lincoln's action or inaction on many of the same occasions that Garrison did, Douglass had a better right to do so because he spoke from a perspective that was fundamentally more sympathetic to politics, and he did so long before the outbreak of war.

The use of force is necessarily circumscribed in a free community, of course. The Constitution, for example, could not go into effect in a state until the people of that state had given their consent. Not that consent can redeem a vicious law, if (as the Garrisonians said) that is what the Constitution was. When Douglass, in announcing his change of opinion about the Constitution, called slavery "a system of lawless violence" that *"never was lawful, and never can be made so"* (SSW, 174), Garrison had an answer ready. "Some are unwilling to admit the possibility of legalizing slavery," he said, "because of its foul and monstrous character. But what iniquity may not men commit by agreement?" Still, in a community where public opinion is all-important, agreement or consent concerning principles of law, if not the application of those principles, is what makes political life possible. Garrison had made this reply to the political abolitionists: "It matters not what is the theory of the government, if the practice of the government be unjust and tyrannical."[15] It did matter, however, if the theory retained its hold on public opinion— it made possible an appeal from the unjust practice to the just theory. Lincoln and Douglass both did this, and Garrison himself frequently appealed to the Declaration of Independence. But Garrison's view of the Constitution as proslavery (with whatever qualification may be implied in the distinction between his own "disunionism" and southern "secessionism") put him at a disadvantage that is evident by comparison with Douglass's political approach.

In his famous 1852 Fourth of July oration, Douglass began by praising the men who effected the separation from Britain:

> Fellow Citizens, I am not wanting in respect for the fathers of this republic. . . . The point from which I am compelled to view them is not, certainly, the most favorable; and yet I cannot contemplate their great deeds with less than admiration. They were statesmen, patriots, and heroes, and for the good they did, and the principles they contended for, I will unite with you to honor their memory. (SSW, 192)

Nevertheless, if the Garrisonians were right, and "the right to hold, and to hunt slaves is a part of that Constitution framed by the illustrious

Fathers of this Republic"—"Then, I dare to affirm, notwithstanding all I have said before, your fathers stooped, basely stooped. . . . And instead of being the honest men I have before declared them to be, they were the veriest imposters that ever practised on mankind. This is the inevitable conclusion" (*SSW*, 203). The Garrisonians were in the position of appealing to the moral principles of the same generation of men that had framed the, in their opinion, wicked Constitution. Having changed his mind about the Constitution, however, Douglass was able to appeal to the legal as well as to the moral principles of the fathers of the American republic. As he said on another occasion, "A chart is one thing, the course of the vessel is another. The Constitution may be right, the Government wrong" (*SSW*, 380). The problem, then, was not the Constitution itself but the interpretation of it that would deny blacks a share in its benefits. Garrison's interpretation of the Constitution was no better than Chief Justice Roger Taney's, Douglass observed at the time the Dred Scott decision was handed down; both Garrison and Taney argued "that the Constitution was designed to secure the blessings of liberty and justice to the people who made it, and to the posterity of the people who made it, but was never designed to do any such thing for the colored people of African descent."[16] These interpreters, however, had to go outside the text of the Constitution to make their argument: "The Constitution knows all the human inhabitants of this country as 'the people.' It makes . . . no discrimination in favor of, or against, any class of the people, but is fitted to protect and preserve the rights of all." In short, Douglass asked that Americans "live up to the Constitution" (*SSW*, 357-58). On the basis of an argument that to Douglass's new way of thinking was far from conclusive, the Garrisonians had deprived themselves of the advantage of appealing from the course of the government at any given moment to the relatively permanent principles of the Constitution. "But how dare any man who pretends to be a friend to the Negro thus gratuitously concede away what the Negro has a right to claim under the Constitution? Why should such friends invent new arguments to increase the hopelessness of his bondage?" (*SSW*, 387).

For all the advantages gained, however, Douglass's change of opinion brought disadvantages too. Douglass describes the change in *My Bondage and My Freedom*:

Upon a reconsideration of the whole subject, I became convinced that there was no necessity for dissolving the "union between the northern and southern states;" that to seek this dissolution was no part of my duty as an abolitionist; that to abstain from voting, was to refuse to exercise a legitimate and powerful means for abolishing slavery; and that the constitution of the United States not only contained no guarantees in favor of slavery, but, on the contrary, it is, in its letter and spirit, an anti-slavery instrument, demanding the abolition of slavery as a condition of its own existence, as the supreme law of the land. (*MBMF,* 396)

The view that the Constitution was antislavery in letter as well as in spirit—that it not only looked to the eventual abolition of slavery but actually demanded it, "as a condition of its own existence"—was taken in the face of the all but universal assumption that the Constitution granted the federal government no power over slavery in the states. Lincoln went so far as to call this assumption "implied constitutional law" in his first inaugural address.[17] Douglass insisted on the "Right and duty of the Federal Government to abolish Slavery everywhere in the United States," but he admitted, in justification of his support for the Republican candidates Frémont and Dayton in 1856, that "this doctrine has been made appreciable but to a few minds, the dwellers in the mountain peaks of the moral world, who catch the first beams of morning, long before the slumberers in the valleys awake from their dreams" (*SSW,* 341). Despite the apparently universal thrust of this metaphor, Douglass evidently had only the North in mind. Although he criticized the Garrisonians on the ground that "to dissolve the Union would be to withdraw the emancipating power from the field" (*SSW,* 352), Douglass could not hope to bring the South around to the view that the Constitution gave this power to the federal government. That being so, Garrison replied, a victory for the political abolitionists would mean the dissolution of the Union anyway.

Supposing—what is not within the scope of probabilities—that we could win over to their view of the Constitution a majority, ay, the entire body of the people of the North, so that they could control the action of Congress through their representatives, and in this manner decree the abolition of slavery throughout the South—could we hope to witness even the enactment of such a decree, (to say nothing of its enforcement,) without its being accompanied by the most fearful consequences?

The South would not only rebel but would have justice on its side in doing so: "such a construction [as the political abolitionists endorsed], if enforced by pains and penalties, would unquestionably lead to a civil war, in which the aggrieved party would justly claim to have been betrayed, and robbed of their constitutional rights."[18]

Garrison's criticism of the constitutional views of the political abolitionists would not seem to touch the moderate antislavery parties such as the Republicans; but his sons, in their biography of their father, append this comment to a similar passage from the *Liberator*: "Let posterity decide how far the South was screwed up to the civil war by this Liberty, Free-Soil, and Republican Party playing fast and loose with the language of the Constitution—covering who could tell what intentions against 'the compact' when once in power on the innocent pretext of checking the further spread of slavery?"[19] From the Garrisonians' point of view, Douglass's position, as weak as they believed it to be, had the advantage of candor over that of the nonextensionists. These parties— so runs the charge—having shown themselves willing to construe the Constitution to their ends by introducing a doubtful distinction between slavery in the states and in the territories, could give no assurance worthy of confidence that they would not set the Constitution aside altogether, given the opportunity. They could not be sincere about upholding the letter of the Constitution as to slavery in the states, if they were genuinely antislavery as they claimed to be. Douglass, however, was open about his intentions: he would use the power of the federal government to overthrow slavery, over the heads of the southern people.

The charge that the Republicans were not to be trusted, however, takes for granted the proslavery character of the Constitution as customarily construed. About the time of his change of opinion, before he had fully made up his mind, Douglass wrote to the political abolitionist Gerrit Smith, "I have about decided to let Slaveholders and their Northern abettors have the Laboring *oar* in putting a proslavery interpretation upon the Constitution. I am sick and tired of arguing on the slaveholders' side of this question" (*SSW,* 171). Surely Douglass was right, in the absence of compelling evidence to the contrary, to argue on freedom's side of the question of constitutional interpretation. The Constitution, after all, was framed as a law by which a free people could govern itself. Douglass found no difficulty in naming constitutional provisions that were implicitly antislavery. Where, he asked, will a reader of the Constitution find a guarantee for slavery?

> Will he find it in the declaration that no person shall be deprived of life, liberty, or property, without due process of law [Fifth Amendment]? Will he find it in the declaration that the Constitution was established to secure the blessing of liberty [Preamble]? Will he find it in the right of the people to be secure in their persons and papers, and houses, and effects [Fourth Amendment]? Will he find it in the clause prohibiting the enactment by any State of a bill of attainder [Article I, section 10]? (*SSW*, 354)

But in his tendency to conflate the Constitution and the Declaration of Independence, Douglass defied the close connection between public opinion and public practice that he noted in *My Bondage and My Freedom*. The support in public opinion for his new interpretation of the Constitution was too slight to bear the weight of his demand for a wholly new public practice.

Gustave de Beaumont, Tocqueville's traveling companion, captures the paradox of slavery in one of the appendixes to his didactic novel *Marie; or, Slavery in the United States:* the institution is both dependent on and deeply resistant to law. Slavery is a creature of law at the same time that it violates the principle of reciprocity that is implicit in the idea of lawful, as opposed to arbitrary, authority. "The law having made a master of one and a slave of the other, creating two beings of an entirely different sort, one feels the impossibility of establishing relations of the slave with the master or of the slave with free men, on a basis of reciprocity; then, in deviating from this rule, the sole equitable basis of human relationships, one falls into complete arbitrariness, and must violate every principle." The master and slave stand in relation to each other very much as two men would stand in the state of nature.

> A salutary principle, consecrated by all wise legislatures, is that in criminal cases the penalties must be fixed by law. . . .
>
> But there is another principle even more sacred than the preceding:

that no one can do justice on his own behalf, and that whoever has been wronged must appeal to the magistrates appointed by law to judge between plaintiff and accused.

This rule is formally violated by the laws of South Carolina and Louisiana, relative to slaves. In the laws of these two states one finds a provision which confers upon the master the discretionary power to punish his slaves, whether by blows of the whip or stick, or by imprisonment; he weighs the offense, condemns the slave, and applies the penalty; he is at once litigant, judge, and executioner.

In the case of slaves, "the principles of common law would be disastrous, and regular forms of justice impossible." That is why those who, while allowing slavery, would ease the condition of the slave by piecemeal reforms are misguided. "Instead of blaming the Americans for their bad treatment of slaves, one should reproach them with slavery itself. The principle being admitted, the consequences people deplore are inevitable." Douglass expresses the same conclusion: "The apologists for slavery often speak of the abuses of slavery; and they tell us that they are as much opposed to those abuses as we are. . . . The answer to that view is, that slavery is *itself* an abuse. . . . Grant that slavery is right; grant that the relation of master and slave may innocently exist; and there is not a single outrage which was ever committed against the slave but what finds an apology in the very necessity of the case."[20]

The Garrisonians stressed the dependence of slavery on law and condemned the Constitution; Douglass, along with other political abolitionists, stressed the lawless nature of slavery and exalted the Constitution as "warrant for the abolition of slavery in every state in the American Union" (*MBMF*, 398). It is easy to see that both sides were partly right—and that the circumstances in which their debate was carried on were unfavorable to a fair assessment of the strengths and weaknesses in the other's views, to say nothing of the views of nonabolitionists. Those circumstances did not discourage doctrinairism. Garrison evidently believed that his own rejection of piecemeal reforms required him to reject politics as well. Douglass did not make this mistake, but his position was hardly more favorable to a comprehensive view of the matter. The abolitionists combined a keen interest in political questions with an almost complete disengagement from practical politics—even

the political abolitionists, whose membership was so small that it was
practically of no consequence.

Douglass's superior political sense saved him from some of the difficulties into which his own arguments might have led him. When apologists for slavery argued that the law distributed burdens and benefits
differently to slaves than it did to freemen but (provided that abuses
could be corrected) not necessarily less advantageously, Douglass
answered that the two cases could not be compared. He would not
"admit that human legislation can rightfully reduce [a man] to slavery,
by a simple vote," or that a slave "abandons the right of self defence" in
favor of protection under law (*SSW*, 280). The advantage of this kind of
argument is that it exposes most clearly the injustice of laws that would
seek to establish slavery. The corresponding disadvantage is that it
deprives antislavery legislation of its intended effect; it puts the slave
outside the legal order, beyond the reach of law. Such unjust laws as
would make one man slave to another are really no laws at all. The
United States could not outlaw what it had no right to recognize as legal
in the first place. But, as Howard Brotz has said, such a doctrinaire position would have been highly uncharacteristic of Douglass. We have also
the testimony of Booker T. Washington on this point: Douglass "was by
temperament a politician, and, like all politicians, more or less of an
opportunist. He was less interested in the theory upon which slavery
should be abolished than he was in the means by which freedom could
be achieved. No doubt he was influenced to a considerable degree, in
the formulation of his views in regard to the Constitution, by his practical sense of what the situation demanded."

Douglass could take a pragmatic attitude concerning even so fundamental a matter as the purchase of his freedom, which he, of course,
regarded as his own by right. When he took advantage of a fund raised
by his friends in England (where Douglass had gone to avoid recapture
after the publication of his *Narrative*) for this purpose, some of his
"uncompromising anti-slavery friends" in the United States "were not
pleased." Those uncompromising friends "thought it a violation of antislavery principles—conceding a right of property in man." Douglass,
however, viewed the matter "simply in the light of a ransom, or money
extorted by a robber"; he "could not see . . . a violation of the rules of
morality" in it. In fact, there was a moral argument in favor of the trans-

action: "I felt that I had a duty to perform—and that was, to labor and suffer with the oppressed in my native land" (*MBMF*, 375-76).[21]

The danger of doctrinairism was real, as is shown by the case of Lysander Spooner, one of those whose writings on the Constitution Douglass cited as having been decisive in changing his opinion. Spooner's treatise *The Unconstitutionality of Slavery* begins by addressing the question, "What is law?" Spooner answers, "Law . . . applied to any object or thing whatever, signifies a natural, unalterable, universal principle, governing such object or thing." Natural law is paramount over "any other rule of conduct, which the arbitrary will of any man, or combination of men, may attempt to establish." Natural law, "inasmuch as it recognizes the natural right of men to enter into obligatory contracts, permits the formation of government, founded on contract"; but the contract of government "must purport to authorize nothing inconsistent with natural justice and men's natural rights." Having found slavery unconstitutional by reason of its deviation from natural justice, it was a short step for Spooner later to find, as it were, the Constitution itself to be unconstitutional. After the war, Spooner wrote a series of pamphlets entitled *No Treason*. Although the war had ended slavery in one sense, Spooner argued that in another sense it had actually increased the number of slaves!

> The principle, on which the war was waged by the North, was simply this: That men may rightfully be compelled to submit to, and support, a government that they do not want; and that resistance, on their part, makes them traitors and criminals.
>
> No principle, that is possible to be named, can be more self-evidently false than this; or more self-evidently fatal to all political freedom. Yet it triumphed in the field, and is now assumed to be established. If it be really established, the number of slaves, instead of having been diminished by the war, has been greatly increased; for a man, thus subjected to a government that he does not want, is a slave.

The people of the North were scarcely better off. Since there was no actual contract between the legislators in Congress and those they affected to represent—Spooner had concluded that the Constitution could not be construed as such—he would eventually deny that this body of men could "by some process or other, become invested with the right *to make laws of their own*—that is, *laws wholly of their own device,* and therefore necessarily distinct from the law of nature, or the principles of natural justice," and compel other men to obey them.[22] Douglass would certainly have dissented from this conclusion, but by insisting that slavery, as "a system of lawless violence," was not only morally inadmissible but actually illegal, he helped to undermine the distinction between law and natural justice that Spooner would do away with altogether.

The distinction in the Republican platform between slavery in the states and slavery in the federal territories represents one application of this broader distinction. The criticism of the Republicans by Garrison's sons, that the distinction between abolition and nonextension gave rise to suspicions of "playing fast and loose with the language of the Constitution," actually justifies the Republicans' conservatism as against the position taken by Douglass. As long as both sections continued to profess allegiance to the Constitution, the best chance that any antislavery party had to overcome the problem of consent lay in their being able to assure the South—in the words of the Republican platform, quoted by Lincoln in his first inaugural address—of "the maintenance inviolate of the rights of the States, and especially the right of each State to order and control its own domestic institutions according to its own judgment exclusively."[23]

Douglass biographer Benjamin Quarles, citing an 1859 letter to Garrison from Hinton Rowan Helper, "who saw the clash between the sections as an economic issue," wrote, "By 1860, economics had caught up with ethics and the two forces had fused to produce a composite Northern mind-set that created a Republican party and a section psychologically prepared for a resort to arms." Such a development was not unwelcome to Douglass; a contest of arms offered another possibility for overcoming the problem of consent. Lincoln's attitude may be judged by his reaction to Helper's provocative book, *The Impending Crisis of the South.* In his Cooper Institute address, Lincoln referred to the book along with John Brown's raid as furnishing the South with an opening to "break up the Republican organization" and, by doing so, possibly "forcing the sentiment which created it out of the peaceful channel of the ballot-box." Other members of his party were not so cautious: the book was endorsed by Horace Greeley and even—though apparently without full knowledge of its contents—by some Republicans in Congress. According to George M. Fredrickson, its reception was "one important factor in converting the South to the view that the Republicans were committed to subverting the slave system in the South"; the book "provides part of the explanation as to why the South found the election of Lincoln intolerable" and seceded thereupon, "without allowing the Republicans to take office and show their true character."[24]

It is unreasonable to expect that a man in Douglass's position—especially sensitive, as he must be, to the wrongs suffered by his own people—would perceive his task in the political situation of the 1850s in quite the same way that Lincoln did his. It is reasonable to expect, however, that he should see those tasks in their proper relation—that he should see, as Herbert Storing has put it, "the dependence of the partial good, the good of blacks, on the good of the whole American community." The clearest sign that Douglass eventually did so is this passage in the final version of his autobiography, *Life and Times of Frederick Douglass*, the first mention of Lincoln in the book:

> It was [the repeal of the Missouri Compromise] which brought Abraham Lincoln into prominence. . . . Pregnant words were now spoken on the side of freedom, words which went straight to the heart of the nation. It was Mr. Lincoln who first told the American people at this crisis that the "Union could not long endure half slave and half free; that they must be all one or the other, that the public mind could find no resting place but in the belief in the ultimate extinction of slavery." These were not the words of an abolitionist—branded a fanatic, and carried away by an enthusiastic devotion to the Negro—but the calm, cool, deliberate utterance of a statesman, comprehensive enough to take in the welfare of the whole country.

Douglass gently ridicules the image of the abolitionist as a fanatic, but his praise of Lincoln's statesmanship is sincere. His own career serves as an illustration of the tension between doctrine that has been formulated with a special, albeit naturally just, end in mind and the comprehensive outlook of a statesman. Douglass's prewar constitutional views are to be seen in the light of his devotion to one specially aggrieved class of Americans; the difficulty is that the Constitution belonged to the "whole country."[25]

Part IV

Conclusion

The Case for Politics

In *giving* freedom to the *slave*, we *assure* freedom to the *free*—honorable alike in what we give, and what we preserve.

Abraham Lincoln, 1862

Chapter 10

Freedom, Political and Economic

Lincoln's refusal to endorse Hinton Helper's book *The Impending Crisis of the South* did not mean that he was unconcerned with the economic question presented by slavery, only that he subordinated that question to the political one. A different relation between economics and politics is implied in the definition of slavery that Allen C. Guelzo has ascribed to Lincoln: "he defined *slavery* as any relationship which forestalled social dynamism and economic mobility, or obstructed 'the paths of laudable pursuit for all.'" This definition is consistent with "indifference to slavery as an injustice to blacks," at least until "the black slave . . . began to emerge in Lincoln's mind as a human being with the same Whiggish aspirations for escape and success" as Lincoln had himself. It is also consistent with indifference to slavery as a status in law because only blacks were legal slaves. If Lincoln "used to be a slave," as he is reported to have said of himself, it was not a change in legal status that made him free. Guelzo apparently follows Richard Hofstadter: "For Lincoln the vital test of a democracy was economic. . . . This belief in opportunity for the self-made man is the key to his entire career . . . it is the core of his criticism of slavery."[1] Lincoln faced a rhetorical difficulty in addressing white audiences on the subject of Negro slavery: his auditors had no fear of being enslaved themselves. To make real to them the danger from a progressive debasement of American institutions under the influence of slavery, Lincoln drew out the similarities between slavery and economic oppression: the resemblance of slave-holders to kings and of "crowned-kings" to "money-kings, and land-kings." In doing so, however, he did not lose sight of the fundamental distinction between these forms of subjection: only slavery was "literal enslavement."[2]

If Lincoln had defined slavery broadly enough to include economic oppression as Thoreau did, he could not have maintained the distinction between legal enslavement and slavery understood as any condition contrary to human dignity. In his essay "Life without Principle," Thoreau wrote, "America is said to be the arena on which the battle of freedom is to be fought; but surely it cannot be freedom in a merely political sense that is meant. Even if we grant that the American has freed him-self from a political tyrant, he is still the slave of an economical and moral tyrant."[3] It does not belittle Thoreau's claim about the imperfect nature of American freedom to point out that legal freedom is a neces-sary condition for economic and moral freedom—and, surely, there is no small difference between being legally the property of another and legally the master of oneself.

Thoreau's ambivalence about northern freedom is evident from his comment about an incident involving Frederick Douglass that he heard described in a lecture by Wendell Phillips. Douglass had announced to an audience in New Bedford his intention to publish an account of his life, in order to put to rest doubts about whether he really had been a slave. In this account, he would give information about himself that would expose him to the risk of being recaptured. His auditors there—and Phillips's in Concord—responded, "He had better not!" Thoreau comments, "we trust [Douglass] will be as superior to degradation from the sympathies of Freedom, as from the antipathies of slavery." In con-ditions of freedom, human beings are threatened by a new form of bondage: slavery to considerations of interest and safety.[4]

Thoreau's view of the degrading effects of free labor was not shared by many reformers. According to Aileen S. Kraditor, in the view of most abolitionists, "the slave deserved priority over the free worker because enslavement was personally more degrading than mere oppression"; "the abolitionists always stressed the degradation rather than the poverty of the slaves." Some free workers may have been as poor as slaves, "but the slave's poverty resulted from his [legal] status."[5] By declining to follow other abolitionists in upholding the distinction between enslavement and oppression, Thoreau conceded to the defenders of slavery more than he would have been willing to avow. The legal turn of mind that many southerners showed in defending their rights did not prevent them from denying the importance of northern workers' legal and political freedoms.[6]

The most sophisticated example of this sort of argument comes from George Fitzhugh. His principal claim is that in denouncing southern institutions the abolitionists were condemning northern ones as well. "If slavery, either white or black, be wrong in principle or practice . . . then is all human government wrong." Efforts underway in the North to reform social institutions with a view to making them freer only served to hasten their collapse. Northern freedom had but engendered a harsher and more destabilizing slavery: "slavery to capital." But Fitzhugh did not succeed in meeting the abolitionists' charges on the same moral plane. In slavery, he wrote, "Liberty has been exchanged by nature for security." The spirit of the exchange is revealed with greater frankness by the writer for the *Edinburgh Review* whom Fitzhugh quotes in *Cannibals All!* "The moral and domestic feelings of the slave are sacrificed, and his intellect is stunted; but in respect of his physical condition he may be a gainer."[7]

In speaking of Americans' economic slavery, Thoreau was certainly not complaining of their poverty. He seems, however, to have been blind to the dignity of free labor: he thought he saw a similar sacrifice of moral feelings and stunting of the intellect among free workers. Frederick Douglass, who had firsthand knowledge of the alternative, did not share Thoreau's blindness. He recognized that a moderate level of wealth serves to foster an enlightened citizenry. Douglass remarked that the condition of blacks in New Bedford was to him "the most astonishing as well as the most interesting thing." His friend Nathan Johnson not only "lived in a neater house" and "dined at a better table" but also "took, paid for, and read, more newspapers" and, consequently, "better understood the moral, religious, and political character of the nation—than nine tenths of the slaveholders in Talbot County, Maryland."[8]

Still, prosperity that extended to workers like Johnson, whose "hands were hardened by toil," was a matter of relatively minor importance to Douglass. As a slave, he had imagined northerners to be "living in the most Spartan-like simplicity," without the luxuries of slaveholders; but that did not make the North a less desirable destination in his eyes. As a boy, he had been shocked by the whipping of "Old Barney," the slave who took care of Colonel Lloyd's horses. "Any supposed inattention to these animals was sure to be visited with degrading punishment"; and Old Barney "was often punished when faultless." "In a free state, a master, thus complaining without cause, of his ostler, might be told—'Sir, I am sorry I cannot please you, but, since I have done the best I can, your remedy is to dismiss me.' Here [in Maryland], however, the ostler must stand, listen and tremble." Observing workers at the port of New Bedford, Douglass "saw no whipping of men; but all seemed to go smoothly on. Every man appeared to understand his work, and went at it with a sober, yet cheerful earnestness, which betokened the deep interest which he felt in what he was doing, as well as a sense of his own dignity as a man."[9]

Guelzo stressed the relation between free wage labor and social mobility—the absence of such mobility counting as slavery. That relation would not have held true equally for all groups, especially not for free blacks. Douglass knew what it was to labor as a slave under the most liberal conditions and to do so as a free wage earner under some of the most illiberal conditions: in New Bedford, the opposition of white mechanics prevented him from practicing the trade he had learned as a slave in Baltimore. Still, he never expressed any reservations about the superiority of free labor—and not only in view of his own subsequent rise to wealth and prominence. Most fugitives probably spent the rest of their lives in much the same way that Douglass spent his first years out of slavery. Days after his arrival in Massachusetts, Douglass happened to notice a pile of coal on the street outside a house, and he asked for and received permission to put it away. When he had finished he was given two silver half-dollars for the work. "To understand the emotion which swelled my heart as I clasped this money, realizing that I had no master who could take it from me—*that it was mine—that my hands were my own,* and could earn more of the precious coin—one must have been in some sense himself a slave."[10] At that moment, Douglass obviously did not regard himself as a slave in any sense.

Douglass's lot at this time was in one respect harder than any northern white worker's. Although he was supporting himself and his family by his own labor, he remained a slave under the law. Residence in a free state was the next best thing to legal status as a freeman, though Douglass was technically still a chattel and subject to recapture. After the war, many southern blacks would find themselves in the contrary predicament. In the late 1880s, Douglass toured South Carolina and Georgia to assess the progress of the freedmen there. After returning home, he took the occasion of an address on the next anniversary of emancipation in the District of Columbia to denounce the rural black's "so-called emancipation as a stupendous fraud" because though "nominally free he is actually a slave." Douglass knew, however, that the emancipation of many other blacks—those in the District, for example, "though there is much that is wrong and unsatisfactory here"—was not merely nominal. The fundamental problem in the rural lower South was not that legal emancipation had been insufficient, but that the law was not being enforced there. A Supreme Court unduly favorable to states' rights was "denying to the government the right to protect the elective franchise of its own citizens." Douglass added, "It was not so meant by Abraham Lincoln."[11]

That Lincoln's views on slavery were sounder than Thoreau's becomes clearer when both are seen in relation to the views of the "mud-sill" theorists, who shared Thoreau's tendency to define slavery in broad extralegal terms. In his 1859 address to the Wisconsin State Agricultural Society, Lincoln characterized the mud-sill theorists as assuming "that whoever is once a *hired* laborer, is fatally fixed in that condition for life; and thence, again, that his condition is as bad as, or worse than, that of a slave."[12] In fact, those theorists went further, insisting that the hired laborer *was* a slave. The term Lincoln used to refer to them had been made popular by James Henry Hammond of South Carolina, who told northern senators in 1858, "your whole hireling class of manual laborers and 'operatives,' as you call them, are essentially slaves." This class "constitutes the very mud-sill of society," the same position occupied in the South by laborers "hired for life." Northern wage earners were slaves in fact, though free in law. One might change laws, but one could not change the natural order of things, and within that order many if not most men were slaves. The mud-sill theorists would represent slavery as an enduring element in human society; and those in the North who, like Thoreau, while hostile to southern pretensions, half-suspected that the mud-sill theorists might be right about the persistence of slavery in some form, naturally could not give their wholehearted support to efforts at reform. According to the "plain statement" of his party's principles that Lincoln made at Quincy in 1858, the Republicans held slavery to be a social as well as a moral and a political wrong. In calling slavery a social wrong, Lincoln was probably thinking of arguments such as Hammond's that denigrated the laborer's contribution to his own well-being. But Lincoln's focus remained on the legal-political institution, even when he took up the claims made for slavery as a superior system of labor.[13]

Lincoln's phrase, "the paths of laudable pursuit," is from the Message to Congress in Special Session, delivered on July 4, 1861.

> This is essentially a People's contest. On the side of the Union, it is a struggle for maintaining in the world that form and substance of government whose leading object is to elevate the condition of men—to lift artificial weights from all shoulders—to clear the paths of laudable pursuit for all—to afford all an unfettered start and a fair chance in the race of life.

One may assume that Lincoln did not expect all to follow the paths of laudable pursuit, however clear they might be. But how broadly did he intend his audience to understand this phase? Was common labor such a pursuit? Guelzo's construction would seem to preclude that possibility—common labor was just the sort of putative slavery that Lincoln himself had escaped from—thus casting doubt on the accuracy of Lincoln's characterization of the war as a "people's contest." There is no doubt that in speaking of "artificial weights," Lincoln had more in mind than the disabilities imposed by slavery, but these disabilities were at the heart of the differences between the Union and its adversaries. In fact, Lincoln was confirming the southern turn toward legal conventionalism, the "deliberate pressing out of view the rights of men and the authority of the people"—noting, for example, that the preamble of the provisional Confederate constitution substitutes for "We, the People," "We, the deputies of the sovereign and independent States."[14]

This theme is taken up again at the conclusion of Lincoln's Annual

Message to Congress from December of 1861, which includes a substantial portion, with slight modification, of his Wisconsin State Agricultural Society address. The difference is in the setting for Lincoln's treatment of the contrast between the rival systems of free and slave labor: the political consequences are made unmistakably clear. Lincoln begins by referring to "the effort to place *capital* on an equal footing with, if not above *labor*, in the structure of government." He ends by warning "those who toil up from poverty" to "beware of surrendering a political power which they already possess, and which, if surrendered, will surely be used to close the door against such as they, and to fix new disabilities and burdens upon them, till all of liberty shall be lost"— until they shall be not only poor but without political rights, which was never the case for Hammond's northern "slaves."[15]

Even the portion of the Wisconsin address that was given over to praise of "thorough cultivation," the larger portion of the whole, had a political significance that was not likely to have been lost on Lincoln's audience. It was obvious, even without his saying so, that the free labor system was more likely to bring about such cultivation and with it the "effect of thorough cultivation upon the farmer's own mind, and, in reaction through his mind, back upon his business." What was true of agriculture was also true of other fields of enterprise. Frederick Law Olmsted's remarks on the economy of Virginia, published a few years before Lincoln's address, included the following observation. Slavery, he wrote,

irresistibly affects the whole industrial character of the people. You may see it in the habits of the free white mechanics and trades-people. All of these must have dealings or be in competition with slaves, and so have their standard of excellence made low, and become accustomed to, until they are content with slight, false, unsound workmanship. You notice in all classes, vagueness in ideas of cost and value, and injudicious and unnecessary expenditure of labour by a thoughtless manner of setting about work. . . .

A man forced to labor under their system is morally driven to indolence, carelessness, indifference to the results of skill, heedlessness, inconstancy of purpose, improvidence, and extravagance. Precisely the opposite qualities are those which are encouraged, and inevitably developed in a man who has to make his living, and earn all his comfort by his voluntarily-directed labour.[16]

Lincoln would have been the last to claim that the people of Wisconsin or any other northern state were the moral superiors of the people of Virginia. The southern people, he said, "are just what we would be in their situation."[17] The chief determinant of that situation, Lincoln makes clear, was the legal-political institution of slavery.

Chapter 11

Between Legalism and the Higher Law

The tendency among Lincoln's opponents to plant themselves wholly upon law or wholly upon natural justice has persisted among writers on the Civil War period. Two modern commentators bring out the difficulties in these approaches with peculiar clarity. M. E. Bradford gives us a view of Lincoln "from the South," a region he regards as filling the historical role of guardian of the American constitutional order. Howard Zinn identifies himself with the tradition of moral-political reformation in American life of which the abolitionists are the outstanding representatives.[1] Both concede that Lincoln was a skillful politician, but they are doubtful about whether that is a good thing to be.

Their Lincolns could hardly be more different. Bradford's was "the American Caesar of his age" whose ultimate objective was "a neo-Puritan war on the powers of darkness," not because Lincoln himself was a moral zealot but because he "burned with ambition to have a 'name' and found in vilification his *modus vivendi*." To Zinn, Lincoln was "the prototype of the political man in power, with views so moderate as to require the pressure of radicals to stimulate action." His stand on slavery "through most of the war" was "so ambiguous and cautious as to make the British abolitionist George Thompson tell Garrison: 'You know how impossible it is at this moment to vindicate, as one would wish, the

155

course of Mr. Lincoln. In no one of his utterances is there an assertion of a great principle—no appeal to right or justice. In everything he does and says, affecting the slave, there is the alloy of expediency."[2] Notwithstanding their different assessments of Lincoln, however, Bradford and Zinn concur in identifying the source of Lincoln's short-comings (a mild word for Bradford's view!) in his political bent.

In Zinn's treatment, the identification is explicit: "The politician, by the very nature of the electoral process, is a compromiser and trimmer, who sets his sails by the prevailing breezes, and without the hard blowing of the radical reformer would either drift actionless or sail along with existing injustice." The nature of the electoral process favors compromise—that is why Thoreau rejected "a democracy, such as we know it." It is unlikely that Zinn is quite as aware to what stark alternatives such a critique of electoral politics leads. At any event, he does not give Lincoln's view of the politician's task but quotes this comment by Wendell Phillips: "The politician dwells in an everlasting now. . . . His office is not to instruct public opinion but to represent it."[3]

Lincoln did understand his office to be one of instructing public opinion—but not "in the thundering tones of anathema and denunciation," which he recognized as a temptation of moral reformers. "When the conduct of men is designed to be influenced, *persuasion,* kind, unassuming persuasion, should ever be adopted." Furthermore, to instruct public opinion was not, in Lincoln's view, necessarily distinct from representing it: by speaking for the "better angels of our nature," he would be doing both. In his first inaugural address, Lincoln stood against the intemperate opinion of the hour; but he did so by standing upon law as reflecting the most durable elements in public opinion.[4]

Zinn relies heavily on Ralph Korngold's *Two Friends of Man* (not *Three,* it will be noted), subtitled *The Story of William Lloyd Garrison and Wendell Phillips and Their Relationship with Abraham Lincoln.* Korngold would have his readers think that Lincoln, in the words chosen as the epigraph to the book, was praising the agitator as one who "goes deeper" than the legislator: "Public sentiment is everything. With public sentiment nothing can fail; without it nothing can succeed. Consequently, he who moulds public sentiment goes deeper than he who enacts statutes and pronounces decisions. He makes statutes and decisions possible or impossible to be executed." Attention to public opinion or sentiment was ground common to these three men, but Korngold's quotation, taken by itself, gives a misleading impression of Lincoln's views. The source of this quote is Lincoln's first Illinois senate campaign debate with Stephen Douglas; it was in reference to Douglas's influence as a leader of his party in Washington that Lincoln made this remark. Moreover, Korngold has omitted a phrase that qualifies the statement with which he begins his quotation: Lincoln actually said, "*In this and like communities,* public sentiment is everything." It is the Constitution that made the Union the sort of community it is—where public sentiment is "everything." To Zinn, however, Lincoln is saved from ignominy only because "it would be wrong to say that Lincoln was completely a politician—his fundamental humanitarianism did not allow that."[5]

Zinn shares the view of politics that was common to those abolitionists who were unable to overcome their distrust of Lincoln. When Lincoln failed to act as they thought he should, he confirmed their low estimation of politics. When, in retrospect, some of Lincoln's actions are difficult to square with such an estimation, Zinn concludes that Lincoln was not completely a politician. These abolitionists thought that the way to influence Lincoln was to appeal directly to what they understood as every politician's all-consuming motive: the desire for reelection. At his January 1863 meeting with the president, Wendell Phillips responded to Lincoln's complaint that "it has been very rare that an opportunity of 'running' this administration has been lost," by telling him, "If we see this administration earnestly working to free the country from slavery and its rebellion, we will show you how we can 'run' it into another four years of power." Had Phillips persisted, Lincoln might have replied to him as he did to congressional Radical Thaddeus Stevens. When Stevens tried to exert pressure on Lincoln by making support for his reelection conditional on a change in the cabinet, Lincoln reportedly told him that he would refuse the office rather than accept it on terms "degrading" to himself.[6]

Bradford's interpretation is more complex. He does not disparage politics as such, but his view of the politician's task is limited by a view of law that rules out many possibilities for reform by political means. He insists on the "difference between legal or political and moral questions in a nation in which basic law is sovereign and not a particular generation of men." Bradford charges Lincoln and the Republicans with failing to uphold this difference. They were guilty of, or guilty of exploiting, "a misunderstanding of the relation of the Constitution to the language concerning equality which appears at the beginning of the Declaration of Independence." Bradford endorses Jefferson Davis's interpretation of that language as expressed in his last speech to the United States Senate: "that men were created equal—meaning the men of the political community." When the speech was given, Davis's state of Mississippi had already decided to secede; interpreting the Declaration of Independence as he did, Davis would have been inconsistent if he had justified his state's independence by reference to natural rights. Rather, he said, the reason for taking this step was "a belief that we are to be deprived in the Union of the rights which our fathers bequeathed to us"—that is to say, legal rights. And Bradford speaks of George III as having "violated his constitutional role as protector and defender . . . of the inherited rights of Englishmen in America." Bradford holds to the "essentially procedural" Taney-Garrison interpretation of the Constitution; he is hostile to the antislavery parties but not to "the honest abolitionists, who simply desired to divide the country or change the Constitution."[7]

Notwithstanding his insistence on the distinction between morality and politics, Bradford's indignation at Lincoln is unmistakable. The matter is not as simple as it had appeared to be. Noting that "much talk of morality surrounded the decision for secession," Bradford attempts to define what he himself calls "constitutional morality." This morality has two requirements, the first of which is "rhetorical civility." Bradford implies that any expression by a northerner of the wrongfulness of slavery would have violated this stricture. Lincoln could not have agreed to suppress his own or others' antislavery views, but one should not conclude that he condemned the South. At the close of the 1858 senatorial campaign Lincoln said, "As I have not felt, so I have not expressed any harsh sentiment towards our Southern bretheren. I have constantly declared, as I really believed, the only difference between them and us, is the difference of circumstances." But the main requirement of constitutional morality, according to Bradford, is "rigid observation of the terms agreed to," along with "a clear awareness that one party to the connection cannot reserve the right to interpret it according to his views and still expect it to bind other parties offended by his construction." Lincoln's strictness on this point distinguished him from the political abolitionists, but Bradford says something else that only appears to be the same, that Lincoln could not have assented to—not as justifying secession, at any rate: "in a free society, the law cannot be maintained or interpreted against the will of a whole people, by compulsion." Although he speaks of the will of a whole people, Bradford clearly has only the southern people in mind; he takes their separateness for granted. As evidence of their will, Bradford offers the words of the "generation of Southern leaders" in the Senate who, following the Republican victory, "could not believe in the advantage of preserving the Constitution within that kind of Union."[8] If this language is set alongside the language previously quoted, that the United States is "a nation in which basic law is sovereign and not a particular generation of men," the difficulty becomes evident.

Bradford attempts to account for the difference between the pre-1854 Lincoln—a "moderate opportunist"—and the "greatly altered" figure of Lincoln's post-Nebraska career—still an opportunist but no longer a moderate one—by reference to changes in Lincoln's part of the North. "By 1854," he argues, "the Midwest was rapidly filling with people who did not understand American history, politics, or constitutional law and with people who had fewer ties with the South. . . . Many of these could see in the South only an analogy to the European societies from which they had fled. In 1854, Lincoln recognized these changes and Stephen Douglas did not." Lincoln would say that the immigrants were correct to perceive an analogy between European despotism and southern slavery (though by all accounts Irish immigration, at least, served to strengthen the Democrats). Let us assume for the moment, however, that Bradford is right: Lincoln saw in these changes little more than a chance to improve his political fortunes, and "he was not about to let it pass." Such a judgment leaves scant basis for distinguishing him from the public men of the South who, according to Bradford, represented their section in its increasing "truculence," and finally in rejecting the Union—scant basis for his claim on their behalf to superior constitutional morality. Bradford's politician begins to resemble Zinn's, the unimpressive figure whose power "is expended on *reading* public opinion rather than on *changing* it"—or rather than on preserving it unchanged in fidelity to the law.[9]

There is no need, however, to accept Bradford's account of Lincoln's return to active politics. There is nothing inherently implausible in Lincoln's self-reported reaction to the repeal of the Missouri Compromise—that at a time when "his profession had almost superseded the thought of politics in his mind," it "aroused him as he had never been before." Even the Reverend Nehemiah Adams, a northerner who was so sympathetic to the South as to gain a favorable notice from George Fitzhugh, considered the repeal to be indefensible. The North ought to consider, Adams wrote in 1854, "that the south was approximating the work of emancipation . . . when the outbreak of northern opposition to slavery, and attempts to emancipate the slaves at once, drove back the south from her purpose, and that all her subsequent attempts at the extension of slavery have been intended as retaliatory acts, or in self-defense." He immediately adds, however, "This is true up to the time of the Nebraska bill and the repeal of the Missouri compromise, measures capable of no defense." In the North since that time, "The hitherto indomitable attachments of party are yielding to the stronger, the uncorrupted sense of violated truth."[10]

The change in Lincoln would have been evident even if he had said nothing about it. Roy P. Basler, the editor of Lincoln's *Collected Works*, writes, "The contrast between Lincoln in 1852 and 1854 is remarkable. . . . From the futile mediocrity of his 'Address before the Springfield Scott Club' he rose to the impassioned seriousness of the 'Speech at Peoria.'" What could account for the change? On the former occasion, Basler surmises, "Lincoln could not, even by choice, find anything worth saying in support of a party which was dying because it strove only to avoid the great issues of the day"; on the latter occasion, he "had simply found a theme worthy of his best." Basler's judgment is consistent with what Lincoln's law partner wrote: lacking "a feeling of confidence in the justice of the cause he represented," Lincoln, notwithstanding his great abilities, "was the weakest man at the bar."[11] As a politician, Lincoln evidently was no different.

But we do not have to rely on the testimony of others—we are in a position to decide for ourselves whether the author of the Peoria speech could have had nothing more in view than his own political prospects. The literary historian Erich Auerbach has introduced a criterion that is applicable in the case of the political Abraham as well as in the case of his biblical namesake. Auerbach argues that the biblical narrator "had to believe in the objective truth of the story of Abraham's sacrifice": "He had to believe in it passionately; or else (as many rationalistic interpreters believed and perhaps still believe) he had to be a conscious liar . . . a political liar with a definite end in view, lying in the interest of a claim to absolute authority." This is also Bradford's interpretation of Lincoln. Auerbach comments, "To me, the rationalistic interpretation seems psychologically absurd."[12] Every reader of Lincoln's postrepeal speeches is invited to consider whether it is not psychologically absurd to suppose that the author of them had such an end in view.

If Lincoln was neither Zinn's man nor Bradford's—if he rejected both the higher law and legalism—what kind of politician was he? These terms, as used here and in the title of this chapter, were suggested by Robert Penn Warren's book-length essay *The Legacy of the Civil War*. Warren speaks of them as "two types of absolutes, the collision of which was an essential part of the picture of the War." He agrees with Wendell Phillips that the politician "dwells in an everlasting now"; but he offers a more realistic assessment of what it meant for someone in Lincoln's position, with Lincoln's political ethic, to dwell there: "Ethics should be, indeed, the measure of politics, but there is an ethic which is somewhat different from that of individual absolutism—an ethic that demands scrutiny of motive, context, and consequences, particularly the consequences to others. This kind of ethic, laborious, fumbling, running the risk of degenerating into expediency, finds its apotheosis in Lincoln."[13]

Warren's is the Lincoln who claimed "not to have controlled events, but confess plainly that events have controlled me." That reference by Lincoln to his war policy may put one in mind of another such reference: "I shall do nothing in malice. What I deal with is too vast for malicious dealing."[14] In the "everlasting now" of events that demanded his attention—many of them likely to appear insignificant from the lofty viewpoint of the moral reformer—Lincoln did not lose sight of the vast matter at issue: the integrity of the Union.

Chapter 12

Lincoln's Defense of Politics

Lincoln's "house divided" doctrine and William Seward's "irrepressible conflict" were both expressions, according to Lincoln, of "the opinion that slavery is a durable element of discord, and that we shall not have peace with it, until it either masters, or is mastered by, the free principle."[1] Lincoln treated the doctrines as equivalent, and perhaps they were—until November 6, 1860. When the election was over, the conflict of principles between the North and the South took on a different character, one that demanded ultimate reconciliation. The challenge for the incoming administration was to preserve the political gains that its party's electoral victory had realized. To do this, it was necessary to preserve the community of the states in its historical integrity. Since the adoption of the Constitution, the history of the Union had been one of uninterrupted growth and prosperity. Seward's language stressed the need for overcoming a threat; Lincoln's stressed the need for overcoming division in Americans' common political house.

With Lincoln's election to the presidency, Americans were confronted, in a more urgent manner than at any time since 1787–1790, with this broad question: Does the Union have a dignity at least equal to that of the states? Republicans believed that it did, but their belief did not necessarily supply them with a ready answer to the immediate prac-

tical question. Voters in the North had elected an administration with a
sectional base of support, in the face of southern threats to break up the
Union if they did so. How far should the incoming administration go to
conciliate the South? Following the outbreak of war, military considerations largely overshadowed political ones in Lincoln's dealings with the
South, even as the president strove to keep slavery a political question.
But political considerations remained paramount in the months
between Lincoln's election and his inauguration, as they continued to
be in his dealings with the border states. During this time, Lincoln resisted pressure to give his support to proposals for compromise on the
central plank of his party's platform, the nonextension of slavery. His
reasons for rejecting such a means to the end of saving the Union mys-
tified even some members of his own party.

In *Lincoln and His Party in the Secession Crisis,* David M. Potter
answers the question as to Lincoln's reasoning in this way: Lincoln rejected
compromise because he did not realize the gravity of the crisis; he badly
overestimated the extent of Unionist sentiment in the South. In a preface written twenty years later, Potter reaffirmed his original conclusion:

> I suggested very strongly . . . that the Crittenden Resolutions [sponsored
> by Senator John J. Crittenden of Kentucky] represented a possible basis
> for compromise, and I presented evidence throughout that the
> Crittenden Plan commanded a great deal of support both in the North
> and in the South—so much, in fact, that if Lincoln had supported it, it
> might have been adopted. I still think the evidence is impressive. . . .
>
> This, of course, means that I believed there was a possible alternative
> to war in 1861. It does not mean that I regarded the crisis as an artificial
> one, or the sources of sectional antagonism as being in any sense super-
> ficial. . . .
>
> The Crittenden Compromise had many of the same qualities and the
> same limitations as the Compromise of 1850. The chief limitation was
> that it did not and could not settle the slavery question. . . .
>
> I am very reluctant to dismiss Crittenden's plan as a stopgap so long
> as we maintain a double standard on the subject of stopgaps. For our
> evaluation of them depends very much upon whose gaps are being
> stopped. Thus no *modus vivendi* with the Soviet Union can be much
> more than a stopgap today, given our basic disagreements with that

country. But we would be prone to regard it as most praiseworthy to
defer a showdown, even for as much as five years.[2]

It is striking that Potter compares the position of the North and the
South in 1861 with that of the United States and the Soviet Union one
hundred years later. He is ready to acknowledge "basic disagreements"
between the sections and to accept the existence of these as a basis for
compromise. In Potter's view, the North and the South had already
ceased to be, if indeed they ever had been, members of one political
community in the most fundamental sense.

Lincoln opposed compromise in the winter of 1860–1861. Yet, in one
important respect, his defense of the Union as a political community
implied an acceptance of compromise—to a point. The Garrisonians
correctly observed that the establishment and maintenance of the Union
required compromising with slavery. One thing was not subject to compromise, in Lincoln's judgment—the Union *was* a political community
in the fundamental sense. But for slavery, no American would have
doubted it. The disagreements between the sections were deep, but they
were not basic. In defining the point up to which compromise was
acceptable and beyond which it was not, Lincoln showed how far his
thinking surpassed that of his critics on both sides. In the secession crisis, he pleased the Radicals and disappointed the states' rights men; in
the Frémont episode nine months later, he pleased the states' rights men
and infuriated the Radicals.[3] In both instances Lincoln defended his
actions on very similar grounds.

Unlike the Radicals, then, Lincoln was not opposed to compromise
as such on the slavery question. In 1854 he had spoken in defense of the
Missouri Compromise, against Stephen Douglas's Nebraska bill, which
opened the territories north of the compromise line to slavery. "Slavery
may or may not be established in Nebraska," Lincoln conceded; but by
its "gross breach of faith" Douglas's bill amounted to a repudiation of
"the SPIRIT of COMPROMISE." In the event that the Missouri Compromise was not restored, "The spirit of mutual concession—that spirit
which first gave us the constitution, and which has thrice saved the
Union—we shall have strangled and cast from us forever." But Lincoln
did not think that further concessions would save the Union in the winter of 1860–1861. On December 10, 1860, he wrote to Illinois's Repub-

lican senator Lyman Trumbull, "The tug has to come, & better now, than any time hereafter."[4] A compromise would not prevent but could only delay the crisis. Reviewing the history of the Nebraska controversy at the start of his senatorial campaign against Douglas in 1858, Lincoln had said,

> We are now far into the *fifth* year, since a policy was initiated, with the *avowed* object, and *confident* promise, of putting an end to slavery agitation.
>
> Under the operation of that policy, that agitation has not only, *not ceased,* but has *constantly augmented.*
>
> In *my* opinion, it will *not* cease, until a *crisis* shall have been reached, and passed.[5]

On December 17, 1860, he wrote to Republican editor Thurlow Weed that in the event of compromise "filibustering for all South of us, and making slave states of it, would follow in spite of us." Lincoln was not in a position to know that these actions would follow, and his view of the likely result of compromise differed from that of many members of his own party. What he did know was that compromise under the circumstances was inadmissible. As he explained in a letter to Republican congressman James T. Hale: "We have just carried an election on principles fairly stated to the people. Now we are told in advance, the government shall be broken up, unless we surrender to those we have beaten, before we take the offices. In this they are either attempting to play upon us, or they are in dead earnest. Either way, if we surrender, it is the end of us, and of the government."[6]

In refusing to offer support to efforts at compromising the territorial issue, Lincoln did not stand primarily on his party's opposition to slavery. He wanted to preserve the Union; but what Lincoln wanted to preserve was not merely the union of thirty-three or thirty-four states in a single government. What he wanted most to preserve was that government itself. Popular government is subject to certain dangers to which the proponents of compromise had not given sufficient thought.

The original draft of Lincoln's first inaugural address includes a section that Lincoln later cut out with the intention of using it in a speech in Kentucky.[7] As it happened, he never gave the speech, and the section was never restored. Most likely, he did not restore it because he thought that pressure for compromise would abate after his inauguration. At any event, this section of the draft inaugural address is Lincoln's fullest statement of his reasons for rejecting compromise. It begins,

> During the winter just closed, I have been greatly urged, by many patriotic men, to lend the influence of my position to some compromise, by which I was, to some extent, to shift the ground upon which I had been elected. This I steadily refused. . . . I thought such refusal was demanded by the view that if, when a Chief Magistrate is constitutionally elected, he cannot be inaugurated till he betrays those who elected him, by breaking his pledges, and surrendering to those who tried and failed to defeat him at the polls, this government and all popular government is already at an end.

Although Lincoln notes that his election had been constitutional, he does not defend his position on constitutional grounds. Nor does he mention slavery or sectional differences. When he refers to popular government, Lincoln is closer to the heart of the matter; but in rejecting compromise he does not present himself as being guided by the will of the American people at that moment. Most Americans were probably not averse to a settlement of the territorial issue that fell short of complete nonextension, and it would have been possible to put any compromise measure to a popular referendum. In fact, Simon Cameron, a prominent Republican who later served in Lincoln's cabinet as his first secretary of war, was on record as favoring this course, and he undoubtedly spoke for others in the party. Lincoln, however, had his own reasons for thinking such a course was unwise. He continues: "Demands for such surrender, once recognized, are without limit, as to nature, extent, and repetition. They break the only bond of faith between public and public servant; and they distinctly set the minority over the majority."[8] A majority of Americans might have accepted compromise rather than see the Union dissolved, but the demands for concessions were not coming from the majority. These demands were coming from a minority whose behavior in this respect was distinctly despotic. Lincoln would not oppose demands that were expressed through legitimate political channels. As he said in one of his few public statements as president-elect, "whatever I might think of the merit of the various

Lincoln's Defense of Politics   167

propositions before Congress, I should regard any concession in the face of menace the destruction of the government itself. . . . But this thing will hereafter be as it is now, in the hands of the people; and if they desire to call a Convention to remove any grievances complained of, or to give new guarantees for the permanence of vested rights, it is not mine to oppose."[9]

The existence of basic disagreements between independent states is not necessarily an obstacle to a satisfactory settlement of other matters. The aims of the states are limited, but the range of acceptable tactics is wide—including the threat of force. Such tactics had no place in the settlement of differences among the states of the Union. The compromises proposed during the secession crisis resemble Douglas's Nebraska measure—another attempt to find middle ground on the issue of slavery in the territories. Both attempts at compromise represented breaches of public faith: in failing to respect the Missouri Compromise in one instance and in failing to respect a constitutionally valid election in the other. Both were in appearance friendly but in fact hostile to the spirit of mutual concession without which politics is impossible.

In his reply to Orville H. Browning's letter defending Frémont's proclamation, Lincoln wrote, "You speak of it as being the only means of *saving* the government. On the contrary it is itself the surrender of the government."[10] Frémont had no right to exercise the powers he had claimed for himself, but he did not lack the means for putting those powers into effect. In this respect, he was in a position analogous to the southern leaders who had the capability, though not the right, to execute their threats to break up the government. In the case of Frémont, as in the previous winter, Lincoln's primary concern was not to preserve the territorial integrity of the Union but to preserve its political integrity. He would save the Union with all its states, if he could; but he would not save it at the cost of the very thing that made the Union worth saving. Lincoln was consistent in refusing to surrender the government to despotism.

With the distinction between political and despotic government in mind, one is in a better position to examine Lincoln's defense of the implied constitutional right of the people of a state and only those people—in ordinary circumstances—to regulate its "domestic institutions."

In his first inaugural address, Lincoln cited, in addition to his party's platform, the formulation of his position on this question from the first debate with Douglas. He had set out the same position more precisely in the third debate: "I hold myself under constitutional obligations to allow the people in all the states without interference, direct or indirect, to do exactly as they please [about slavery], and I deny that I have any inclination to interfere with them, even if there were no such constitutional obligation."[11]

In a moral sense, the right of the people in a state to do as they pleased about slavery was no right at all.

> When the white man governs himself that is self-government; but when he governs himself, and also governs *another* man, that is *more* than self-government—that is despotism. If the negro is a *man,* why then my ancient faith teaches me that "all men are created equal"; and that there can be no moral right in connection with one man's making a slave of another.

Nothing in the constitutional distinction between states and territories made slavery in the states any less despotic. But if Lincoln was disinclined to do what the Constitution forbade—interfere with slavery in the states—even in the event that the Constitution had permitted it, he must have thought he understood the reason for the prohibition and approved of that reason. The framers' reason, as Lincoln understood it, was stated with impressive clarity by the Agrarian writer Frank Lawrence Owsley: "The knowledge gained from experience as English colonists demonstrated irrefutably to these men that government from a great distance, by legislators not equally affected by their laws with the people for whom they were legislating, was ignorant government because it had no understanding of the local situation; and it was despotic government because the opinion and wishes of the people for whom the laws were passed were not considered or even known." When Douglas made this view of American self-government the basis for an objection to the free-soil position, however, Lincoln replied:

> [Douglas] shows us that when it was in contemplation for the colonies to break off from Great Britain, and set up a new government for them-

selves, several of the states instructed their delegates to go for the measure, PROVIDED EACH STATE SHOULD BE ALLOWED TO REGULATE ITS DOMES-
TIC CONCERNS IN ITS OWN WAY. I do not quote; but this in substance. This
was right. I see nothing objectionable in it. I also think it probable that it
had some reference to the existence of slavery amongst them. I will not
deny that it had. But had it, in any reference, to the carrying of slavery
into NEW COUNTRIES? That is the question.

Following Calhoun, the southern Democrats went further: they argued
that they were constitutionally entitled to protection for their human
property in the territories (Lincoln's "new countries"). Owsley departed
from Lincoln's understanding of the framers' reasoning when he represented it to be the basis not only of "State rights" but also of "State sovereignty," which underlaid the southern insistence on equal rights for
slavery in the federal territories—the common property of all the
states—even if the settlers in the territories did not want it.[12]

Upon the question of state sovereignty hinged the matter of whether
the United States was, as Lincoln expressed it in his first inaugural address,
"a government proper," with the dignity that is implied by that phrase,
or an "association of States in the nature of contract merely." If Lincoln
seems hasty in disposing of the historical evidence for state sovereignty,
one must remember what he thought was at stake. Lincoln's inauguration was not the occasion for him to argue the matter, but his own view
could not have been in doubt. Stopping in Indianapolis on his way to
Washington, Lincoln said, "What is the particular sacredness of a State?
... Now, I ask the question ... where is the mysterious, original right, from
principle, for a certain district of country with inhabitants, by merely
being called a State, to play tyrant over all its own citizens, and deny the
authority of everything greater than itself." In his message to Congress of
July 4, 1861, Lincoln set forth his own view of the Union as he had not
permitted himself to do at his inauguration four months earlier:

This relative matter of National power, and State rights, as a principle, is
no other than the principle of *generality*, and *locality*. Whatever concerns
the whole, should be confided to the whole—to the general government;
while, whatever concerns *only* the State, should be left exclusively, to the
State. This is all there is of original principle about it. Whether the

National Constitution, in defining boundaries between the two, has applied the principle with exact accuracy, is not to be questioned. We are all bound by that defining, without question.[13]

In Lincoln's judgment, slavery as a moral question could never be a matter of merely local concern: national approval was implied in permitting its extension into new territories. According to Lincoln's understanding of the Constitution, regulation of the actual institution of slavery *was* a local concern, to be left to the people of the states where it existed. Implicit in the idea of the United States as "a government proper," however, was the possibility that extraordinary circumstances might compel the general government to assume extraordinary powers.

The Emancipation Proclamation represented just such an assumption of power. The decree carried considerable danger, as its author was aware. The kind of Union that the Southern Agrarians preferred—Calhoun's association of sovereign states, each compacting with the rest for strictly limited ends—would have ruled out any extraordinary assumption of power by the executive, but it would also have ruled out much else that was less readily subject to criticism.[14] It would have deprived the Union of its genuinely political character.

Garrison biographer Henry Mayer characterized the Emancipation Proclamation as "an uncertain foundation for social transformation." As a military measure, and one of questionable legality, the Proclamation had obvious weaknesses.[15] Lincoln knew better than Garrison what an uncertain foundation it was. The president could not have been more explicit than when he compared the Proclamation to an operation to remove a limb: "By general law life *and* limb must be protected; yet often a limb must be amputated to save a life; but a life is never wisely given to save a limb. I felt that measures, otherwise unconstitutional, might become lawful, by becoming indispensable to the preservation of the constitution, through the preservation of the nation."[16] Lincoln had concluded that the circumstances justified otherwise unconstitutional measures; but he knew that the end of slavery would require a transformation of southern society that could not be imposed successfully from without, by force of arms. For this reason, the very weaknesses of the Proclamation were an advantage in disguise inasmuch as they left room for politics—a much less uncertain foundation—to continue.

Mayer points to a puzzling feature in Lincoln's message to Congress of December 1, 1862, in which he made good on his purpose, announced in the preliminary emancipation proclamation, "upon the next meeting of Congress to again recommend the adoption of a practical measure tendering pecuniary aid to the free acceptance or rejection of all slave-states, so called . . . which . . . may then have voluntarily adopted, or thereafter may voluntarily adopt, immediate, or gradual abolishment of slavery within their respective limits." When Lincoln made his recommendation, he did so in the form of three proposed constitutional amendments, reasoning that the "requisite three-fourths of the States [for ratification] will necessarily include seven of the Slave states. Their concurrence, if obtained, will give assurance of their severally adopting emancipation, at no very distant day, upon the new constitutional terms. This assurance would end the struggle now, and save the Union forever." Some of the states still in rebellion as of the date of the message would have to ratify the amendments, and the Emancipation Proclamation was set to take effect at the start of January. Mayer comments, "It was evident, if the president meant to achieve serious discussion of his proposed amendment[s], that he would have to renege on his promise to issue a permanent emancipation decree on January 1, 1863." It is possible that Lincoln intended no more than to indicate the course that he would have preferred to follow in addressing the slavery problem, though he recognized it as impracticable; but what are we to make of what even Mayer, who doubts Lincoln's sincerity, calls the "unmatched heights of eloquence" attained in the close of his message to Congress?

> The dogmas of the quiet past, are inadequate to the stormy present. The occasion is piled high with difficulty, and we must rise with the occasion. As our case is new, so we must think anew, and act anew. We must dis-enthrall our selves, and then we shall save our country.
>
> Fellow-citizens, *we* cannot escape history. We of this Congress and this administration, will be remembered in spite of ourselves. No personal significance, or insignificance, can spare one or another of us. The fiery trial through which we pass, will light us down, in honor or dishonor, to the latest generation. We *say* we are for the Union. The world will not forget that we say this. We know how to save the Union. The

world knows we do know how to save it. We—even *we here*—hold the power, and bear the responsibility. In *giving* freedom to the *slave,* we *assure* freedom to the *free*—honorable alike in what we give, and what we preserve. We shall nobly save, or meanly lose, the last best, hope of earth. Other means may succeed; this could not fail. The way is plain, peaceful, generous, just—a way which, if followed, the world will forever applaud, and God must forever bless.

Could Lincoln have attained such heights of eloquence on behalf of a plan that he knew was certain to fail? Mayer writes, "Posterity has chosen to read Lincoln's closing words as a reference to the promised proclamation of January 1, 1863, rather than to the thirty-seven-year deferral (with compensation) that he proposed in December 1862."[17] Mayer is right to be dissatisfied with this interpretation, but he misses the real significance of Lincoln's proposal. When Lincoln said, "In *giving* freedom to the *slave,* we *assure* freedom to the *free*," he meant that by inducing the southern states to give up slavery, Congress and the administration would be acting to preserve constitutional relations throughout the Union, by political means. Lincoln was renewing the appeal in favor of voluntary emancipation that he had made to border state representatives the previous May and again in July; but now he was addressing his appeal to the whole Congress and through it to the American people.

The most plausible answer, then, to the puzzle of Lincoln's intention in the December 1862 message is that he was looking beyond January 1, 1863, mindful of how far the emancipation to be effected by his proclamation fell short of a definitive abolishment of slavery in a transformed southern society. In a letter dated January 8, 1863, Lincoln suggested that the states still in rebellion against the Union might receive compensation from the federal government, if they would accept the abolishment of slavery and make their own provisions to institute a system of free labor in its place. "Let them adopt systems of apprenticeship for the colored people, conforming substantially to the most approved plans of gradual emancipation; and, with the aid they can have from the general government, they may be nearly as well off, in this respect, as if the present trouble had not occurred, and much better off than they can possibly be if the contest continues persistently." More surprising was

Lincoln's revival of the offer two years later, at the time of the Hampton Roads peace conference.[18] His reelection had indicated that the northern public was willing to maintain the contest of arms until a final victory; and a proposed constitutional amendment abolishing slavery had just passed Congress. The end of slavery now appeared virtually certain, but it made no small difference to Lincoln how the end would come. He wanted the people of the South to take the initiative—to accept that slavery was ended and to reassume their place in the Union before they were forced to return to it. Alexander Stephens, one of the Confederate delegates at Hampton Roads, reported that Lincoln told him,

> Stephens, if I were in Georgia . . . I'll tell you what I would do if I were in your place. I would go home and get the governor of the state to call the legislature together and get them to recall all the troops from the war, elect senators and members to Congress, and ratify this constitutional amendment *prospectively,* so as to take effect, say, in five years. . . . Whatever may have been the views of your people before the war, they must be convinced now that slavery is doomed. It cannot last long in any event, and the best course, it seems to me, for your public men to pursue would be to adopt such a policy as will avoid, as far as possible, the evils of immediate emancipation.

Lincoln also told Stephens that "he would be willing to be taxed to remunerate the southern people for their slaves. He believed the people of the North were as responsible for slavery as the people of the South, and if the war should then cease, with the voluntary abolition of slavery by the states, he should be in favor, individually, of the government paying a fair indemnity for the loss to the owners."[19]

As it happened, it was the freedmen themselves who paid the penalty for the nation's failure to effect emancipation politically. In 1880 Frederick Douglass observed, "History does not furnish an example of emancipation under conditions less friendly to the emancipated class than this American example. Liberty came to the freedmen of the United States not in mercy, but in wrath—not by moral choice but by military necessity—not by the generous action of the people among whom they were to live, and whose good will was essential to the success of the measure, but by strangers, foreigners, invaders, trespassers, aliens, and enemies." That was how many in the South had come to see their northern countrymen, and under the circumstances they were partly right. Douglass was speaking, as he had done many times, on the anniversary of emancipation in the British West Indies, which had been peaceful, though not voluntary: London had imposed the measure on its colonies. "What though it was not American," Douglass asked, "what though it was not republican, but monarchical"?[20] Lincoln, however, could not regard this difference as lightly as Douglass seemed to. Dangers to freedom lay on the side of "monarchical" forwardness as well as on the side of "republican" complacency.

Unlike the abolitionists, Lincoln did not see the question presented by slavery in terms of a simple pair of alternatives: either one was on the side of the slave and consequently insisted on his immediate and unconditional release from bondage, or one was on the side of the slave-holder. Rather, Lincoln suggested that his own point of view was more comprehensive. As early as 1838, Lincoln had called attention to the possibility that the demise of Americans' liberal form of government might come about through "emancipating slaves" as well as "enslaving freemen." He referred to this possibility again in 1845: "I hold it to be a paramount duty of us in the free states, due to the Union of the states, and perhaps to liberty itself (paradox though it may seem) to let the slavery of the other states alone." In a society "where slavery was already widely spread and deeply seated," Lincoln said in 1852, even a wise statesman could not perceive "how it could be at *once* eradicated, without producing a greater evil, even to the cause of human liberty itself."[21]

Similarly, when Lincoln warned in 1856 that "State equality"—the Calhoun doctrine of the Union—was threatening to supplant human equality as the "central idea" of the American republic, he did not speak of these as competing ideas: the equality of men *includes* the equality of the states. State equality represented an impoverished version of Americans' original idea of equality. Referring to the division of the antislavery vote in the presidential election just held, Lincoln said,

Let every one who really believes, and is resolved, that free society is not, *and shall not be,* a failure, and who can conscientiously declare that in the past contest he has done only what he thought best—let every such one have charity to believe that every other one can say as much. . . . Let past differences, as nothing be; and with steady eye on the real issue, let us reinaugurate the good old "central ideas" of the Republic. . . . We shall again be able not to declare, that "all States as States, are equal," nor yet that "all citizens as citizens are equal," but to renew the broader, better declaration, including both these and much more, that "all *men* are created equal."[22]

The dependence of citizen equality on natural human equality is clear: it is because human beings are equal by nature in the decisive respects that their governments may not arbitrarily institute distinctions among them, unjustly elevating some citizens and degrading others. The dependence of state equality on natural human equality is less clear, but it is nevertheless intelligible.

State equality means, for example, that Pennsylvania and its much smaller neighbor Delaware are entitled to the same number of senators—apparently in defiance of the natural equality of their respective people. Lincoln's remark, however, suggests the appearance of inequality is misleading. The states enjoy a degree of equality as members of a larger political community. The constitutional equality of states within the Union rests on a different basis from the equality of sovereign states considered by themselves: sovereign states are equal inasmuch as none recognizes an authority higher than itself. In truth, of course, such states are anything but equal. Out of the Union, a sovereign Delaware could not long maintain its independence against a sovereign and hostile Pennsylvania. Equal representation in the Senate reflects the efforts of delegates to the Constitutional Convention to make their plan of union acceptable to the people of all the states, large and small alike. *Federalist* No. 62, which takes up this point, quotes from the letter that was sent to Congress with the proposed constitution, over Washington's signature: the provision for equal representation in the Senate is "a part of the Constitution which is allowed on all hands to be the result, not of theory, but 'of a spirit of amity, and that mutual deference and concession which the peculiarity of our political situation rendered indispensable.'" State equality resulted from a prior decision for union, with acceptance of the political necessities that such a decision would impose. A similar point can be made about the clauses in the Constitution related to slavery.[23]

The real alternative to "a government proper" of all the states, then, was two or more sectional confederacies, in which liberty would be less secure—this is the argument of the opening numbers of *The Federalist,* which Lincoln adapted to the circumstances of 1860–1861. In the face of possible disunion, Publius stressed the danger of conflict between alien confederacies; in the face of actual disunion, Lincoln stresses the superiority of laws to treaties as a means of establishing terms of intercourse.

> We cannot remove our respective sections from each other. . . . They cannot but remain face to face; and intercourse, either amicable or hostile, must continue between them. Is it possible then to make that intercourse more advantageous, or more satisfactory, *after* separation than *before?* Can aliens make treaties easier than friends can make laws? Can treaties be more faithfully enforced between aliens, than laws can among friends?[24]

It would prove easy for the states that seceded from the Union at this time to unite on the basis of a constitution outwardly much like the old one, but all possibilities were open, and the act of secession itself had in Lincoln's view set a fatal precedent for further acts of disobedience.

Measuring Lincoln by the standard of what are today called *human rights* risks distorting his achievement: this was not exactly Lincoln's standard. To apply such a standard is to assume too rigid a distinction between human rights and citizen rights—precisely the mistake committed by both the abolitionists and the most ardent defenders of states' rights. Writing at the time of the First World War, Lord Charnwood used the same term in describing Lincoln's purpose, but evidently with a broader signification:

> When he was President and Civil War was raging, many good men in the North mistook him and thought him half-hearted, because he persisted in his respect for the rights of the slave States so long as there seemed to be a chance of saving the Union in that way. . . . But . . . his forbearance with slavery cost him real pain, and we shall misread both his policy as President and his character as a man if we fail to see that in the bottom of his mind he felt this forbearance to be required by the *very same prin-*

ciples which roused him against the extension of the evil. . . . Negro slavery was not the only important issue, nor was it an isolated issue. What
really was in issue was the continuance of the nation . . . a nation founded
by the Union of self-governing communities, some of which lagged far
behind the others in applying in their own midst the elementary principles of freedom, but yet a nation actuated from its very foundation in
some important respects by the acknowledgement of human rights.

Lincoln looked to the ultimate extinction of slavery as a matter of
national policy, but he would not hasten the event by any gratuitously
provocative measure. His extinctionism is distinguished from abolitionism by having as its primary object not the abolition of a vicious
institution but the preservation of a wholesome government—a government that southerners, too, valued, even if they were slow to apply
the principles on which it was based.[25]

Tocqueville observed, paraphrasing Aristotle's definition of political
rule, "The man who obeys violence bows and demeans himself; but
when he submits to the right to command that he recognizes in someone like him, he raises himself in a way above the very one who com-
mands him."[26] By the time of Lincoln's rise to prominence, northerner
and southerner alike had grown reluctant to recognize such a right in the
other as "someone like him." "What have we in common with them?"
Garrison once asked in reference to the people of the South. "Are not
their principles, their pursuits, their policies, their interests, their
designs, their feelings, utterly diverse from ours?"[27] According to
Calhoun's theory of the Union, the government in Washington, being no
more than a "common agent" of the states, has no right to rule them; it
is actuated not by the acknowledgment of human rights but by an obligation "so to exercise its powers as to give, as far as may be practicable,
increased stability and security to the domestic institutions of the States
that compose the Union." Fitzhugh accepted this theory in its most
important features and developed them still further: his assertion of
"State nationality" was an attempt to impart some naturalness to what
evidently struck him as the highly artificial division of the territory of
the United States into distinct sovereignties. It is clear, however, that the
more natural the states should become in this respect—the more like little nations—the less natural a union of such states must be.[28]

Behind southerners' reluctance to acknowledge a reciprocal right to rule in their northern fellow citizens lay their far deeper reluctance to acknowledge anything like it in their own slaves. The recognition of such a right in another person means recognizing the right in that other to be ruled politically, as opposed to despotically. Political rule is based on the presupposition of a nature common to rulers and ruled, and it reflects a relatively high degree of confidence in the capability of human beings to rule themselves. This is the philosophical content in Lincoln's defense of politics. Lincoln knew that the capability of self-government could not be taken for granted—the crisis over slavery was a test, and without a doubt other tests would follow—but he understood, as his opponents did not, that rejecting politics means giving up the cause as hopeless in advance.

On November 10, 1864, Lincoln used the occasion of a serenade to reflect on the circumstances of the recent election, an election that returned him to office for a second term of which he would serve only six weeks. Reading from a prepared text, he admitted that by dividing the loyal population in a "political war," the election had imperiled the war to suppress the rebellion. Nevertheless, Lincoln pronounced the election to have been "a necessity" and even to have "done good"; victory over the rebellion would be deprived of its meaning if it should be achieved at the cost of self-government. "We can not have free government without elections; and if the rebellion could force us to forego, or postpone a national election, it might fairly claim to have already conquered and ruined us." The end of the military contest was to preserve the conditions under which political contests are possible. As it happened, events "demonstrated that a people's government can sustain a national election, in the midst of a great civil war." Lincoln also made this observation for the benefit of his supporters, to assuage any bitterness lingering from the campaign—an observation that reveals his attitude toward the larger conflict: "In any future great national trial, compared with the men of this, we shall have as weak, and as strong; as silly and as wise; as bad and good. Let us, therefore, study the incidents of this, as philosophy to learn wisdom from, and none of them as wrongs to be revenged."[29]

Epilogue

Political Temperament

In an 1851 essay, "The Fugitive-Slave Law," Orestes Brownson noted that "the feeling on the subject is deepest in those very states [in the Lower South] from which the fewest slaves escape, or are likely to escape." He explained this odd fact as follows: the southern people "insist on the law," not in consideration of the value of the slaves otherwise lost, but "because it is constitutional, because in executing it we give them assurance that we are willing and able to abide by our constitutional engagements, and are not disposed to abuse the power of the federal government, now passing, once for all, into our hands."[1] The Fugitive Slave Law kept slavery before the eyes of the nation at a time when the actual institution was confined below the Mason-Dixon Line. Brownson evidently wanted to impress on his northern readers a sense of the reasonableness of such an obligation from a national point of view. In doing so, however, he wrote as if the deep feeling of slaveholders concerning the subject was a reflection of their sagacity. More likely, they saw northern defiance of the Fugitive Slave Law as an expression of disdain toward themselves—and they fully returned the sentiment.

Although he was inflexibly opposed to any further extension of the South's characteristic institution, Abraham Lincoln bore no feelings of ill will toward the southern people. Lincoln did not expect southerners and their allies to concur in his party's view of slavery as a wrong, but he called on them "as national men" to consider whether sectional harmony was likely to be restored on any basis other than the one proposed by the Republicans. Slavery, he said, was the "only thing that has ever threatened the perpetuity of the Union"—the "only thing which has ever menaced the destruction of the government under which we live."[2]

Lincoln's approach to the slavery question was not primarily moral in the usual sense but political. It was an approach that well suited his temperament. In the words of Don E. Fehrenbacher, although Lincoln shared the abolitionists' antislavery goals, "the author of the single greatest reform in American history, was not himself a reformer by nature. . . . Crusades just did not suit his temperament. He was by no means a cynic, but he tended to accept the world as he found it." In another place, Fehrenbacher quotes from Lord Charnwood's biography: Lincoln "accepted the institutions to which he was born, and he enjoyed them." (Charnwood observes, for example, that Lincoln from early on showed an attraction to the "somewhat unholy business of party management.") Herbert Croly, a proponent of reform in the early twentieth century whose hero was Lincoln, nevertheless said of him, "He had none of the moral strenuousness of the reformer, none of the exclusiveness of a man, whose purposes and ideas were consciously perched higher than those of his neighbors."[3]

The abolitionists' attacks invited a defensive, even self-righteous response from many otherwise moderate southerners; they also made it more likely that men of a temperament quite unlike Lincoln's would rise to prominence in southern politics. There is an implied contrast with Lincoln in Robert Penn Warren's description of Jefferson Davis. After returning a hero from the Mexican War, Davis "was soon appointed senator. But the game of politics he had not learned (and never did learn): the deal; the nature of combinations; easy fellowship; compromise; the slipperiness of logic; humor; patience; generosity." The word *appointed* is significant: the Mississippi legislature made Davis a senator without the kind of vigorous partisan contest that would mark Lincoln's campaign for the Senate in 1858. Allen Tate, who like Warren was one of the Twelve Southerners that collaborated in *I'll Take My Stand*, wrote that "a man who had served a full political apprenticeship could never have fallen into [the] error" of supposing that "so rapid and so unearned a rise to leadership" as Davis had experienced "was due to personal merit so great that men could not fail to recognize it." Consequently, "when people disagreed with him he felt personally insulted." (Whether Davis would ever have submitted to such a political apprenticeship is another question.) According to Warren, Davis "lacked the indefinable sense for 'handling' men, the intuitive understanding of others"; in Tate's judgment, he "could not manage men, and he was too great a character to let men manage him: that is the tragedy of his career."[4]

The reader may judge whether Lincoln was guilty of "slipperiness of logic." There is admittedly a potential for slipperiness of a sort in politicians' need to accept and accommodate themselves to conditions in the world as they find it. As Warren has noted in another part of his characterization of the "game of politics," there is also a quality of generosity in that acceptance. The best politicians accommodate themselves—but not too closely.

George Fitzhugh was the rare southerner who did not simply condemn the abolitionists in turn but actually tried to open a dialogue with them. (He even subscribed to the *Liberator*.) Fitzhugh thought he discerned in the character of the reformer a tendency to find fault with the world—reversing the formula of Alexander Pope's "Essay on Man," the reformer is inclined to think that "Whatever is, is *wrong*." But Fitzhugh's acceptance of conditions in his world is difficult to distinguish from abject surrender to them. He was less than generous in his estimation of the human ability to reason about justice and to undertake appropriate reforms. Eugene D. Genovese, a sympathetic critic, finds Fitzhugh "dangerously close to cynicism" in rejecting all possibility of progress. A newspaper writer in New Haven, Connecticut, where Fitzhugh spoke in 1855, reported that many in the audience were "amused" by the novelty of Fitzhugh's arguments, but "a few were saddened that a man whom nature evidently intended for a genial gentleman . . . should have the end of his production thwarted by the mere fact of tropical location under the influences of slavery."[5]

Through many trials Frederick Douglass retained something of his faith in "the power of truth over the conscience of even a slaveholder," but as he grew older his view of the slavery problem grew more complex. He records this exchange with John Brown, which took place in

1847 when Douglass was still a disciple of Garrison: "When I suggested that we might convert the slaveholders, he became much excited, and said that could never be, he knew their proud hearts and that they would never be induced to give up their slaves, until they felt a big stick about their heads." From the time of this meeting, Douglass says, "while I continued to write and speak against slavery, I became all the same less hopeful of its peaceful abolition."[6] In time, however, Douglass became more receptive to a political alternative that combined something of Brown's "big stick" with something of the Garrisonian idea of moral conversion.

Douglass seems to have been temperamentally suited for political life; in fact, he served in a number of nonelective offices under Republican presidents after the war. Reviewing a life, then in its seventh decade, in which there had been many incidents, both in and out of slavery, that would have embittered a lesser man, Douglass wrote,

> It may possibly be inferred from what I have said of the prevalence of prejudice, and the practice of proscription, that I have had a very miserable sort of life, or that I must be remarkably insensible to public aversion. Neither inference is true. I have neither been miserable because of the ill-feeling of those about me, nor indifferent to popular approval, and I think, upon the whole, I have passed a tolerably cheerful and even joyful life.

Douglass mentions three reasons he had lived a joyful life in spite of prejudice and proscription: first, "there have been raised up for me friends of both colors to cheer and strengthen me in my work"; second, "I have had the wit to distinguish between what is merely artificial and transient and what is fundamental and permanent, and resting on the latter, I could cheerfully encounter the former"; and third, "I have been greatly helped to bear up under unfriendly conditions . . . by a constitutional tendency to see the funny side of things, which has enabled me to laugh at follies that others would soberly resent."[7]

Douglass did not doubt that slavery was one of the "artificial and transient" things. After the institution had been destroyed in the United States, and more than forty years after his own escape from bondage, Douglass would be reunited with his former master Thomas Auld, who was then over eighty years old and close to the end of his life. This visit, Douglass wrote, was "by serious-minded men regretted as a weakening of my lifelong testimony against slavery." Douglass, however, was not inclined to judge his old master harshly on this occasion. "We had both been flung, by powers that did not ask our consent, upon a mighty current of life, which we could neither resist nor control. By this current he was a master, and I a slave, but now our lives were verging towards a point where differences disappear."[8]

This example of generosity may be set alongside that of the president who, after nearly four years of "terrible war," in which he had faced, according to William Lloyd Garrison, his onetime opponent, who was in a position to know, "perils and trials unknown to any man, in any age of the world, in official station," could, without suspicion of pretence, call on his countrymen to show both "firmness in the right" and "charity for all."[9]

Notes

Preface

1. Emancipation Proclamation, in *The Collected Works of Abraham Lincoln,* ed. Roy P. Basler et al., 6:28–31 (hereafter cited as *CW*); Richard Hofstadter, *The American Political Tradition and the Men Who Made It,* 169; *Frederick Douglass: Selected Speeches and Writings,* ed. Philip S. Foner, 560 (hereafter cited as *SSW*). On the scope of the Emancipation Proclamation, see Steve Crockett, "On Becoming Free."

2. *Congressional Globe,* 37th Cong., 3d sess., Appendix, 45, 47; Gettysburg Address, *CW,* 7:23. Grider had been present to hear Lincoln make his last appeal to border state representatives on July 12, 1862; afterward he signed a letter stating the views of the majority in rejecting Lincoln's proposal (*CW,* 5:317–19; John G. Nicolay and John Hay, *Abraham Lincoln: A History,* 6:111–12).

3. Harry V. Jaffa, *Crisis of the House Divided: An Interpretation of the Issues in the Lincoln-Douglas Debates,* v.

4. In his more recent study, Jaffa includes a consideration of John C. Calhoun and Alexander H. Stephens, by way of assigning them their proper places in European and American intellectual history. He links Calhoun with Rousseau and the German idealists, for example, and both Calhoun and Stephens with the "mid-nineteenth-century faith in science" (*A New Birth of Freedom: Abraham Lincoln and the Coming of the Civil War,* 86, 224, 427).

5. These essays appear in *Toward a More Perfect Union: Writings of Herbert J. Storing,* ed. Joseph M. Bessette. The question of politics and moral reform in reference to slavery is also treated briefly in another essay in the same collection, "The Role of Government in Society."

6. Storing, *Toward a More Perfect Union,* 155–56.

Chapter 1.   A Divided Lincoln?

1. Don E. Fehrenbacher, *Prelude to Greatness: Lincoln in the 1850s*, 3. Although Fehrenbacher places Lincoln "very close to dead center" in the Republican Party of 1860, Fehrenbacher does perceive an ambivalence in Lincoln's discussions of slavery, "the same ambivalence that had characterized his earlier discussions" (147–48).

2. First Inaugural Address, March 4, 1861, *CW*, 4:263–64. For the source of Lincoln's self-quotation, see First Debate with Stephen A. Douglas, at Ottawa, August 21, 1858, *CW*, 3:16. In his October 16, 1854, speech at Peoria, Lincoln had said, "I wish to MAKE and to KEEP the distinction between the EXISTING institution, and the EXTENSION of it, so broad, and so clear, that no honest man can misunderstand me, and no dishonest one, successfully misrepresent me" (*CW*, 2:248).

3. Henry David Thoreau, "Slavery in Massachusetts," in *Reform Papers*, ed. Wendell Glick, 103.

4. John C. Calhoun, *Union and Liberty: The Political Philosophy of John C. Calhoun*, ed. Ross M. Lence, 468.

5. Douglass, "The True Ground upon Which to Meet Slavery," *SSW*, 333; Henry Mayer, *All on Fire: William Lloyd Garrison and the Abolition of Slavery*, 218; *Recollected Words of Abraham Lincoln*, ed. and comp. Don E. Fehrenbacher and Virginia Fehrenbacher, 384. Two much smaller antislavery parties, forerunners of the Republican Party, were the Liberty Party and the Free Soil Party (see Donald Bruce Johnson, comp., *National Party Platforms*, 1:4–8, 13–14).

6. George Fitzhugh, *Cannibals All! or, Slaves without Masters*, ed. C. Vann Woodward, 7–8. The phrase Fitzhugh quotes is from the Virginia Declaration of Rights of 1776 (see Philip B. Kurland and Ralph Lerner, eds., *The Founders' Constitution*, 1:6–7).

7. Speech in Independence Hall, February 22, 1861, *CW*, 4:240.

8. Robert W. Johannsen, *Lincoln, the South, and Slavery: The Political Dimension*, 68; Editorial, "Mr. Lincoln—Mr. Seward's Speech," *Louisville Daily Journal*, August 22, 1860, in *Southern Editorials on Secession*, ed. Dwight L. Dumond, 164–67; Speech at Peoria, *CW*, 2:256; "A House Divided": Speech at Springfield, June 16, 1858, *CW*, 2:461; Lincoln to John A. Gilmer, December 15, 1860, *CW*, 4:151–53. The editorial was presumably written by George D. Prentice; see Lincoln's letter to him, October 29, 1860, *CW*, 4:134–35.

9. Johannsen, *Lincoln, the South, and Slavery*, 68; Phillips quoted in Hofstadter, *American Political Tradition*, 194; Oliver Johnson, *William Lloyd Garrison and His Times*, 311, 435, 448.

10. James M. McPherson, *Abraham Lincoln and the Second American Revolution*, 130; Johnson, *William Lloyd Garrison and His Times*, 435; Lincoln to Horace Greeley, August 22, 1862, *CW*, 5:388–89; Lincoln to Albert G. Hodges, April 4, 1864, *CW*, 7:281–82; Annual Message to Congress, December 3, 1861, *CW*, 5:49.

11. Speech at Peoria, *CW*, 2:276, 255; Speech at Springfield, July 17, 1858, *CW*, 2:520; Speech at Chicago, July 10, 1858, *CW*, 2:501; William Lloyd

Garrison, *Selections from the Writings and Speeches of William Lloyd Garrison*, 311; Lincoln to George Robertson, August 15, 1855, *CW*, 2:318.

12. Don E. Fehrenbacher, *Lincoln in Text and Context: Collected Essays*, 108; Lord Charnwood, *Abraham Lincoln*, 59.

13. Speech at Peoria, *CW*, 2:273. In the first issue of the *Liberator*, Garrison wrote, "Tell a man whose house is on fire, to give a moderate alarm; tell him to moderately rescue his wife from the ravisher; . . . but urge me not to use moderation in a cause like the present" (*Selections from the Writings and Speeches of William Lloyd Garrison*, 63).

14. Fehrenbacher, *Lincoln in Text and Context*, 127–28.

15. Hofstadter, *American Political Tradition*, 146–47, 151; Speech at Springfield, June 26, 1857, *CW*, 2:409.

16. Speech in the U.S. House of Representatives on Internal Improvements, June 20, 1848, *CW*, 1:488; First Inaugural Address, *CW*, 4:264.

17. Eugene D. Genovese, *The World the Slaveholders Made: Two Essays in Interpretation*, 119; Fitzhugh, *Cannibals All!* 257. Hartz himself acknowledges that what he calls the Reactionary Enlightenment was "the great imaginative moment in American political thought . . . when America almost got out of itself, as it were, and looked with some objectivity on the liberal formula it has known since birth" (*The Liberal Tradition in America: An Interpretation of American Political Thought since the Revolution*, 176). Edmund Wilson's *Patriotic Gore: Studies in the Literature of the American Civil War* also includes a section on Fitzhugh; Wilson correctly emphasizes Fitzhugh's unconventionality but overlooks the deeper consistency between his views and those of other southern interpreters of the Constitution. The most thorough treatment since Genovese's is by Robert J. Loewenberg, "John Locke and the Antebellum Defense of Slavery." Loewenberg errs, however, in reading Fitzhugh as if he had been primarily a political theorist. Fitzhugh was addressing a practical question (using theoretical arguments, to be sure): Shall southern society be reformed?

18. Genovese, *World the Slaveholders Made*, 146; Lincoln to Joshua F. Speed, August 24, 1855, *CW*, 2:323; Speech at Cincinnati, Ohio, September 17, 1859, *CW*, 3:442; George Fitzhugh, *Sociology for the South; or, The Failure of Free Society*, 94, 225. Harvey Wish wrote that the idea "expressed in *Sociology for the South* that the United States would ultimately cease to be divided as between liberty and slavery, and become one thing or the other . . . was ultimately translated during 1858 into the superb prose of the future Emancipator." It seems much more likely, however, that Lincoln arrived at the same conclusion independently (*George Fitzhugh, Propagandist of the Old South*, 150–51).

19. William H. Herndon and Jesse W. Weik, *Herndon's Life of Lincoln: The History and Personal Recollections of Abraham Lincoln as Originally Written by William H. Herndon and Jesse W. Weik*, ed. Paul M. Angle, 297–98.

Chapter 2.   Stephen A. Douglas
The Missing Constitutional Basis

1. Even Lincoln's "Second Lecture on Discoveries and Inventions" is in part a satire on the Young America movement that promoted the leadership of Douglas over the "old fogies" of the Democratic Party. See Nicolay and Hay, *Abraham Lincoln: A History,* 1:130–32, 335–37.

2. Jaffa begins part 4 of *Crisis of the House Divided,* which is devoted to making the case for Lincoln, by referring to the possibility that leading Republicans, impressed by Douglas's defiance of the Buchanan administration and the southern wing of his own party in the dispute over the proposed proslavery Lecompton Constitution for Kansas, might have accepted his leadership of a free-soil coalition: "Douglas had brought the majority of the free-soil North to the point of accepting popular sovereignty, and it was precisely this imminent possibility that Abraham Lincoln regarded as the greatest disaster that could befall the American people." Later, in the same part, Jaffa wrote that "Lincoln held that the attempted betrayal of Kansas by the Lecompton fraud was an outcome of the betrayal of principle embodied in the Kansas-Nebraska Act," of which Douglas was the author (276, 297).

3. Eulogy on Henry Clay, July 6, 1852, *CW,* 2:130.

4. Fehrenbacher, *Prelude to Greatness,* 94–95.

5. See especially Lincoln's reply to Douglas in their last debate, held in Alton, October 15, 1858, *CW* 3:310–11, from which the epigraph to this section has been taken.

6. Speech at Kalamazoo, Mich., August 27, 1856, *CW,* 2:361. The newspaper report that is the source for this speech omits the negative, which is clearly required by the sense of the passage.

7. Fragment on Sectionalism, *CW,* 2:350. I have corrected Lincoln's erratic spelling in this citation.

8. Jaffa, *Crisis of the House Divided,* 49, 51, 50.

9. Nebraska bill quoted by Lincoln, *CW,* 2:462.

10. Douglas quoted by Lincoln, *CW,* 2:406; Jaffa, *Crisis of the House Divided,* 317; Speech at Springfield, June 26, 1857, *CW,* 2:407.

11. Paul M. Angle, ed., *The Complete Lincoln-Douglas Debates of 1858,* 54–55; Speech at Springfield, July 17, 1858, *CW,* 2:241; Speech at Peoria, *CW,* 2:255.

12. Douglas quoted in Jaffa, *Crisis of the House Divided,* 53; Seventh Debate with Douglas, *CW,* 3:297.

13. Thoreau, "Resistance to Civil Government," in *Reform Papers,* 86–87.

14. Thoreau, "Slavery in Massachusetts," 96, 108, and "Resistance to Civil Government," 87. Wendell Glick, editor of the *Reform Papers,* raises the possibility that Thoreau may have had Frederick Douglass in mind when he wrote this essay because he spelled the last word in the quotation *Douglassii.* This possibility is difficult to reconcile with the context, and I have accepted the emendation made by the editor of the Modern Library edition of Thoreau's writings.

15. Sixth Debate with Douglas, at Quincy, October 13, 1858, *CW,* 3:276, 254–55. Lincoln's example of southern candor was Preston Brooks, the South

Carolinian who had gained notoriety for his assault on Massachusetts senator Charles Sumner.

16. The quotation is from Stephens's "Cornerstone" speech, see Henry Cleveland, *Alexander H. Stephens in Public and Private, with Letters and Speeches before, during, and since the War,* 723.

Chapter 3.   Alexander H. Stephens
Slavery, Secession, and the Higher Law

1. Cleveland, *Alexander H. Stephens in Public and Private,* 722; Jaffa, *A New Birth of Freedom,* 216.

2. Cleveland, *Alexander H. Stephens in Public and Private,* 128. For the relevant portion of Seward's speech, see George E. Baker, ed., *The Life of William Henry Seward, with Selections from His Works,* 254–55.

3. Jaffa, *A New Birth of Freedom,* 247–48; Cleveland, *Alexander H. Stephens in Public and Private,* 126. In *Southern Statesmen of the Old Régime: Washington, Jefferson, Randolph, Calhoun, Stephens, Toombs, and Jefferson Davis,* William P. Trent paraphrases Stephens's view as follows: "If Washington and Jefferson opposed slavery, it must have been because they really had not understood the institution" (179).

4. Thomas E. Schott, *Alexander H. Stephens of Georgia: A Biography,* 310, 306; Cleveland, *Alexander H. Stephens in Public and Private,* 696.

5. Lincoln's view bears some resemblance to the doctrine of "constitutional aspiration" (see Herman Belz, *Abraham Lincoln, Constitutionalism, and Equal Rights in the Civil War Era,* 88–90).

6. Speech to the Springfield Scott Club, August 14 and 26, 1852, *CW,* 2:156. Lincoln would repeat this position in 1860: "I agree with Seward in his 'Irrepressible Conflict,' but I do not endorse his 'Higher Law' doctrine" (Endorsement on the margin of the *Missouri Democrat,* May 17, 1860, *CW,* 4:50).

7. Cleveland, *Alexander H. Stephens in Public and Private,* 149.

8. William W. Freehling and Craig M. Simpson, eds., *Secession Debated: Georgia's Showdown in 1860,* 15.

9. Ibid., 119, 121–22, 143.

10. Jaffa, *A New Birth of Freedom,* 221, 223.

11. Speech at Edwardsville, *CW,* 3:93; Fragment on slavery, *CW,* 2:222–23. See Jaffa, *Crisis of the House Divided,* 337, 336.

12. Cleveland, *Alexander H. Stephens in Public and Private,* 649.

13. Ibid., 721; Lincoln to Stephens, December 22, 1860, *CW,* 4:160.

14. *CW,* 4:160; Stephens to Lincoln, December 30, 1860, in Cleveland, *Alexander H. Stephens in Public and Private,* 151.

15. Lincoln to John A. Gilmer, *CW,* 4:152; First Inaugural Address, *CW,* 4:268–69. Stephens may also have been considered for a cabinet position; see *CW,* 4:155.

16. Cleveland, *Alexander H. Stephens in Public and Private,* 153; Fragment on the Constitution and the Union, ca. January 1861, *CW,* 4:169.

17. Cleveland, *Alexander H. Stephens in Public and Private,* 301; Seventh Debate with Douglas, *CW,* 3:311.

18. Freehling and Simpson, eds., *Secession Debated,* xvii.

19. Jaffa, *Crisis of the House Divided,* 337.

20. Speech at Steubenville, Ohio, February 14, 1861, *CW,* 207.

Chapter 4.   John C. Calhoun
The Politics of Interest

1. Charnwood, *Abraham Lincoln,* 72; Seventh Debate with Douglas, *CW,* 3:301; Eulogy on Henry Clay, *CW,* 2:130.

2. Arthur Styron, *The Cast-Iron Man: John C. Calhoun and American Democracy,* 359; Alexander H. Stephens, *A Constitutional View of the Late War between the States: Its Causes, Character, Conduct and Results,* 1:341.

3. H. Lee Cheek Jr., *Calhoun and Popular Rule: The Political Theory of the "Disquisition" and "Discourse,"* 22. For another consideration of Calhoun as a "man of theory-and-practice," who was "at or near the center of the national political stage for forty tumultuous years," see Ralph Lerner, "Calhoun's New Science of Politics," 193–224.

4. Cheek, *Calhoun and Popular Rule,* 77–79. Thomas R. Dew concludes his "Review of the Debate [on Emancipation] in the Virginia Legislature of 1831 and 1832," with the statement that "the time for emancipation has not yet arrived, *and perhaps it never will*" (32; the emphasis is mine). One who credits Calhoun with prescience is Jefferson Davis. The three divisions of opinion on the disposition of the territories that Davis describes in his memoir of Calhoun correspond more closely to the political circumstances of 1860 than to those of 1850 ("Life and Character of the Hon. John Caldwell Calhoun," 23).

5. August O. Spain, *The Political Theory of John C. Calhoun,* 35, 94.

6. The first volume of Calhoun's *Works* contains: *A Disquisition on Government* (1–107) and *A Discourse on the Constitution and Government of the United States* (111–406).

7. Senator James Henry Hammond expressed the same view more explicitly in his "Mud-Sill" speech: "Society precedes government; creates it, and ought to control it" (122). See also Fitzhugh, *Sociology for the South,* 26.

8. "The confederacy had failed; and it was absolutely necessary that something should be done to save the credit of the Union, and to guard against confusion and anarchy" (*Works,* 1:287).

9. Ibid., 2:630. A different version of Calhoun's remarks can be found in Calhoun, *Union and Liberty,* 467.

10. Guy Story Brown, *Calhoun's Philosophy of Politics: A Study of "A Disquisition on Government,"* 302. Brown notes the resemblance between the Roman plebeians and the American slaves, but he admits that Calhoun "once replied to a repeated assertion of the innate fragility and insecurity of the institution of slavery in the South by saying that it might last 'forever among us' if left undisturbed by outside intervention" (428n30).

11. Address at Cooper Institute, New York City, February 27, 1860, *CW,* 3:541.

12. Jaffa, *A New Birth of Freedom,* 432, 438–39.

13. Carl L. Becker, *The Declaration of Independence: A Study in the History of Political Ideas,* 254–55.

14. Trent, *Southern Statesman,* 181–82; Edmund Burke, "Speech to the Electors of Bristol," in Kurland and Lerner, eds., *The Founders' Constitution,* 1:195.

15. Trent, *Southern Statesmen,* 186. Trent passes a similar judgment on Alexander Stephens: "He did check his people"; but "to grasp American history as a whole . . . and to lead his people along new paths, was beyond his power, and beyond that of any man then living in the South" (215).

16. Alexis de Tocqueville, *Democracy in America,* 342n47; Ralph Lerner, *The Thinking Revolutionary: Principle and Practice in the New Republic,* 187n6. Slavery was practically excluded from Britain itself by the 1772 ruling of Lord Mansfield in the Somerset case, which prevented the forcible repatriation of slaves to the colonies. For the text of the Somerset ruling ("Sommersett's Case"), see Kurland and Lerner, eds., *The Founders' Constitution,* 4:525.

17. Burke, "Speech to the Electors of Bristol," 1:195.

18. Lerner, *Thinking Revolutionary,* 187; Tocqueville, *Democracy in America,* 190, 216, 342.

19. Tocqueville, *Democracy in America,* 144.

20. Speech at Peoria, *CW,* 2:270.

21. Address at a Sanitary Fair, Baltimore, Md., April 18, 1864, *CW,* 7:301–2.

22. For examples, see *CW,* 2:266, 274–75, 501, and 520.

23. Storing, "Slavery and the Founders," *Toward a More Perfect Union,* 143.

24. Calhoun had in mind such a case as the use of the federal mails to circulate abolitionist literature. He concluded the passage, "Without this restriction, most of the reserved powers of the States,—and, among them, those relating to their internal police, including the health, tranquillity, and safety of their people—might be made abortive, by the laws passed by Congress, to carry into effect the delegated powers; especially in regard to those regulating commerce, and establishing post-offices and post-roads." For Calhoun's discussion of this question, see his "Speech on the Circulation of Incendiary Papers," *Works,* 2:525–28.

25. Speech at Kalamazoo, *CW,* 2:364; Lincoln to Anton C. Hesing, Henry Wendt, and Alexander Fisher, *CW,* 2:475.

Chapter 5.   George Fitzhugh
The Turn to History

1. Speech at a Republican Banquet, Chicago, December 10, 1856, *CW,* 2:385. The word *slave* or *slavery* appears in just three of twenty-eight chapter headings in *Sociology for the South,* and only six of the thirty-seven chapter headings in *Cannibals All!* contain either word.

2. Richard J. Ellis presents evidence that Fitzhugh was correct to see the abolitionist program as going beyond the abolition of chattel slavery (*The Dark Side of the Left: Illiberal Egalitarianism in America*, 19–25). The breadth of Fitzhugh's argument is obscured somewhat by omissions from the index to the only edition of his work in print. For references to Aristotle, the most significant of these omissions, see 12–13, 21, 26, 53, 71, 159–60, and 191–94 in the Belknap edition of *Cannibals All!*

3. John G. Nicolay, *The Outbreak of Rebellion*, 11; Wish, *George Fitzhugh*, 292. In a letter to his friend Holmes, dated April 11, 1855, Fitzhugh was even more pointed, classing Calhoun with Locke, Rousseau, and Jefferson, among others, in denying that human beings are naturally social (quoted in Wish, 118–19). In 1857, however, in another essay for *De Bow's Review*, "The Politics and Economics of Aristotle and Mr. Calhoun," Fitzhugh praised the *Disquisition on Government*, noting similarities with the *Politics*.

4. Friedrich Nietzsche, *On the Advantage and Disadvantage of History for Life*, 7, 47.

5. Lincoln made the same point: biblical slavery was "the Slavery of the *white* man—of men without reference to color" (Speech at Cincinnati, *CW*, 3:445).

6. Fragment on the Constitution and the Union, *CW*, 4:169.

7. Speech in Independence Hall, *CW*, 4:240.

8. Wish, *George Fitzhugh*, 289, 298; [James Fitzjames Stephen], "A Practical Man."

9. C. Vann Woodward, "George Fitzhugh, *Sui Generis*," in *Cannibals All!* xvii.

10. Sir Henry Maine, *Ancient Law*, 96. Lincoln identified the common root of slavery and of kingship in "the same old serpent that says you work and I eat, you toil and I will enjoy the fruits of it" (Speech at Chicago, *CW*, 2:500).

11. Address at Cooper Institute, *CW*, 3:537.

12. For details of Fitzhugh's trip to the North, see John Hope Franklin, *A Southern Odyssey: Travelers in the Antebellum North*, 217–23, 260–61.

13. Wayne Ambler, "Aristotle on Nature and Politics: The Case of Slavery," 390.

14. Aristotle, *Politics*, bk. 1, chaps. 1 and 2. The words quoted as Aristotle's "celebrated justification of slavery" by the writer for the *Edinburgh Review* are from bk. 1, chap. 2 of the *Politics*. References not otherwise identified are to this chapter, which also contains Aristotle's account of the origin of society in the family.

15. Tocqueville, *Democracy in America*, vol. 2, pt. 3, chaps. 8, 10, and 12.

16. Aristotle, *Politics*, bk. 3, chap. 9. The classicist Basil L. Gildersleeve attests that at the outbreak of war "the people of the Southern States were practically of one mind as to the seat of the paramount obligation [that is, in the states]. Adherence to the Union was a matter of sentiment, a matter of interest" (*The Creed of the Old South: 1865–1915*, 22).

Chapter 6. The Attack on Locke

1. Speech at Peoria, *CW*, 2:266; Fitzhugh, *Sociology for the South*, 178–79.
2. Fitzhugh, *Sociology for the South*, 177, 182.
3. Fitzhugh, "Revolutions of '76 and '61 Contrasted," 38.
4. Ibid., 40; John Locke, *Second Treatise of Government: An Essay Concerning the True Original, Extent, and End of Civil Government*, §95, in *Two Treatises of Government*, ed. Peter Laslett.
5. Laslett, *Two Treatises*, 336n, 316n.
6. Fitzhugh, "Revolutions of '76 and '61 Contrasted," 40.
7. *The Frederick Douglass Papers*, ed. John W. Blassingame et al., ser. 1, 2:165, 165n9. See Gregg D. Crane, "Douglass's Natural Rights Constitutionalism."
8. In his 1852 Fourth of July oration, Douglass asked, "Would you have me argue that man is entitled to liberty? That he is the rightful owner of his own body? You have already declared it" (*SSW*, 196).
9. Frederick Law Olmsted, *The Cotton Kingdom: A Traveller's Observations on Cotton and Slavery in the American Slave States, Based upon Three Former Volumes of Journeys and Investigations by the Same Author*, ed. Arthur M. Schlesinger, xvii, xviii, 100. Olmsted greatly admired Douglass: "There are no white men in the United States that display every attribute of a strong and good soul better than some of the freed slaves. What would Frederick Douglass have been had he failed to escape . . . ? What has he become since . . . ? All the statesmanship and kind mastership of the South has done less, in fifty years, to elevate and dignify the African race, than he in ten" (*A Journey in the Seaboard Slave States, with Remarks on Their Economy*, 133). See John David Smith, "Introduction," in the Penguin edition of Douglass, *My Bondage and My Freedom*.
10. Fitzhugh, *Cannibals All!* 249.
11. Thoreau, *Reform Papers*, 89.
12. Fitzhugh, *Cannibals All!* 71–72, 214–15, and *Sociology for the South*, 33.
13. Fitzhugh classed Locke among the political philosophers who have followed the example of Plato's "visionary schemes" ("Politics and Economics of Aristotle and Mr. Calhoun," 164).
14. For Mrs. Freeland's reaction to the arrest of Henry and John Harris, and Douglass's comment on this subject, see Douglass, *My Bondage and My Freedom*, 294. Elsewhere Douglass acknowledges the truth in her charge (279).
15. Harvey Wish, "Introduction," in *Ante-Bellum: Writings of George Fitzhugh and Hinton Rowan Helper on Slavery*, 21; Genovese, *World the Slaveholders Made*, 130–31.
16. Maine, *Ancient Law*, 99–100.
17. Douglass, *My Bondage and My Freedom*, 326–29.
18. Ibid., 325–26; First Debate with Douglas, *CW*, 3:16.
19. Temperance Address, February 22, 1842, *CW*, 1:277; Lincoln to Joshua F. Speed, *CW*, 2:322.
20. Speech at Peoria, *CW*, 2:266; Hofstadter, *American Political Tradition*, 170.

Chapter 7.   Henry David Thoreau
The Question of Political Engagement

1. Speech at Elwood, Kans., December 1 [November 30?], 1859, *CW*, 3:496. There is some doubt as to the correct date of the speech.

2. Glick quoted in Stanley Edgar Hyman, "Henry Thoreau Once More," 176. I have been unable to identify the source of this quotation.

3. Speech at a Republican Banquet, *CW*, 2:385; Bob Pepperman Taylor, *America's Bachelor Uncle: Thoreau and the American Polity*, 114, 164n83; Thoreau, "Resistance to Civil Government," 84.

4. Nick Aaron Ford, "Henry David Thoreau, Abolitionist," 359; Henry Seidel Canby, *Thoreau*, 383. Canby had written, "Henry Thoreau was never an Abolitionist, although at last, and somewhat reluctantly, he associated himself with the Abolitionist organizations."

5. Thoreau, *Walden and Other Writings of Henry David Thoreau*, ed. Brooks Atkinson, 155. By the time these words were published, Congress had passed a measure abolishing the slave trade in the District of Columbia, as part of the Compromise of 1850. Thoreau, however, had resumed paying the poll tax even earlier, in 1849 (Canby, *Thoreau*, 235).

6. Thoreau, *Walden and Other Writings of Henry David Thoreau*, 7.

7. Ibid., 155; Thoreau, "Resistance to Civil Government," 71, 79. Thoreau refers to this essay when he explains why he has omitted a detailed account of the prison episode from *Walden:* he has "elsewhere related" what happened on that occasion. For the textual history of "Resistance to Civil Government," see the editorial appendix to *Reform Papers*, 313–21.

8. Ford supplies what he understands to be the connection between slavery and the Mexican War: the war was "undertaken primarily to extend the boundaries of slavery" ("Henry David Thoreau, Abolitionist," 361).

9. Page references in parenthetical citations in this chapter are to the following essays: "Resistance to Civil Government" (63–90); "Slavery in Massachusetts" (91–109); "A Plea for Captain John Brown" (111–38); and "Reform and the Reformers" (181–97).

10. Eugene O'Connor, trans., *The Essential Epicurus*, 83 (Vatican Sayings, #62). In "Slavery in Massachusetts," Thoreau makes this criticism of the Epicurean posture: "Suppose you have a small library, with pictures to adorn the walls—a garden laid out around—and contemplate scientific and literary pursuits, &c., and discover all at once that your villa, with all its contents, is located in hell, and that the justice of the peace has a cloven foot and a forked tail—do not these things suddenly lose their value in your eyes?" (107).

11. Taylor, *America's Bachelor Uncle*, 110, 161n56; *SSW*, 375. Much the same point is made by Nancy L. Rosenblum: Thoreau "lauded John Brown's uncompromisingness, his self-certainty and intolerance, and not his efficacy as a social reformer" ("Thoreau's Militant Conscience," 97).

12. Thoreau does except Garrison's *Liberator,* which later printed the text of the address.

13. Leo Stoller, "Civil Disobedience: Principle and Politics," 41, and *After*

Walden: Thoreau's Changing Views on Economic Man, 151; Joseph Wood Krutch, *Henry David Thoreau,* 239. Douglass said in 1882, "John Brown began the war that ended slavery and made this a free republic." Quarles, who quoted this statement, wrote that Douglass was "delighted" at the outbreak of war between the states because "now the full might of an aroused North was to be hurled against the slaveholders" (Benjamin Quarles, *Frederick Douglass,* 185, 187).

14. Stoller, *After Walden,* 150, and "Civil Disobedience: Principle and Politics," 41; Henry D. Thoreau, *Correspondence,* ed. Walter Harding and Carl Bode, 611.

15. Phillip Booth's poem entitled "Letter from a Distant Land" captures this side of Thoreau better than any scholarly commentary could. The poem updates Thoreau's assertion in the form of a question, "When were the good and the brave ever in a majority?" (*Reform Papers,* 131).

16. Temperance Address, *CW,* 1:273; Taylor, *America's Bachelor Uncle,* 114, 164n86 (the emphasis is mine); Protest in Illinois Legislature on Slavery, March 3, 1837, *CW,* 1:75.

Chapter 8. William Lloyd Garrison
From Disunionist to Lincoln Emancipationist

1. *Liberator,* May 12, 1865; Wendell P. Garrison and Francis J. Garrison, *William Lloyd Garrison, 1805–1879: The Story of His Life Told by His Children,* 4:132n1; Lincoln to Horace Greeley, *CW,* 5:388. Garrison had been invited by the Lincoln administration to be present when the Union flag was again raised over Fort Sumter, four years to the day after the fort was surrendered to the Confederacy.

2. Orestes Brownson, "The Fugitive-Slave Law," 17:20.

3. Garrison and Garrison, *William Lloyd Garrison, 1805–1879,* 4:44–45.

4. Mayer, *All on Fire,* 563–64, 566; Fehrenbacher, *Lincoln in Text and Context,* 195; J. G. Randall, *Lincoln the Liberal Statesman,* 20; Johnson, *William Lloyd Garrison and His Times,* 311; Jefferson Davis, *The Rise and Fall of the Confederate Government,* 2:182 (quoted in James M. McPherson, "Foreword," in the Da Capo edition of Davis's work).

5. Lincoln to Horace Greeley, *CW,* 5:388, 389n2; Speech at Peoria, *CW,* 2:276; Lincoln to August Belmont, July 31, 1862, *CW,* 5:350.

6. See Emancipation Proclamation—First Draft, July 22, 1862, *CW,* 5:336–38.

7. *Liberator,* September 26 and December 26, 1862, January 9, 1863.

8. Charles M. Segal, ed., *Conversations with Lincoln,* 238. A somewhat different account of this meeting appears in Lincoln, *Recollected Words of Abraham Lincoln,* 119–20.

9. In 1847 Judge John A. Campbell of Alabama wrote to Calhoun: "Garrison and Phillips say that the Constitution of the U.S. is a pro–slavery contract—containing powerful and stringent securities for the slaveholder. . . . Their remedy is to make a *revolution.* Now all this is better to me than the course of those other men who deny your rights or who disregard them while claiming to be

the friends of the Constitution" (*Correspondence of John C. Calhoun,* ed. J. Franklin Jameson, 1143). See William E. Cain, "Introduction," in Garrison, *William Lloyd Garrison and the Fight against Slavery: Selections from "The Liberator."*

10. Garrison and Garrison, *William Lloyd Garrison, 1805–1879,* 4:15, 19.

11. *Liberator,* September 26, 1862. The previous December Garrison had removed the "Covenant with Death" motto from the banner of the *Liberator* and replaced it with "Proclaim Liberty throughout the land, to all the inhabitants thereof."

12. Mayer, *All on Fire,* 549.

13. Garrison, *William Lloyd Garrison and the Fight against Slavery,* 171–72.

14. "Proclamation Revoking General Hunter's Order of Military Emancipation of May 19, 1862," *CW,* 5:223.

15. Garrison and Garrison, *William Lloyd Garrison, 1805–1879,* 4:62n1.

16. John Jay Chapman, *William Lloyd Garrison,* 2nd ed., in *The Selected Writings of John Jay Chapman,* ed. Jacques Barzun, 71–72.

17. In his review of *My Bondage and My Freedom,* Garrison wrote that its latter portion, which touches on the break with the Garrisonians, was "reeking with the virus of personal malignity" toward his old associates. Readers of the book will likely find themselves agreeing with Philip S. Foner that "it is difficult to understand on what Garrison based his sharp attack" ("Introduction to the Dover Edition," in Douglass, *My Bondage and My Freedom,* xi–xii.

18. Chapman, *William Lloyd Garrison,* 87–90.

19. Mayer, *All on Fire,* 264, 444.

20. Ibid., 414; Chapman, *William Lloyd Garrison,* 88; Thoreau, *Reform Papers,* 64. "The Abolitionists, in the main, were impracticable people; Garrison in the end proved otherwise" (Charnwood, *Abraham Lincoln,* 43).

21. Chapman, *William Lloyd Garrison,* 74; *Spectator* editorialist quoted in John Hope Franklin, *The Emancipation Proclamation,* 60; *Liberator,* September 26, 1862.

22. Mayer, *All on Fire,* 527; Lincoln to John C. Frémont, September 2, 1861, *CW,* 4:506; Lincoln to Orville H. Browning, September 22, 1861, *CW,* 4:531–32. See also Nicolay and Hay, *Abraham Lincoln: A History,* 4:423–25.

23. *National Intelligencer,* September 23 and 26, 1862, in Herbert Mitgang, ed., *Abraham Lincoln, A Press Portrait: His Life and Times from the Original Newspaper Documents of the Union, the Confederacy, and Europe,* 302–3, 308–10 (see also Franklin, *Emancipation Proclamation,* 53); *CW,* 5:222–23. The editorialist could not believe that the preliminary emancipation proclamation was seriously meant because it was susceptible to the same objections that Lincoln himself had voiced to the Chicago delegation just days before, which were not obviated by invoking the president's constitutional authority.

24. Chapman, *William Lloyd Garrison,* 74; Lincoln to Orville H. Browning, *CW,* 4:532.

25. Remarks to a Delegation of Progressive Friends, *CW,* 5:278.

26. Garrison and Garrison, *William Lloyd Garrison, 1805–1879,* 4:52–53; *CW,* 5:278; Speech at Springfield, June 15, 1858, *CW,* 2:461–62; Message to

Congress in Special Session, *CW,* 4:439; Reply to Emancipation Memorial Presented by Chicago Christians, *CW,* 5:423–24.

27. Preliminary Emancipation Proclamation, September 22, 1862, *CW,* 5:435, 434n5; Lincoln to Salmon P. Chase, September 2, 1863, *CW,* 6:428–29.

28. Mayer, *All on Fire,* 444, 616–17.

29. *SSW,* 406. Douglass was speaking on the anniversary of West Indies emancipation, so a comparison between the British and American governments naturally suggested itself.

30. Garrison and Garrison, *William Lloyd Garrison, 1805–1879,* 4:119–20.

31. The "European observer," Massimo d'Azeglio, was quoted in Franklin, *Emancipation Proclamation,* 110–11; Lincoln to George Robertson, *CW,* 2:318.

Chapter 9.   Frederick Douglass
Antislavery Constitutionalism and the Problem of Consent

1. *SSW,* xiii–xiv, 618.

2. *The Life and Writings of Frederick Douglass,* ed. Philip S. Foner, 3:110; Storing, "The Case against Civil Disobedience," in *Toward a More Perfect Union,* 248.

3. *SSW,* 126. Some blacks favored colonization, among them Martin R. Delany, who was Douglass's coeditor at his newspaper *North Star* from 1847 to 1849. In 1852 Delany published *The Condition, Elevation, Emigration, and Destiny of the Colored People of the United States* (see Howard Brotz, ed., *African-American Social and Political Thought, 1850–1920,* 37–101).

4. David E. Schrader, "Natural Law in the Constitutional Thought of Frederick Douglass," 72.

5. Speech at Peoria, *CW,* 2:264; First Inaugural Address, *CW,* 4:264.

6. Schrader, "Natural Law," 78; *CW,* 4:264; Brotz, ed., *African-American Social and Political Thought,* 29–30. Brotz includes Booker T. Washington in this judgment.

7. James Madison, *Notes of Debates in the Federal Convention of 1787,* 648. This statement is quoted in the notes added with Lincoln's approval to the published text of his Cooper Institute address; see *CW,* 3:545.

8. Douglass, *My Bondage and My Freedom,* 397.

9. Garrison, *William Lloyd Garrison and the Fight against Slavery,* 106.

10. For Tocqueville's views on the power of public opinion in a democracy, see *Democracy in America,* vol. 1, pt. 2, chap. 7, and vol. 2, pt. 1, chap. 2. John G. Nicolay presents a striking instance of this power. After Lincoln's election, when secessionists confronted the people of the South with the question whether they would submit to rule by the Republicans, "a false shame and the inexorable tyranny of Southern public opinion made many a voter belie the honest convictions of his heart, and answer No, when at the very least he would gladly have evaded the inquiry." If Nicolay is wrong about the extent of pro-Union sentiment in the lower South, nevertheless his account has psychological plausibility (*Outbreak of Rebellion,* 2, 8–9).

11. Douglass, *Life and Times of Frederick Douglass,* 454–59. For further information about Edward [Colston] Marshall and other members of the Marshall family, see James Grant Wilson and John Fiske, eds., *Appleton's Cyclopaedia of American Biography,* 4:225.

12. Douglass, *Narrative of the Life of Frederick Douglass, An American Slave,* ed. Benjamin Quarles, 35–36.

13. Ibid., 118.

14. Douglass, *Life and Times of Frederick Douglass,* 229.

15. "The United States Constitution," in *Selections from the Writings and Speeches of William Lloyd Garrison,* 303, 313.

16. The same point is made, without reference to Douglass, by William M. Wiecek (*The Sources of Antislavery Constitutionalism in America, 1760–1848,* 247–48).

17. *CW,* 4:270.

18. "The United States Constitution," *Selections from the Writings and Speeches of William Lloyd Garrison,* 306, 310.

19. Garrison and Garrison, *William Lloyd Garrison, 1805–1879,* 3:116n1. The reference is to the original Liberty Party of the early 1840s, as distinct from the party of the same name with which Douglass was later associated. The original party was not pledged to the goal of abolition but to "the absolute and unqualified divorce of the General Government from Slavery" (Johnson, comp., *National Party Platforms,* 1:4).

20. Gustave de Beaumont, "Note on the Social and Political Condition of the Negro Slaves and of Free People of Color," in *Marie; or, Slavery in the United States: A Novel of Jacksonian America* (App. A), 193, 197–98, 199; "Inhumanity of Slavery: Extract from a Lecture on Slavery, at Rochester, N.Y., December 8, 1850," *MBMF* (App.), 436.

21. Booker T. Washington, *Frederick Douglass,* 131–32. Douglass does say that he would not have consented to the payment for his freedom if he had been "a private person, having no other relations or duties than those of a personal and family nature" (*MBMF,* 376).

22. Lysander Spooner, *The Unconstitutionality of Slavery,* 1–8; *No Treason* No. 1, iii; "Letter to Thomas F. Bayard," 3. In listing his constitutional authorities in "Change of Opinion Announced," Douglass had put Spooner's name first (*SSW,* 173–74).

23. *CW,* 4:263.

24. Quarles, *Frederick Douglass,* 186; Address at Cooper Institute, *CW,* 3:541; George M. Fredrickson, "Introduction," in *The Impending Crisis of the South: How to Meet It,* by Hinton Rowan Helper, xix.

25. Storing, "Frederick Douglass," in *Toward a More Perfect Union,* 173; *Life and Times of Frederick Douglass,* 294–95.

Chapter 10. Freedom, Political and Economic

1. Allen C. Guelzo, *Abraham Lincoln, Redeemer President,* 9, 121, 184;

Hofstadter, *American Political Tradition,* 135.

2. Address before the Wisconsin State Agricultural Society, September 30, 1859, *CW,* 3:481. "All of [Lincoln's] economic agendas in the Illinois legislature had been aimed at breaking up economic slavery of the Jacksonian sort. It did not, however, drive him into militant criticism of the American republic's most institutionalized version of slavery . . . the literal enslavement of African-Americans" (Guelzo, *Abraham Lincoln, Redeemer President,* 124).

3. Thoreau, "Life without Principle," *Reform Papers,* 174. Tocqueville noted similar shortcomings; see Lerner, *Thinking Revolutionary,* 174–91.

4. Thoreau, "Wendell Phillips before Concord Lyceum," *Reform Papers,* 60–61. In fact, Douglass prudently went abroad after the publication of his *Narrative,* returning only after he had purchased his freedom. Henry S. Canby seems to have had passages like this one, critical of "Yankee" self-concern, in mind when he wrote, "If he had been able to disregard the ugly fact of slavery, Thoreau would have found the plantation life of the old South in closer accord with his philosophy than Concord ways of living" (*Thoreau,* 483n3).

5. Aileen S. Kraditor, *Means and Ends in American Abolitionism: Garrison and His Critics on Strategy and Tactics, 1834–1850,* 247. It was the distinction between slavery and oppression that led abolitionists as a group to keep the nascent labor movement at arm's length. David Donald alleges class bias, but he discounts the abolitionists' own words, relying instead on sociological analysis ("Toward a Reconsideration of Abolitionists," 19–36).

6. August O. Spain wrote, "Southerners accepted the charge that slavery was exploitation, but asserted also that all human exploitation was in essence slavery" (*The Political Theory of John C. Calhoun,* 231).

7. Fitzhugh, *Cannibals All!* 72, 159, 254, 258.

8. Douglass, *Narrative,* 150.

9. Ibid., 149–50; Douglass, *My Bondage and My Freedom,* 112–14.

10. Douglass, *Life and Times of Frederick Douglass,* 209–10.

11. *SSW,* 712–15.

12. *CW,* 3:478.

13. James Henry Hammond, "'Mud-Sill' Speech," 123; Sixth Debate with Douglas, *CW,* 3:254–55.

14. *CW,* 4:438.

15. Ibid., 5:51–53.

16. Ibid., 3:475; Olmsted, *The Cotton Kingdom,* 103–4.

17. Speech at Peoria, *CW,* 2:255.

Chapter 11. Between Legalism and the Higher Law

1. The remarks in this chapter are based on Zinn's essay "Abolitionists, Freedom-Riders, and the Tactics of Agitation," and on two essays by M. E. Bradford, "A Long Farewell to Union: The Southern Valedictories of 1860–1861" and "Lincoln and the Language of Hate and Fear: A View from the South," in his *Against the Barbarians, and Other Reflections on Familiar Themes.*

While "A Long Farewell to Union" does not mention Lincoln by name, Bradford clearly has him in mind: in concluding he refers to Alexander Stephens's remark on Lincoln, "The Union with him in sentiment, rose to the sublimity of a religious mysticism" (Stephens, *Constitutional View of the Late War*, 2:448). Bradford also quotes from Stephens's letter to Lincoln dated December 30, 1860, again without naming the source.

2. Bradford, *Against the Barbarians*, 242, 245; Zinn, "Abolitionists, Freedom-Riders, and the Tactics of Agitation," 438–39, 441.

3. Zinn, "Abolitionists, Freedom-Riders, and the Tactics of Agitation," 439, 438.

4. Temperance Address, *CW*, 1:273; *CW*, 4:271.

5. Ralph Korngold, *Two Friends of Man: The Story of William Lloyd Garrison and Wendell Phillips and Their Relationship with Abraham Lincoln*, ix; *CW*, 3:27; Zinn, "Abolitionists, Freedom-Riders, and the Tactics of Agitation," 440. I have corrected Korngold's substitution of *models* for *moulds* in the Lincoln quotation.

6. Segal, ed., *Conversations with Lincoln*, 238, 338.

7. Bradford, *Against the Barbarians*, 245, 237, 219–20; Davis, *Rise and Fall of the Confederate Government*, 1:191.

8. Bradford, *Against the Barbarians*, 217–19; *CW*, 3:334.

9. Bradford, *Against the Barbarians*, 230, 244–45; Zinn, "Abolitionists, Freedom-Riders, and the Tactics of Agitation," 442.

10. Autobiography written for John L. Scripps, *CW*, 4:67; Nehemiah Adams, *A South-side View of Slavery; or, Three Months at the South*, 125; Fitzhugh, *Cannibals All!* 66.

11. Roy P. Basler, "Lincoln's Development as a Writer," 18–19; Herndon and Weik, *Herndon's Life of Lincoln*, 272.

12. Erich Auerbach, *Mimesis: The Representation of Reality in Western Literature*, 14.

13. Robert Penn Warren, *The Legacy of the Civil War*, 20, 32.

14. Lincoln to Albert G. Hodges, *CW*, 7:282; Lincoln to Cuthbert Bullitt, July 28, 1862, *CW*, 5:436.

Chapter 12. Lincoln's Defense of Politics

1. Notes for Speeches at Columbus and Cincinnati, *CW*, 3:426–27.

2. "Preface to the 1962 Edition," in David M. Potter, *Lincoln and His Party in the Secession Crisis*, xviii–xx.

3. For the Frémont episode, see Lincoln to Orville H. Browning, *CW*, 4:531–33.

4. Speech at Peoria, *CW*, 2:271–72 (Lincoln is referring to the Missouri crisis, the nullification crisis, and the crisis over lands acquired from Mexico); Lincoln to Lyman Trumball, *CW*, 4:150.

5. "A House Divided," *CW*, 2:461.

6. Lincoln to Thurlow Weed, *CW*, 4:154; Lincoln to James T. Hale, *CW*, 4:172.

7. Fragment of a Speech Intended for Kentuckians, *CW*, 4:201n3.

8. Ibid., 4:200–201; Potter, *Lincoln and His Party*, 180.

9. Remarks Concerning Concessions to Secession, *CW,* 4:176.

10. Lincoln to Orville H. Browning, *CW,* 4:531–32. Browning himself was a conservative—Lincoln wrote, "coming from you, I confess it astonishes me"—but he joined with abolitionists and Radicals on this occasion in criticizing Lincoln's handling of Frémont. James McPherson quotes from Lincoln's letter to Browning in such a way as to leave the impression that by "saving the government" Lincoln meant forestalling secession by the border states, which is precisely what he did not mean (*Abraham Lincoln and the Second American Revolution,* 128).

11. Third Debate with Douglas, at Jonesboro, September 15, 1858, *CW,* 3:116–17.

12. Speech at Peoria, *CW,* 2:266, 267; Frank Lawrence Owsley, "The Foundations of Democracy," 85. For the southern Democratic position on slavery in the territories—largely endorsed by the Supreme Court in the Dred Scott decision—see the resolutions introduced in the Senate by Calhoun, December 27, 1837 (*Congressional Globe,* 25th Cong., 2d sess., Appendix, 55).

13. First Inaugural Address, *CW,* 4:265; Speech from the Balcony of the Bates House, Indianapolis, *CW,* 4:195–96; Message to Congress in Special Session, *CW,* 4:435.

14. According to Andrew Lytle, the constitutional Union "came to an end at the hands of those who said they were fighting to save it" (*From Eden to Babylon: The Political and Agrarian Essays of Andrew Nelson Lytle,* ed. M. E. Bradford, 155).

15. Mayer, *All on Fire,* 549. "A question might be raised whether the proclamation was legally valid. It might be added that it only aided those who came into our lines and that it was inoperative as to those who did not give themselves up, or that it would have no effect upon the children of the slaves born hereafter" (Response to a Serenade, February 1, 1865, *CW,* 8:254).

16. Lincoln to Albert G. Hodges, *CW,* 7:281. Compare James McPherson's reference to the "diseased limb of slavery": the limb in question was, in fact, the Constitution (*Abraham Lincoln and the Second American Revolution,* 129).

17. *CW,* 5:434, 536–37; Mayer, *All on Fire,* 543–44.

18. Lincoln to John A. McClerand, January 8, 1863, *CW,* 6:49. "A proposal from Lincoln to qualify the abolition of slavery, and, after the loss of hundreds of thousands of lives, to pay off the slaveholders whose secession had triggered the war in the first place, seems so bizarre in February of 1865 that the natural reaction might be to question whether Lincoln could ever really have made it. But all the evidence, from Seward as well as Stephens, suggests that this is pretty much what Lincoln did" (Guelzo, *Abraham Lincoln, Redeemer President,* 408).

19. *Recollected Words of Abraham Lincoln,* 421–22. The source is Stephens's *Constitutional View of the Late War.*

20. This speech is printed as an appendix to Douglass's autobiography, *Life and Times of Frederick Douglass,* 496–97, 503.

21. Address before the Young Men's Lyceum of Springfield, January 27, 1838, *CW,* 1:114; Lincoln to Williamson Durley, *CW,* 1:348; Eulogy on Henry Clay, *CW,* 2:130.

22. Speech at a Republican Banquet, *CW*, 2:385.

23. Alexander Hamilton, John Jay, and James Madison, *The Federalist*, ed. Robert Scigliano, 396. For the full text of the letter, see Kurland and Lerner, eds., *The Founders' Constitution*, 1:195. In this connection the example of the Anti-Federalist Melancton Smith is instructive. In the New York ratifying convention he called the three–fifths clause of the proposed constitution "utterly repugnant to his feelings," because the "very operation of it was to give certain privileges to those people who were so wicked as to keep slaves." The next day, however, he announced that he was "persuaded we must yield the point, in accommodation to the southern states" (Herbert J. Storing, ed., *The Anti-Federalist: Writings by the Opponents of the Constitution*, 336, 337–38).

24. First Inaugural Address, *CW*, 4:269.

25. Charnwood, *Abraham Lincoln*, 96. Robert Faulkner makes the same point by adapting one of Lincoln's favorite metaphors for explaining the status of slavery in the Constitution: that of a man who "hides away a wen or cancer, which he dares not cut out at once, lest he bleed to death; with the promise, nevertheless, that the cutting may begin at the end of a given time" (*CW*, 2:274; for other examples, see *CW*, 3:313, 4:5–6, 11, and 5:327). Faulkner wrote, "The health of a largely free country was more important [to Lincoln] than the cure of a particular disease—even if the test of health became a willingness to fight the disease when it showed symptoms of dominating" (Robert K. Faulkner, "Lincoln and the Constitution," 181).

26. Tocqueville, *Democracy in America*, 227; Aristotle, *Politics*, bk. 3, chap. 13: under political rule "a citizen is one who shares in the government, and also in his turn submits to be governed."

27. Garrison and Garrison, *William Lloyd Garrison, 1805–1879*, 3:50. T. R. R. Cobb, one of the participants in the Milledgeville debate on secession, wrote of northerners in an 1860 letter to his wife, "They are *different* people from us, whether better or worse and *there is no love* between us. Why then continue together?" (Schott, *Alexander H. Stephens of Georgia*, 296).

28. *Congressional Globe*, 25th Cong., 2d sess., Appendix, 55; Fitzhugh, "Small Nations." In Fitzhugh's estimation, the Calhoun school did not fully comprehend the "origin, character, and anatomical naturalness and necessity of *State nationality*" (568).

29. Response to a Serenade, November 10, 1864, *CW*, 8:100–102.

Epilogue

1. Brownson, "The Fugitive-Slave Law," 17:25.

2. Speech at Cincinnati, *CW*, 3:460.

3. Don E. Fehrenbacher, "Introduction," in *Abraham Lincoln: A Documentary Portrait through His Speeches and Writings*, xxiii; Fehrenbacher, *Lincoln in Text and Context*, 108; Charnwood, *Abraham Lincoln*, 59; Herbert Croly, *The Promise of American Life*, 90.

4. Robert Penn Warren, *Jefferson Davis Gets His Citizenship Back*, 47, 51;

Allen Tate, *Jefferson Davis: His Rise and Fall,* 76.

5. Fitzhugh, *Cannibals All!* 130; Franklin, *Southern Odyssey,* 220 (quoting Wish, *George Fitzhugh,* 134); Genovese, *World the Slaveholders Made,* 164.

6. Douglass, *Narrative,* 66, and *Life and Times of Frederick Douglass,* 275.

7. Douglass, *Life and Times of Frederick Douglass,* 462–63. The following pages are devoted to "the famous Free-Soil Convention" held the following year, which Douglass attended.

8. Douglass, *Life and Times of Frederick Douglass,* 441–42.

9. Garrison, *William Lloyd Garrison and the Fight against Slavery,* 171; Second Inaugural Address, March 4, 1865, *CW,* 8:333.

Works Cited

Adams, Nehemiah. *A South-side View of Slavery; or, Three Months at the South.* 1854. Reprint. Miami: Mnemosyne Publishing Co., 1969.

Ambler, Wayne. "Aristotle on Nature and Politics: The Case of Slavery." *Political Theory* 15 (1987): 390–410.

Angle, Paul M., ed. *The Complete Lincoln-Douglas Debates of 1858.* Chicago: University of Chicago Press, 1991.

Aristotle. *Politics and Economics.* Translated by Edward Walford. London: Henry G. Bohn, 1853.

Auerbach, Erich. *Mimesis: The Representation of Reality in Western Literature.* Translated by Willard R. Trask. Princeton: Princeton University Press, 1953.

Baker, George E., ed. *The Life of William Henry Seward, with Selections from His Works.* New York: Redfield, 1855.

Basler, Roy P. "Lincoln's Development as a Writer." In *Abraham Lincoln: His Speeches and Writings,* edited by Roy P. Basler. New York: Da Capo Press, 1990.

Beaumont, Gustave de. *Marie; or, Slavery in the United States: A Novel of Jacksonian America.* 1835. Translated by Barbara Chapman, 1958. Reprint with a new introduction. Baltimore: Johns Hopkins University Press, 1999.

Becker, Carl L. *The Declaration of Independence: A Study in the History of Political Ideas.* New York: Vintage Books, 1958.

Belz, Herman. *Abraham Lincoln, Constitutionalism, and Equal Rights in the Civil War Era.* New York: Fordham University Press, 1998.

Booth, Phillip. "Letter from a Distant Land." In *Thoreau: A Collection of Critical Essays,* edited by Sherman Paul. Englewood Cliffs, N.J.: Prentice-Hall, 1962.

Bradford, M. E. *Against the Barbarians, and Other Reflections on Familiar Themes.* Columbia: University of Missouri Press, 1992.

Brotz, Howard, ed. *African-American Social and Political Thought, 1850–1920.* 1966. Reprint with a new introduction. New Brunswick, N.J.: Transaction Publishers, 1992.

Brown, Guy Story. *Calhoun's Philosophy of Politics: A Study of "A Disquisition on Government."* Macon, GA: Mercer University Press, 2000.

Brownson, Orestes. "The Fugitive-Slave Law." In *The Works of Orestes A. Brownson,* edited by Henry Brownson. 20 vols. Detroit: T. Nourse, 1882–1887.

Calhoun, John C. *Correspondence of John C. Calhoun.* Edited by J. Franklin Jameson. Washington, D.C.: American Historical Association, 1899.

——— . *Union and Liberty: The Political Philosophy of John C. Calhoun.* Edited by Ross M. Lence. Indianapolis: Liberty Fund, 1992.

——— . *The Works of John C. Calhoun.* Edited by Richard K. Crallé. 6 vols. New York: D. Appleton, 1853–1854.

Canby, Henry Seidel. *Thoreau.* Boston: Houghton Mifflin, 1939.

Chapman, John Jay. *William Lloyd Garrison,* 2nd ed. In *The Selected Writings of John Jay Chapman,* edited by Jacques Barzun. New York: Farrar, Straus and Cudahy, 1957.

Charnwood, Lord. *Abraham Lincoln.* 1916. Lanham, Md.: Madison Books, 1996.

Cheek, H. Lee, Jr. *Calhoun and Popular Rule: The Political Theory of the "Disquisition" and "Discourse."* Columbia: University of Missouri Press, 2001.

Cleveland, Henry. *Alexander H. Stephens in Public and Private, with Letters and Speeches before, during, and since the War.* Philadelphia: National Publishing Co., 1866.

Congressional Globe. 46 vols. Washington, D.C., 1833–1873.

Crane, Gregg D. "Douglass's Natural Rights Constitutionalism." In *Approaches to Teaching "Narrative of the Life of Frederick Douglass,"* edited by James C. Hall. New York: Modern Language Association of America, 1999.

Crockett, Steve. "On Becoming Free." *St. John's Review* 44 (1997): 23–50.

Croly, Herbert. *The Promise of American Life.* New York: Capricorn Books, 1964.

Davis, Jefferson. "Life and Character of the Hon. John Caldwell Calhoun." In *John C. Calhoun: A Profile,* edited by John L. Thomas. New York: Hill and Wang, 1968.

———. *The Rise and Fall of the Confederate Government.* 2 vols. 1881. Reprint with a new foreword by James M. McPherson. New York: Da Capo Press, 1990.

Dew, Thomas R. "Review of the Debate in the Virginia Legislature of 1831 and 1832." In *Slavery Defended: The Views of the Old South,* edited by Eric L. McKitrick. Englewood Cliffs, N.J.: Prentice-Hall, 1963.

Donald, David H. "Toward a Reconsideration of Abolitionists." In *Lincoln Reconsidered: Essays on the Civil War Era.* New York: Alfred A. Knopf, 1965.

Douglass, Frederick. *Frederick Douglass: Selected Speeches and Writings.* Edited by Philip S. Foner. Chicago: Lawrence Hill Books, 1999.

———. *The Frederick Douglass Papers.* Series One: Speeches, Debates, and Interviews, edited by John W. Blassingame et al. 5 vols. New Haven: Yale University Press, 1979–1992.

———. *Life and Times of Frederick Douglass.* 1892. Reprint. New York: Bonanza Books, 1962.

———. *The Life and Writings of Frederick Douglass.* Edited by Philip S. Foner. 4 vols. New York: International Publishers, 1952.

———. *My Bondage and My Freedom.* 1855. Reprint with a new introduction by Philip S. Foner. New York: Dover Publications, 1969.

———. *Narrative of the Life of Frederick Douglass, an American Slave.* Edited by Benjamin Quarles. Cambridge: Belknap Press of Harvard University Press, 1960.

Dumond, Dwight L., ed. *Southern Editorials on Secession.* New York: The Century Co., 1931.

Ellis, Richard J. *The Dark Side of the Left: Illiberal Egalitarianism in America.* Lawrence: University Press of Kansas, 1998.

Faulkner, Robert K. "Lincoln and the Constitution." In *The Revival of Constitutionalism,* edited by James W. Muller. Lincoln: University of Nebraska Press, 1988.

Fehrenbacher, Don E. "Introduction." In *Abraham Lincoln: A Documentary Portrait through His Speeches and Writings.* Stanford: Stanford University Press, 1964.

———— . *Lincoln in Text and Context: Collected Essays.* Stanford: Stanford University Press, 1987.

———— . *Prelude to Greatness: Lincoln in the 1850s.* Stanford: Stanford University Press, 1962.

Fitzhugh, George. *Cannibals All! or, Slaves without Masters.* 1857. Reprint. Edited by C. Vann Woodward. Cambridge: Belknap Press of Harvard University Press, 1960.

———— . "The Politics and Economics of Aristotle and Mr. Calhoun." *De Bow's Review* 23 (1857): 163–72.

———— . "Revolutions of '76 and '61 Contrasted." *De Bow's Review,* After the War Series, 4 (1867): 36–42. Originally published in *Southern Literary Messenger* 37 (1863): 718–26.

———— . "Small Nations." *De Bow's Review* 29 (1860): 561–69.

———— . *Sociology for the South; or, The Failure of Free Society.* Richmond, Va.: A. Morris, 1854.

Ford, Nick Aaron. "Henry David Thoreau, Abolitionist." *New England Quarterly* 19 (1946): 359–71.

Franklin, John Hope. *The Emancipation Proclamation.* Wheeling, Ill.: Harlan Davidson, 1995.

———— . *A Southern Odyssey: Travelers in the Antebellum North.* Baton Rouge: Louisiana State University Press, 1976.

Fredrickson, George M. "Introduction." In *The Impending Crisis of the South: How to Meet It,* by Hinton Rowan Helper. Cambridge: Belknap Press of Harvard University Press, 1968.

Freehling, William W., and Craig M. Simpson, eds. *Secession Debated: Georgia's Showdown in 1860.* New York: Oxford University Press, 1992.

Garrison, Wendell P., and Francis J. Garrison. *William Lloyd Garrison, 1805–1879: The Story of His Life Told by His Children.* 4 vols. 1889. Reprint. New York: Arno Press, 1969.

Garrison, William Lloyd. *Selections from the Writings and Speeches of William Lloyd Garrison.* 1852. Reprint. New York: Negro Universities Press, 1968

———. *William Lloyd Garrison and the Fight against Slavery: Selections from "The Liberator."* Edited by William E. Cain. Boston: Bedford Books, 1995.

Genovese, Eugene D. *The World the Slaveholders Made: Two Essays in Interpretation.* 1969. Reprint with a new introduction. Hanover, N.H.: Wesleyan University Press, 1988.

Gildersleeve, Basil L. *The Creed of the Old South, 1865–1915.* Baltimore: Johns Hopkins University Press, 1915.

Guelzo, Allen C. *Abraham Lincoln, Redeemer President.* Grand Rapids, Mich.: William B. Eerdmans, 1999.

Hamilton, Alexander, John Jay, and James Madison. *The Federalist: A Commentary on the Constitution of the United States.* Edited by Robert Scigliano. New York: The Modern Library, 2000.

Hammond, James Henry. "'Mud-Sill' Speech." In *Slavery Defended: The Views of the Old South,* edited by Eric L. McKitrick. Englewood Cliffs, N.J.: Prentice-Hall, 1963.

Hartz, Louis. *The Liberal Tradition in America: An Interpretation of American Political Thought since the Revolution.* San Diego: Harcourt Brace, 1991.

Herndon, William H., and Jesse W. Weik. *Herndon's Life of Lincoln: The History and Personal Recollections of Abraham Lincoln as Originally Written by William H. Herndon and Jesse W. Weik.* Edited by Paul M. Angle. New York: Da Capo Press, 1983.

Hofstadter, Richard. *The American Political Tradition and the Men Who Made It.* 1948. Reprint. New York: Vintage Books, 1989.

Hyman, Stanley Edgar. "Henry Thoreau Once More." In *Thoreau in Our Season,* edited by John H. Hicks. Amherst: University of Massachusetts Press, 1966.

Jaffa, Harry V. *Crisis of the House Divided: An Interpretation of the Issues in the Lincoln-Douglas Debates.* 1959. Reprint with a new preface. Chicago: University of Chicago Press, 1982.

———. *A New Birth of Freedom: Abraham Lincoln and the Coming of the Civil War.* Lanham, Md.: Rowman and Littlefield, 2000.

Johannsen, Robert W. *Lincoln, the South, and Slavery: The Political Dimension.* Baton Rouge: Louisiana State University Press, 1991.

Johnson, Donald Bruce, comp. *National Party Platforms.* 2 vols. Urbana: University of Illinois Press, 1978.

Johnson, Oliver. *William Lloyd Garrison and His Times.* 1881. Reprint. Miami: Mnemosyne Publishing Co., 1969.

Korngold, Ralph. *Two Friends of Man: The Story of William Lloyd Garrison and Wendell Phillips and Their Relationship with Abraham Lincoln.* Boston: Little, Brown, 1950.

Kraditor, Aileen S. *Means and Ends in American Abolitionism: Garrison and His Critics on Strategy and Tactics, 1834–1850.* New York: Pantheon Books, 1969.

Krutch, Joseph Wood. *Henry David Thoreau.* New York: William Sloane Associates, 1948.

Kurland, Philip B., and Ralph Lerner, eds. *The Founders' Constitution.* 5 vols. Chicago: University of Chicago Press, 1986.

Lerner, Ralph. "Calhoun's New Science of Politics." In *John C. Calhoun: A Profile,* edited by John L. Thomas. New York: Hill and Wang, 1968.

————. *The Thinking Revolutionary: Principle and Practice in the New Republic.* Ithaca, N.Y.: Cornell University Press, 1987.

Liberator. Boston. 1831–1865.

Lincoln, Abraham. *The Collected Works of Abraham Lincoln.* Edited by Roy P. Basler et al. 9 vols. New Brunswick, N.J.: Rutgers University Press, 1953–1955.

————. *Recollected Words of Abraham Lincoln.* Edited and compiled by Don E. Fehrenbacher and Virginia Fehrenbacher. Stanford: Stanford University Press, 1996.

Locke, John. *The Second Treatise of Government: An Essay Concerning the True Original, Extent, and End of Civil Government.* In *Two Treatises of Government,* edited by Peter Laslett. Cambridge: Cambridge University Press, 1988.

Loewenberg, Robert J. "John Locke and the Antebellum Defense of Slavery." *Political Theory* 13 (1985): 266–91.

Lytle, Andrew Nelson. *From Eden to Babylon: The Political and Agrarian Essays of Andrew Nelson Lytle.* Edited by M. E. Bradford. Washington, D.C.: Regnery Gateway, 1990.

Madison, James. *Notes of Debates in the Federal Convention of 1787.* 1840. Reprint. Athens: Ohio University Press, 1966.

Maine, Sir Henry. *Ancient Law.* Everyman's Library. New York: E. P. Dutton, n.d.

Mayer, Henry. *All on Fire: William Lloyd Garrison and the Abolition of Slavery.* New York: St. Martin's Press, 1998.

McPherson, James M. *Abraham Lincoln and the Second American Revolution.* New York: Oxford University Press, 1991.

Mitgang, Herbert, ed. *Abraham Lincoln, a Press Portrait: His Life and Times from the Original Newspaper Documents of the Union, the Confederacy, and Europe.* 1971. Reprint with a new introduction. New York: Fordham University Press, 2000.

Nicolay, John G. *The Outbreak of Rebellion.* 1881. Reprint. New York: Da Capo Press, 1995.

Nicolay, John G., and John Hay. *Abraham Lincoln: A History.* 10 vols. New York: The Century Co., 1890.

Nietzsche, Friedrich. *On the Advantage and Disadvantage of History for Life.* Translated by Peter Preuss. Indianapolis: Hackett, 1980.

O'Connor, Eugene, trans. *The Essential Epicurus.* Buffalo, N.Y.: Prometheus, 1993.

Olmsted, Frederick Law. *The Cotton Kingdom: A Traveller's Observations on Cotton and Slavery in the American Slave States. Based upon Three Former Volumes of Journeys and Investigations by the Same Author.* 1861. Reprint. Edited by Arthur M. Schlesinger. New York: Da Capo Press, 1996.

———. *A Journey in the Seaboard Slave States, with Remarks on Their Economy.* New York: Dix and Edwards, 1856.

Owsley, Frank Lawrence. "The Foundations of Democracy." In *Who Owns America? A New Declaration of Independence,* edited by Herbert Agar and Allen Tate. 1936. Reprint with new foreword. Wilmington, Del.: ISI Books, 1999.

Potter, David M. *Lincoln and His Party in the Secession Crisis.* 1942. Reprint with a new preface. New Haven: Yale University Press, 1962.

Quarles, Benjamin. *Frederick Douglass.* New York: Da Capo, 1997.

Randall, J. G. *Lincoln the Liberal Statesman.* New York: Dodd, Mead and Co., 1947.

Redpath, James, ed. *Echoes of Harper's Ferry.* 1860. Reprint. New York: Arno Press, 1969.

Rosenblum, Nancy L. "Thoreau's Militant Conscience." *Political Theory* 9 (1981): 81–110.

Schott, Thomas E. *Alexander H. Stephens of Georgia: A Biography.* Baton Rouge: Louisiana State University Press, 1988.

Schrader, David E. "Natural Law in the Constitutional Thought of Frederick Douglass." In *Frederick Douglass: A Critical Reader,* edited by Bill E. Lawson and Frank M. Kirkland. Oxford: Blackwell Publishers, 1999.

Segal, Charles M., ed. *Conversations with Lincoln.* 1961. Reprint with a new preface. New Brunswick, N.J.: Transaction Publishers, 2002.

Smith, John David. "Introduction." In *My Bondage and My Freedom,* by Frederick Douglass. New York: Penguin, 2003.

Spain, August O. *The Political Theory of John C. Calhoun.* New York: Octagon Books, 1980.

Spooner, Lysander. "A Letter to Thomas F. Bayard, Challenging His Right—And that of All the Other So-Called Senators and Representatives in Congress—To Exercise Any Legislative Power Whatever Over the People of the United States." Boston, 1882.

——— . *No Treason* No. 1. Boston, 1867.

——— . *The Unconstitutionality of Slavery.* Boston: Bela Marsh, 1860.

[Stephen, James Fitzjames]. "A Practical Man." *Saturday Review* 1 (1856): 434.

Stephens, Alexander H. *A Constitutional View of the Late War between the States: Its Causes, Character, Conduct and Results.* 2 vols. 1868–1870. Reprint. New York: Kraus Reprint Co., 1970.

Stoller, Leo. *After Walden: Thoreau's Changing Views on Economic Man.* Stanford: Stanford University Press, 1966.

——— . "Civil Disobedience: Principle and Politics." In *Thoreau in Our Season,* edited by John H. Hicks. Amherst: University of Massachusetts Press, 1966.

Storing, Herbert J., ed. *The Anti-Federalist: Writings by the Opponents of the Constitution.* Chicago: University of Chicago Press, 1985.

——— . *Toward a More Perfect Union: Writings of Herbert J. Storing.* Edited by Joseph M. Bessette. Washington, D.C.: AEI Press, 1995.

Styron, Arthur. *The Cast-Iron Man: John C. Calhoun and American Democracy.* New York: Longmans, Green, 1935.

Tate, Allen. *Jefferson Davis: His Rise and Fall.* Nashville: J. S. Sanders, 1998.

Taylor, Bob Pepperman. *America's Bachelor Uncle: Thoreau and the American Polity.* Lawrence: University Press of Kansas, 1996.

Thoreau, Henry D. *Correspondence.* The Writings of Henry D. Thoreau. Edited by Walter Harding and Carl Bode. New York: New York University Press, 1958.

————. *Reform Papers.* The Writings of Henry D. Thoreau. Edited by Wendell Glick. Princeton: Princeton University Press, 1973.

————. *Walden and Other Writings of Henry David Thoreau.* Edited by Brooks Atkinson. New York: The Modern Library, 1937.

Tocqueville, Alexis de. *Democracy in America.* Translated by Harvey C. Mansfield and Delba Winthrop. Chicago: University of Chicago Press, 2000.

Trent, William P. *Southern Statesmen of the Old Régime: Washington, Jefferson, Randolph, Calhoun, Stephens, Toombs, and Jefferson Davis.* New York: Thomas Y. Crowell, 1897.

Warren, Robert Penn. *Jefferson Davis Gets His Citizenship Back.* Lexington: University Press of Kentucky, 1980.

————. *The Legacy of the Civil War.* Cambridge: Harvard University Press, 1961.

Washington, Booker T. *Frederick Douglass.* Philadelphia: G. W. Jacobs, 1906.

Wiecek, William M. *The Sources of Antislavery Constitutionalism in America, 1760–1848.* Ithaca, N.Y.: Cornell University Press, 1972.

Wilson, Edmund. *Patriotic Gore: Studies in the Literature of the American Civil War.* New York: Oxford University Press, 1962.

Wilson, James Grant, and John Fiske, eds. *Appleton's Cyclopaedia of American Biography.* 1888. Reprint. Detroit: Gale Research, 1968.

Wish, Harvey. *George Fitzhugh, Propagandist of the Old South.* Baton Rouge: Louisiana State University Press, 1943.

————. "Introduction." In *Ante-Bellum: Writings of George Fitzhugh and Hinton Rowan Helper on Slavery.* New York: Capricorn Books, 1960.

Woodward, C. Vann. "George Fitzhugh, *Sui Generis.*" In *Cannibals All! or, Slaves without Masters.* 1857. Reprint. Edited by C. Vann Woodward. Cambridge: Belknap Press of Harvard University Press, 1960.

Zinn, Howard. "Abolitionists, Freedom-Riders, and the Tactics of Agitation." In *The Antislavery Vanguard: New Essays on the*

Abolitionists, edited by Martin Duberman. Princeton: Princeton University Press, 1965.

Index

Abolitionism: and Bible, 29; and charges of expediency against Lincoln, 8; and criticisms of democratic politics, 19; and dissolving the Union, 63, 137–38; and Douglas, 19; and Douglass, ix–x, 89, 126; and Emancipation Proclamation, 105–10; federal mails for circulation of abolitionist literature, 191n24; Fitzhugh on, 63, 81, 192n2; and free versus slave labor, 148–49; and Garrison, 105; and higher law, 15–16; and labor movement, 199n5; Lincoln's reservations about, 9, 104, 118–19; moral suasionists versus political or voting abolitionists, 89, 140–41; and natural law, 126, 127; and other reform movements, 55; and Republican Party, 106–7; and slavery in states, 111; and slavery in territories, 2; and Thoreau, ix, 2, 89–90, 94, 100, 117, 194n4; and U.S. Constitution, 34, 111, 158; versus Lincoln's slavery extinctionism, 5, 7, 177. *See also* Emancipation; Emancipation Proclamation; and specific abolitionists

Adams, Rev. Nehemiah, 160
Aesthetic Papers, 9
Alexander II, Czar, 123–24
American Anti-Slavery Society, 110
American Revolution, 61, 62
Ancient Law (Maine), 64–65
Aristotle: on family, 68, 70, 74; Fitzhugh on, 65–66, 69, 70, 192n3; on governmental function, 38; influence of, on Calhoun, 38; on justice, 68; on members of league or alliance, 72; on political rule, 177; on slavery, 66, 67, 68, 71, 192n14; on society, 65–66, 70
— work: *Politics*, 66, 70, 192n3, 192n14
Auerbach, Erich, 160–61

Basler, Roy P., 160
Beaumont, Gustave de, 139–40
Becker, Carl L., 47
Benning, Henry L., 29
Bible, 29, 56, 57, 97, 192n5
Blacks: alleged inferiority of, 18–19, 29–30, 56, 57, 63, 67. *See also* Slavery
Booth, Phillip, 195n15
Bradford, M. E., 155–61, 199–200n1

215

government, 75–78, 82, 83; on
equality, 75; on family, 76–78;
Fitzhugh on, 65, 69, 73–83, 192n3,
193n13; influence of, on Calhoun,
40–41, 73; and justice, 52; and natural rights, 38; on patriarchy, 76–77;
and Plato, 193n13; on property,
78–79; and social contract theory,
66, 74–75; and socialism, 68
— work: *Second Treatise of Government,*
75–79, 83
Loewenberg, Robert J., 187n17
Lycurgus, 61
Lytle, Andrew, 201n14

Maine, Henry, 64–65, 81
Mansfield, Lord, 191n16
Marie; or, Slavery in the United States
(Beaumont), 139–40
Marshall, Edward, 132
Marshall, John, 132
Mayer, Henry, 3, 106–7, 112, 116–18,
123, 170–72
McPherson, James M., 6, 201n10, 201n16
Mexican War, 27, 91, 92, 95, 194n8
Milledgeville speech (Stephens), 27–28,
34
Minority: Calhoun on, 47; Thoreau on
majority versus, 93–94, 97–99, 103,
195n15
Missouri Compromise, 20, 144, 160,
164, 167
Mormons, 69
Moses, 61
Mud-sill theorists, 151–52
My Bondage and My Freedom (Douglass),
128–34, 136–37, 139–42, 196n17

Narrative of the Life of Frederick Douglass
(Douglass), 128, 141, 199n4
National Intelligencer, 119
Natural law: and Calhoun, 47; Chapman
on, 115–16; and Declaration of Independence, 17; and doctrine of equality in Declaration of Independence,
3, 10, 15; and Locke, 38; Schrader on
abolitionists and, 126; and slavery
defense, 25–27, 29; Spooner on, 142

Newman, Francis, 123
Nicolay, John G., 55–56, 197n10
Nietzsche, Friedrich, 56
Norris, Moses, 132
North Star, 197n3
No Treason (Spooner), 142
Numa, 61

Olmsted, Frederick Law, 79–80, 153–54,
193n9
Oneida community, 69
Owsley, Frank Lawrence, 168, 169

Parker, Theodore, 9
Parliament, British, 49, 50
Peoria speech (Lincoln), 160, 164
Phillips, Wendell, 5, 109, 113, 115, 123,
148, 156, 157, 161, 195n9
Plato, 193n13
"A Plea for Captain John Brown"
(Thoreau), 9, 88–89, 99–102
Politics (Aristotle), 66, 70, 192n3, 192n14
Polk, James, 27
Pope, Alexander, 181
Positive law: and Declaration of Inde-
pendence, 17; and secession, 29
Postal service, 191n24
Potter, David M., 163–64
Property, Locke on, 78–79
Public opinion: Douglass on, 129–32;
Korngold on, 156–57; Lincoln on,
88, 156–57; in South and secession,
197n10; Tocqueville on, 131

Quarles, Benjamin, 143, 195n13

Randall, J. G., 107
Redpath, James, 9
"Reform and the Reformers"
(Thoreau), 100–101
Reformation, 61
Republican Party: and abolitionism,
106–7; as conservatives, 65; and
defense of Union, 162–63; forerunners of, 186n5; Garrison on, 138;
and Lincoln, 14, 20, 65, 186n1; and
nonextension of slavery in territories,
163; and presidential election of